SUPERSIZING THE MIND

PHILOSOPHY OF MIND

Series Editor
David J. Chalmers, Australian National University

Supersizing the Mind

Embodiment, Action,
and Cognitive Extension

Andy Clark

OXFORD
UNIVERSITY PRESS

2011

OXFORD
UNIVERSITY PRESS

Oxford University Press, Inc., publishes works that further
Oxford University's objective of excellence
in research, scholarship, and education.

Oxford   New York
Auckland   Cape Town   Dar es Salaam   Hong Kong   Karachi
Kuala Lumpur   Madrid   Melbourne   Mexico City   Nairobi
New Delhi   Shanghai   Taipei   Toronto

With offices in
Argentina   Austria   Brazil   Chile   Czech Republic   France   Greece
Guatemala   Hungary   Italy   Japan   Poland   Portugal   Singapore
South Korea   Switzerland   Thailand   Turkey   Ukraine   Vietnam

Published by Oxford University Press, Inc.
198 Madison Avenue, New York, New York 10016

www.oup.com

Oxford is a registered trademark of Oxford University Press

Library of Congress Cataloging-in-Publication Data
Clark, Andy, 1957–
Supersizing the mind : embodiment, action, and cognitive
extension / Andy Clark.
   p. cm. — (Philosophy of mind)
ISBN 978-0-19-533321-3 (Hbk)
        978-0-19-977368-8 (Pbk)
1. Philosophy of mind.   2. Mind and body.
3. Distributed cognition.   I. Title.
BD418.3.C532 2008
128'.2—dc22   2007051359

Printed in the United States of America

For my mother, Christine Clark, the gentle Londoner
who taught me to imagine, explore, and care

Hands and feet, apparatus and appliances of all kinds are as much a part of it [thinking] as changes in the brain. Since these physical operations (including the cerebral events) and equipments are a part of thinking, thinking is mental, not because of a peculiar stuff which enters into it or of peculiar non-natural activities which constitute it, but because of what physical acts and appliances do: the distinctive purpose for which they are employed and the distinctive results which they accomplish.

—John Dewey, *Essays in Experimental Logic*

Foreword

David Chalmers

A month ago, I bought an iPhone. The iPhone has already taken over some of the central functions of my brain. It has replaced part of my memory, storing phone numbers and addresses that I once would have taxed my brain with. It harbors my desires: I call up a memo with the names of my favorite dishes when I need to order at a local restaurant. I use it to calculate, when I need to figure out bills and tips. It is a tremendous resource in an argument, with Google ever present to help settle disputes. I make plans with it, using its calendar to help determine what I can and can't do in the coming months. I even daydream on the iPhone, idly calling up words and images when my concentration slips.

Friends joke that I should get the iPhone implanted into my brain. But if Andy Clark is right, all this would do is speed up the processing and free up my hands. The iPhone is part of my mind already.

Clark is a connoisseur of the myriad ways in which the mind relies on the world to get its work done. The first part of this marvelous book explores some of these ways: the extension of our bodies, the extension of our senses, and, crucially, the use of language as a tool to extend our thought. The second part of the book defends the thesis that, in at least some of these cases, the world is not serving as a mere instrument for the mind. Rather, the relevant parts of the world have become parts of my mind. My iPhone is not my tool, or at least it is not wholly my tool. Parts of it have become parts of me.

This is the thesis of the extended mind: when parts of the environment are coupled to the brain in the right way, they become parts of the mind. The thesis has a long history: I am told that there are hints of it in Dewey, Heidegger, and Wittgenstein. But no one has done as much to give life to the idea as Andy Clark. In a series of important books and articles—*Being There, Natural-Born Cyborgs,* "Magic Words: How Language Augments Human Computation," and many others—he has explored the many ways in which the boundaries between mind and world are far more flexible than one might have thought. This book is his major statement of the philosophical picture that undergirds the view.

Andy invited me to write this foreword because of my role in coauthoring an article, "The Extended Mind" (included as an appendix to this book), that has come to serve as a sort of flagship philosophical statement for this picture of the mind. This paper was written when Andy and I were colleagues at Washington University in 1995 and was published in *Analysis* in 1998. Now that a decade has passed, Andy suggested that I might offer a retrospective perspective on that article while saying something about my own views on the topic. I am more than happy to do this, though no one should feel any obligation to read what I have to say. Readers who are not already familiar with the issues might want to first look at the rest of the book, or at least at the appendix, before returning to this foreword.

It will come as no surprise to anyone who knows Andy's work to hear that the inspiration behind the original article was all his. In March 1995, Andy handed me a short article that he had written, called "Mind and World: Breaching the Plastic Frontier." This article already contained many of the key theses and arguments that appear in "The Extended Mind." It contained the key thought-experiment comparing Tetris players who rotate images inside and outside the head. It also contained the crucial Parity Principle, which held that if a process in the world works in a way that we should count as a cognitive process if it were done in the head, then we should count it as a cognitive process all the same. I had some ideas about how to further develop and argue for the thesis, and we ended up working together on an expanded and renamed paper.

The original article contained a notorious footnote, saying "The authors are listed in order of their degree of belief in the central thesis." Some have taken this to imply that I reject the extended mind thesis and was working as a sort of hired gun in service of someone else's cause. In fact, I find the thesis very attractive. If anything, I am more confident of the thesis than I was a decade ago, having seen it survive the many objections that have been raised to it without too much trouble. (I agree with almost everything in Andy's authoritative treatment of these objections in part II of this book.) But I do not think the matter is completely cut and dried.

I am not worried by the most common objections to the thesis: the fact that external cognitive processes work differently from internal cognitive processes, the threat that the mind will extend too far into the world, and the threat that the core role of the brain will be lost, for example. And I certainly do not think that there is anything privileged about skin and skull as boundaries for the mind.

Still, I think that there is one potentially principled place where the opponent of the extended mind can resist. This is an appeal to the dual boundaries of perception and action. It is natural to hold that perception is the interface where the world affects the mind, and that action is the interface where the mind affects the world. If so, it is tempting to hold that what precedes perception and what follows action is not truly mental. And one might use this to draw a principled distinction between the cases of Otto (the Alzheimer's patient who uses a notebook as memory) and Inga (the ordinary subject who uses her brain). To interact with his notebook Otto must read it and write in it, requiring perception and action, where there is no such requirement for Inga. If so, then the boundaries above would place the notebook outside the mind.

We consider this sort of worry briefly in "The Extended Mind," suggesting that Otto's access to the notebook need not be seen as perceptual. But this is surely too quick: there is no denying that Otto sees the notebook and reads from it, just as there is no denying that Otto reaches for the notebook and writes in it. So there is certainly perception and action taking place here. A better reply might be to note that there can be inner perception (when one reads from a mental image, say) and mental action (when one makes a mental note, say). Then Otto's perception and action could be seen as of a piece with these. But an opponent could reasonably respond that Otto's interaction with the notebook involves real perception and real action (where these might be glossed as sensory perception and physical action, or in terms of the right sort of perceptual and agentive experience, or in some other way), of a sort not present in cases of inner perception and mental action. And it could be suggested that real perception and real action mark a plausible boundary for the mental.

Perhaps the best reply for the proponent of the extended mind is to reject the proposed boundary. We touch on this reply in the "The Extended Mind," saying that just because the Terminator retrieves information by reading it from a screen, this does not mean that the information is not truly part of its memory. One can more generally hold that the difference between real perception and inner perception, or between real action and mental action, is not sufficiently robust or important to ground a mental/nonmental distinction. Still, an opponent could hold the line, saying that if the Terminator has to retrieve the information by reading it, then he did not truly believe it beforehand. And perhaps this opponent would have commonsense psychology on his or her side. If so, then perhaps this is one point where the "commonsense functionalism" that Clark favors in this book, individuating mental states by the roles that commonsense psychology assigns to them, counts against the extended mind thesis.

At this point, I think the proponent of the extended mind should not be afraid of a little revisionism. Even if commonsense psychology marks a distinction here, the question still arises of whether this is an important distinction that ought to be marked in this way. One can argue, as we do, that Otto's extended state involving the notebook functions in explanation in very much the way that beliefs function in psychological explanation. If so, then it ought to be classified as a belief, whether or not it is so classified by common sense. And it is a familiar philosophical move to argue that if a state shares the most important explanatory features of a belief, then it really is a belief.

Still, this strategy will work only if the involvement of perception and action makes no important difference to the explanatory role of Otto's extended state. And this is not so clear. For at least some explanatory purposes, these things seem to make a difference. After all, one can ask a crucial question: why did Otto reach for his notebook? This seems to be a perfectly good psychological question about the explanation of action. And the natural answer is: he wanted to get to the museum, he did not know its location, and he believed that the notebook contained the information. In this explanatory structure, we speak naturally as if Otto lacked the extended belief. On the other hand, for many other explanatory purposes, the mediating role of perception and action seems quite unimportant. We can ask why Otto walked north and explain this in terms of his extended standing belief about the museum's location, in just the same way that we explain Inga's movements in terms of her beliefs.

I take the moral here to be that the classification of states can depend on our explanatory purposes. When we are interested in explaining Otto's large-scale behavior, it is natural to say that his beliefs are extended, with his interactions with his notebook serving as a sort of uninteresting background constant. When we are interested in explaining Otto's local-scale interactions with his notebook, it is natural to deny that he has the extended belief and to hold that the relevant actions are explained by internal beliefs. As Clark suggests in his concluding chapter, we can flip back and forth between both ways of looking at things. We have a sort of Necker Cube effect, with mental states counting as extended or not depending on our perspective and our purposes.

As this Necker Cube flips, various things flip along with it. Otto's access to the notebook flips from an act of perception to an act of memory retrieval. His writing in the notebook flips from a physical action to a mental action. We might thus flip from regarding Otto's cognitive system as local to regarding it as extended, and we might even flip our perspective on Otto himself in a similar way. And importantly, Otto's state before opening the notebook flips from ignorance to knowledge.

This duality of perspectives can naturally be accommodated in various stories about the way mental terms like "believe" and "know" function. One such story holds that that ascriptions such as "Otto believes that the museum is on 53rd Street" are sensitive to contextual factors including explanatory purposes. In a context where one is explaining Otto's travels, the ascription is true. In a context where one is explaining his interactions with his notebook, the ascription is false. One can find a similar dependence on explanatory purposes in nonextended cases. Say that someone has to think for a moment before responding that 7 times 8 is 56. If we ask why they hesitated, we might reasonably say that they did not know the answer and had to think about it. But if we are asked why they got all the questions right, we might say that it is because they knew all the values in the multiplication table.

Other semantic stories are possible. One could give an account where the extended belief and knowledge ascriptions are always true, and when we say that Otto reached for his notebook because he did not know the address, we say something that is useful but strictly speaking false. One could also give an account where the extended belief and knowledge ascriptions are always false, so that our explanation of Otto's actions in terms of extended beliefs are at best metaphorically true. Or one could suggest that the reference of terms like "belief" is indeterminate between the two notions. If so, then the original extended belief ascriptions may be neither true nor false, but there will be precisified versions that fall on each side.

Ultimately, however, I think that issues about what really counts as a belief and about how the term "belief" functions are terminological questions that, while interesting, can mask the deeper point. If someone insists that they use the term "believe" in such a way that it picks out states realized in the space between perception and action, then one can allow them to use the term this way if they like. The deeper point is that extended states can function in explanation in very much the same way that beliefs function, and they should be regarded as sharing a deep and important explanatory kind with beliefs. This explanatory unification is the real underlying point of the extended mind thesis.

In "The Extended Mind," the only extended elements of the mind that we argued for were beliefs and cognitive processes: in particular standing beliefs (like Inga's belief about the museum's location), and cognitive processes such as mental rotation. It is natural to ask whether the extended mind thesis might itself be extended. What about extended desires, extended reasoning, extended perception, extended imagination, and extended emotions? I think that there is something to be said for each of these. Perhaps the camera on my iPhone can serve as an extended perceptual mechanism. And perhaps one might have something akin to an extended mood, if not an extended emotion, when one's environment is always nudging one toward happiness or sadness. Clark discusses many such cases throughout the book, including extended perceptual mechanisms in chapter 2 and extended mechanisms of attention in chapter 3.

But then, what about the big question: extended consciousness? The dispositional beliefs, cognitive processes, perceptual mechanisms, and moods considered above all extend beyond the borders of consciousness, and it is plausible that it is precisely the nonconscious part of them that is extended. I think there is no principled reason why the physical basis of consciousness could not be extended in a similar way. It is probably so extended in some possible worlds: one could imagine that some of the neural correlates of consciousness are replaced by a module on one's belt, for example. There may even be worlds where what is perceived in the environment is itself a direct element of consciousness: my paper "Perception and the Fall from Eden" tells a fable about one such world.

Still, I think it is unlikely that any everyday process akin to Otto's interaction with his notebook will yield extended consciousness, at least in our world. Certainly, relatives of the Otto/Inga argument do not seem to extend to consciousness. The original argument crucially yields a twin case, involving Otto and Twin Otto, who are physical duplicates with different beliefs. An argument for extended consciousness would require twins with different states of consciousness: Olga and Twin Olga are internal duplicates, but what it is like to be Olga differs from what it is like to be Twin Olga. But no matter how hard one tries to construct an Otto-style story that works like this, the story does not seem to succeed. Perhaps part of the reason is that the physical basis of consciousness requires direct access to information on an extremely high bandwidth. Perhaps some future extended system, with high-bandwidth sensitivity to environmental information, might be able to do the job. But our low-bandwidth conscious connection to the environment seems to have the wrong form as it stands.

In recent years, a few philosophers have argued that the basis of conscious states lies partly outside the head. Some of these arguments, such as those of Dretske (1996), Fisher (2007), and Martin (2004), turn on considerations quite different from the sort of two-way coupling between organism and environment that is at the heart of the extended mind thesis. The resulting views are interesting and challenging, but they are largely independent of the active externalism of the extended mind thesis. Others, including Hurley (1998) and Noë (2006), have argued that the two-way coupling extends to consciousness. But these arguments do not seem to yield a twin case of the sort discussed above, so they do not rule out the supervenience of consciousness on the internal. At best, as Clark suggests in chapter 8, they yield a weaker sort of dependence of consciousness on the environment. I tentatively conclude that the extension of the mind is compatible with retaining an internal conscious core.

What general picture of the mind does the extended mind thesis rest on? It has sometimes been suggested that the thesis requires functionalism about the mental, where all mental states are defined by the causal roles that they play. This cannot be quite right: I think that functionalism about consciousness is implausible, for example, but this implausibility does not affect the arguments for the extended mind thesis. One might support the view by invoking an attenuated functionalism: say, one where certain mental states (such as dispositional beliefs) are defined by their causal relations to conscious states, to behavior, and to other elements of the cognitive network. I find such a picture attractive myself, but strictly speaking even this picture is not required for all the argument to go through. All one needs is the very weak functionalism captured in the Parity Principle: roughly, if a state plays the same causal role in the cognitive network as a mental state, then there is a presumption of mentality, one that can only be defeated by displaying a relevant difference between the two (and not merely the brute difference between inner and outer). Combined with the observation that there are no relevant differences in the relevant cases—an observation that does not require functionalism for its support—the thesis follows.

Likewise, the extended mind thesis is compatible with both physicalism and dualism about the mental. It is compatible with connectionist and classical views, with computational and noncomputational approaches, and even with internalism and externalism in the traditional debates over mental content (as we suggest in "The Extended Mind"). So I do not think that the extended mind thesis requires much in the way of theoretical presupposition at all. Instead, it is an independently attractive view of the mental.

Ultimately, the proof is in the pudding. The deepest support for the view comes from the explanatory insights that the extended mind perspective yields. And those insights are just what this book provides. In case after case, in domain after domain, Andy Clark brings out the many ways in which the extended view of the mind can productively reconfigure our thinking about the relationship between mind and world. After absorbing this picture, nothing will ever look quite the same way again. And if Clark is right, then the absorption has already started. Just opening his book may have turned you into a smarter, deeper, and more insightful person.

Canberra, November 2007

Acknowledgments

I owe a sincere debt of thanks to those who read and commented on early versions of this work and/or the arguments it presents, especially (though in no particular order) Robert Rupert, Fred Adams, Ken Aizawa, Mike Wheeler, Robert Wilson, Teed Rockwell, Mark Rowlands, Alva Noë, Larry Shapiro, John Sutton, Richard Menary, and Susan Hurley. Susan Hurley passed away in August 2007, during the very final stages of this project. Her enthusiasm, engagement, and critical contributions did much to frame and advance the debate, and I have no words to capture my sense of personal and intellectual loss. Thanks are due to Richard Menary, who organized two wonderful conferences at the University of Hertfordshire, in 2001 and again in 2006, devoted to work on the extended mind. John Sutton brought the topic to two fantastic workshops on memory, mind, and media, held at Sydney in 2004. Shaun Gallagher organized a truly rewarding interdisciplinary conference called Cognition: Embodied, Embedded, Enactive, Extended, held in October 2007 at the University of Central Florida. Thanks to all the speakers and participants at those meetings. Special thanks to David Chalmers, who shares part of the blame for the original extended mind story that lies at the heart of this treatment and who (apart from also writing the splendid foreword) offered invaluable input at all stages of production. Thanks to Robert McIntosh, Tim Bayne, Thomas Schenk, Michael Tye, Matthew

Nudds, Mog Stapleton, Zoe Drayson, Michele Merritt, Julian Kiverstein, and Tillmann Vierkant for stimulating exchanges on (variously or all together) consciousness, technology, and cognitive extension; to all the participants in the Perception, Action, and Consciousness: Sensorimotor Dynamics and Dual Vision conference held at Bristol in July 2007; and to Harry Halpin, Dave Cochran, and all the members of the Edinburgh PPIG (Philosophy, Psychology, and Informatics Reading Group). Thanks to my editor at Oxford University Press, Peter Ohlin, for endless support, encouragement, and patience, and to Christine Dahlin at Oxford University Press for her wonderful help with the illustrations and final copy. Thanks, too, to Joachim Lyon for discussions of the topics and for his invaluable work on the index. I am indebted to Olaf Sporns and Chen Yu for introducing me to work on the self-structuring of information flows. As ever, my greatest intellectual debt is to Daniel Dennett, whose work and views are without a doubt the major, if sometimes subterranean, influence on all that I write. Thanks, too, to Tom Roberts and Dave Ward, whose doctoral work on consciousness and sensorimotor models helped shape and inform the treatments of consciousness and sensorimotor contingency theory. Pierre Steiner provided the quote from Dewey that opens the text, and Harry Halpin the 'mind as mashup' slogan that wraps it up. Extreme and heartfelt thanks are due to Christine Clark and to Pepa (Josefa Toribio). Thanks to Ian Davies, Nigel Davies, Gill Banks, Miguel Toribio, and Lee Swindley for essential doses of play and pleasure. Thanks, too, to Lolo the cat who continued to provide embodied and, often rather snugly, embedded desktop presence.

Some of the material that appears here is based on, or appeared as parts or fragments of, published papers. Thanks to the editors, presses, and copyright holders for permission to reproduce selections and passages from the following pieces:

"Beyond the Flesh: Some Lessons from a Mole Cricket." *Artificial Life* 11 (2005): 233–244.

"Cognitive Complexity and the Sensorimotor Frontier." *Proceedings of the Aristotelian Society*, Supp. Vol. 80 (2006): 43–65.

"Coupling, Constitution and the Cognitive Kind: A Reply to Adams and Aizawa." To appear in R. Menary, ed., *The Extended Mind*. Aldershot, UK: Ashgate.

"Curing Cognitive Hiccups." *Journal of Philosophy* 104, no. 4 (2007): 163–192.

"Material Symbols." *Philosophical Psychology* 19, no. 3 (2006): 1–17.

"Memento's Revenge: The Extended Mind, Re-visited." To appear in R. Menary, ed., *The Extended Mind*. Aldershot, UK: Ashgate.

"Pressing the Flesh: A Tension in the Study of the Embodied, Embedded Mind?" *Philosophy and Phenomenological Research* 76, no. 1 (January 2008): 37–59.

"Re-inventing Ourselves: The Plasticity of Embodiment, Sensing, and Mind." *Journal of Medicine and Philosophy* 32 no. 3 (2007): 263–282.

"Time and Mind." *Journal of Philosophy* 95 no. 7 (1998): 354–376.

Sources of figures are credited in the captions.

The first draft of this book was completed under the AHRC Research Leave Scheme, Award # 130000R39525. Thanks to Edinburgh University for a semester of sabbatical leave directly preceding the period of that award. The final version was completed with invaluable support from the AHRC, under the ESF Eurocores CNCC scheme, for the CONTACT (Consciousness in Interaction) project, AH/E511139/1.

Contents

Introduction: BRAINBOUND Versus EXTENDED

Consider this famous exchange between the Nobel Prize–winning physicist Richard Feynman and the historian Charles Weiner.[1] Weiner, encountering with a historian's glee a batch of Feynman's original notes and sketches, remarked that the materials represented "a record of [Feynman's] day-to-day work." But instead of simply acknowledging this historic value, Feynman reacted with unexpected sharpness:

> "I actually did the work on the paper," he said.
>
> "Well," Weiner said, "the work was done in your head, but the record of it is still here."
>
> "No, it's not a *record*, not really. It's *working*. You have to work on paper and this is the paper. Okay?" (from Gleick 1993, 409)

Feynman's suggestion is, at the very least, that the loop into the external medium was integral to his intellectual activity (the "working") itself. But I would like to go further and suggest that Feynman was actually *thinking* on the paper. The loop through pen and paper is part of the physical machinery responsible for the shape of the flow of thoughts and ideas that we take, nonetheless, to be distinctively those of Richard Feynman. It reliably and robustly provides a functionality which, were it provided by goings-on in the head alone, we would have no hesitation in designating as part of the cognitive circuitry.

Such considerations of parity, once we put our bioprejudices aside, reveal the outward loop as a functional part of an extended cognitive machine. Such body- and world-involving cycles are best understood, or so I shall argue, as quite literally extending the machinery of mind out into the world—as building extended cognitive circuits that are themselves the minimal material bases for important aspects of human thought and reason. Such cycles *supersize* the mind.

Similar intuitions, as we shall later see, can be pumped by appeal to many other aspects of human behavior, such as the role of bodily gesture in the unfolding of thought (chap. 6). If such bodily and extrabodily loops are indeed integral to certain forms of intelligent activity, we need to understand when and why this can be so and just what (if anything) this might mean for our general model of mind, reason, and agency. Do such examples really lend support to the radical "supersized" vision, or are they better accommodated in some much more deflationary way?

Human minds, it can hardly be doubted, are at the very least in deep and critically important contact with human bodies and with the wider world.[2] Human sensing, learning, thought, and feeling are all structured and informed by our body-based interactions with the world around us. Thus, when Esther Thelen,[3] a leading proponent of the embodied perspective, writes that "to say that cognition is embodied means that it arises from bodily interactions with the world," no sensible person is likely to disagree. Clearly, there is more to this than meets the eye. Here is how the quote continues:

> From this point of view, cognition depends on the kinds of experiences that come from having a body with particular perceptual and motor capacities that are inseparably linked and that together form the matrix within which memory, emotion, language, and all other aspects of life are meshed. The contemporary notion of embodied cognition stands in contrast to the prevailing cognitivist stance which sees the mind as a device to manipulate symbols and is thus concerned with the formal rules and processes by which the symbols appropriately represent the world. (2000, 4)

In this much-quoted passage, we begin to glimpse some of the key elements of a more radical view. But even here, there are plenty of claims with which no one is likely to take issue. As active sensors of our world, possessed of bodies with specific shapes and characters, it is relatively unsurprising if what we think, do, and perceive all turn out to be *in some sense* deeply intertwined. Nor is it all that surprising if much of higher cognition turns out to be in some sense *built on* a substrate of embodied perceptuomotor capacities. But the notion of "meshing" that Thelen deploys should give us pause, suggesting as it does a kind of ongoing intermingling of cognitive activity with the perceptuomotor matrix from which it putatively emerges.

Meshing and intermingling are likewise prominent in John Haugeland's benchmark assertion that

> if we are to understand mind as the locus of intelligence, we cannot follow Descartes in regarding it as separable in principle from the body and the world...Broader approaches, freed of that prejudicial commitment, can look again at perception and action, at skillful involvement with public equipment and social organization, and see not principled separation but all sorts of close coupling and functional unity...Mind, therefore, is not incidentally but *intimately* embodied and *intimately* embedded in its world. (1998, 236–237)

What this passage makes clear is that the core claim at issue is not primarily a claim about development and learning. Nor is it about the undoubted role of body and world in fixing the contents of thought or in determining the sequence of thoughts or even in determining what kinds of thing we find it worth thinking about. Rather, what is at issue is something to do with the separability of mind, body, and world, at least for the purposes of understanding mind as the "locus of intelligence." What Haugeland is selling is a radical package deal aimed at undermining a simple, but arguably distortive, model of mind. This is the model of mind as essentially inner and, in our case, always and everywhere neurally realized. It is, to put it bluntly, the model of mind as brain (or perhaps brain and central nervous system): a model increasingly prevalent in a culture where just about everything to do with thinking seems to be accompanied by some kind of image of the brain. Call this model BRAINBOUND.

According to BRAINBOUND, the (nonneural) body is just the sensor and effector system of the brain, and the rest of the world is just the arena in which adaptive problems get posed and in which the brain–body system must sense and act. If BRAINBOUND is correct, then all human cognition depends directly on neural activity alone. The neural activity itself may, of course, in turn depend on worldly inputs and gross bodily activity. But that would be merely what Hurley (1998, 10–11) usefully dubs "instrumental dependence," as when we move our head or eyes and get a new perceptual input as a result. All that really matters as far as the actual mechanisms of human cognition are concerned, BRAINBOUND asserts, is what goes on in the brain.

Maximally opposed to BRAINBOUND is a view according to which thinking and cognizing[4] may (at times) depend directly and noninstrumentally upon the ongoing work of the body and/or the extraorganismic environment. Call this model EXTENDED.[5] According to EXTENDED, the actual local operations that realize certain forms of human cognizing include inextricable tangles of feedback, feed-forward, and feed-around loops: loops that promiscuously criss-cross the boundaries of brain, body, and world. The local mechanisms of mind, if this is correct, are not all in the head. Cognition leaks out into body and world.

That may sound like a strange idea. But it is hardly stranger, I think, than the commonplace idea that the activity of *brain-meat* realizes all that matters about human cognition. In questioning BRAINBOUND, I shall not in any way be questioning the basic materialist vision of mind as emerging fully and without residue from physical goings-on. Any added strangeness flows merely from the fact that some of the relevant goings-on, if EXTENDED is correct, don't stay neatly in the brain. They don't even stay neatly within the biological body. On the contrary, they prove perfectly and productively able to span brain, body, and world. Of course, not all physical goings-on (not even all the physical goings-on that interact, one way or another, with the unfolding activity of our neural and bodily apparatus) are plausibly cast as parts of the machinery of mind. One goal of this book is to ask when and where an extended perspective is indicated and to show what we gain by adopting it.

Another goal is to show that it matters. It matters that we recognize the very large extent to which individual human thought and reason are not activities that occur solely in the brain or even solely within the organismic skin-bag. This matters because it drives home the degree to which environmental engineering is also self-engineering. In building our physical and social worlds, we build (or rather, we massively reconfigure) our minds and our capacities of thought and reason.

It matters, too, for the sciences of the mind. For although both the biological brain and the whole embodied organism each stand as perfectly good, and strategically crucial, units for cognitive scientific investigation, I hope to show that they are not the *only* such units. There is, as we shall see, important science emerging (and much more that remains to be done) that targets hybrid ensembles of neural, bodily, and environmental elements.

In closing, let me say a few words about the structure of this book. The backdrop to this exploration, and the central target of many of the critical engagements we shall consider, is a paper called "The Extended

Mind." The paper was coauthored with David Chalmers and appeared in *Analysis* back in 1998. That piece, which lays out the original (and still the central) arguments in favor of EXTENDED, is reproduced in full as the appendix to this book. Readers unfamiliar with the original paper should probably read the appendix as well as the "executive summary" of those arguments found in chapter 4 (sec. 4.8).

The general structure of the book is as follows. Part I is largely concerned with displaying a variety of empirical considerations and exemplars. These serve to frame, and in some ways lend a kind of indirect support to, an extended perspective. Some of these foreground the role of the active body, and others focus on the role of the local environment, where this includes the role of "material symbols" such as words on the page and speech sounds in the air. Part II then considers a wide range of critical worries and objections concerning the claims about cognitive extension, and it introduces some new arguments, examples, and case studies in response. Part III describes some limitations on the scope of EXTENDED and asks just how it fits into the broader explanatory framework of the sciences of mind.

I

FROM EMBODIMENT TO COGNITIVE EXTENSION

1

The Active Body

1.1   A Walk on the Wild Side

Honda's Asimo (see fig. 1.1) is billed, perhaps rightly, as the world's most advanced humanoid robot. Boasting a daunting 26 degrees of freedom (2 on the neck, 6 on each arm, and 6 on each leg), Asimo is able to navigate the real world, reach, grip, walk reasonably smoothly, climb stairs, and recognize faces and voices. The name Asimo stands (a little clumsily perhaps) for Advanced Step in Innovative Mobility. And certainly, Asimo is an incredible feat of engineering, still relatively short on brainpower but high on mobility and maneuverability.

As a walking robot, however, Asimo is far from energy efficient. For a walking agent, one way to measure energy efficiency is by the so-called specific cost of transport (Tucker 1975)—namely, "the amount of energy required to carry a unit weight a unit distance."[1] The lower the number, the less energy is required to shift a unit of weight a unit of distance. Asimo rumbles in with a specific cost of transport of about 3.2, whereas we humans display a specific metabolic cost of transport of about 0.2. What accounts for this massive difference in energetic expenditure?

Whereas robots like Asimo walk by means of very precise, and energy-intensive, joint-angle control systems, biological walking agents make maximal use of the mass properties and biomechanical couplings

3

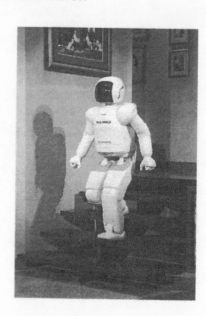

FIGURE 1.1   Honda's Asimo robot.
(http://asimo.honda.com/gallery.aspx;
by permission of Honda Corporation)

present in the overall musculoskeletal system and walking apparatus itself. Wild walkers thus make canny use of so-called passive dynamics, the kinematics and organization inhering in the physical device alone (McGeer 1990). Pure passive-dynamic walkers are simple devices that boast no power source apart from gravity and no control system apart from some simple mechanical linkages such as a mechanical knee and the pairing of inner and outer legs to prevent the device from keeling over sideways. Yet despite (or perhaps because of) this simplicity, such devices are capable, if set on a slight slope, of walking smoothly and with a very realistic gait. The ancestors of these devices are, as Collins, Wisse, and Ruina (2001) nicely document, not sophisticated robots but children's toys, some dating back to the late 19th century. These toys stroll, walk, or waddle down ramps or when pulled by string (see fig. 1.2). Such toys have minimal actuation and no control system. Their walking is a consequence not of complex joint-movement planning and actuating but of basic morphology (the shape of the body, the distribution of linkages and weights of components, etc.). Behind the passive-dynamic approach thus lies the compelling thought that

> locomotion is mostly a natural motion of legged mechanisms, just as swinging is a natural motion of pendulums. Stiff-legged walking toys naturally generate their comical walking motions. This suggests that human-like motions might come naturally to human-like mechanisms. (Collins, Wisse, and Ruina 2001, 608)

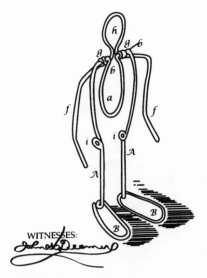

FIGURE 1.2   Fallis's (1888) clever implementation of counterswinging arms. The entire toy is made from two pieces of wire. Each wire makes up a leg, a bearing, an axle, and an arm. One wire also has a head and the other a body of sorts. (S. Collins, M. Wisse and A. Ruina, "A Three-dimensional Passive-dynamic Walking Robot with Two Legs and Knees," *The International Journal of Robotics Research* 20, no. 7 [July 2001]: 607–615, © 2001 Sage Publications, by permission)

Collins, Wisse, and Ruina (2001) built the first such device to mimic humanlike walking by adding curved feet, a compliant heel, and mechanically linked arms to the basic design pioneered by McGeer (1990). In action (see fig. 1.3), the device exhibits good, steady motion and is described by its creators as "pleasing to watch" (McGeer 1990, 613). By contrast, robots that make extensive use of powered operations and joint-angle control tend to suffer from "a kind of rigor mortis [because] joints encumbered by motors and high-reduction gear trains...make joint movement inefficient when the actuators are on and nearly impossible when they are off" (607).

What, then, of powered locomotion? Once the body itself is "equipped" with the right kind of passive dynamics, powered walking can be brought about in a remarkably elegant and energy-efficient way. In essence, the tasks of actuation and control have now been massively reconfigured so that powered, directed locomotion can come about by systematically pushing, damping, and tweaking a system in which passive-dynamic effects still play a major role. The control design is delicately geared to utilize all the natural dynamics of the passive baseline, and the actuation is consequently efficient and fluid.

Some of the core flavor of such a solution is captured by the broader notion of "ecological control,"[2] where an ecological control system is one in which goals are not achieved by micromanaging every detail of the desired action or response but by making the most of robust,

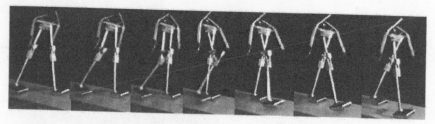

FIGURE 1.3   Pure passive dynamic walker in action. (S. Collins, M. Wisse, and A. Ruina, "A Three-dimensional Passive-dynamic Walking Robot with Two Legs and Knees," *The International Journal of Robotics Research* 20, no. 7 [July 2001]: 607–615, © 2001 Sage Publications, by permission)

reliable sources of relevant order in the bodily or worldly environment of the controller. In such cases,

> part of the "processing" is taken over by the dynamics of the agent-environment interaction, and only sparse neural control needs to be exerted when the self-regulating and stabilizing properties of the natural dynamics can be exploited. (Pfeifer et al. 2006, 7)

A nice example is the use of sparse, well-timed control signals to support the "rolling and rising" motion (see fig. 1.4) of a robot that must raise itself up from a prone position (Kuniyoshi et al. 2004). Another is Iida and Pfeifer's (2004) work on the running robot Puppy. Puppy has springs (roughly mimicking some of the special properties of a muscle-tendon system) connecting the lower and upper parts of each leg, has pressure sensors on each foot, and benefits from just a few built-in powered oscillatory movements. These simple inbuilt oscillatory movements nonetheless lead, in the special context provided by the sprung body, to fluent running and scampering behavior. Even the simple fact that Puppy has aluminum legs and feet plays an "adaptive" role, for it leads to small amounts of slippage on most surf aces. This might seem like a bad thing, but reducing the slippage by adding rubber pads to the feet caused the robot to begin to fall over: The subtle slippage was actually playing a stabilizing role, effectively enabling the robot to rapidly search for a stable way to proceed (see Pfeifer and Bongard 2007, 96–100, 125–128, for discussion).

In subsequent chapters, we shall encounter ecological control style solutions for problems ranging all the way from perceptuomotor

FIGURE 1.4 Sparse but well-timed control signals enable fluent, energy-efficient roll and rise motion. (Work by Kuniyoshi et al. [2004]; figure from Y. Ohmura, by permission)

response to reflection, recall, and deliberation. To capture such effects, Pfeifer and Bongard (2007) invoke the Principle of Ecological Balance.[3] This principle states

> first...that given a certain task environment there has to be a match between the complexities of the agent's sensory, motor, and neural systems...second....that there is a certain balance or task-distribution between morphology, materials, control, and environment. (123)

The "matching" of sensors, morphology, motor system, materials, controller, and ecological niche yields a spread of responsibility for efficient adaptive response in which "not all the processing is performed by the brain, but certain aspects of it are taken over by the morphology, materials, and environment [yielding] a 'balance' or task-distribution between the different aspects of an embodied agent" (see Pfeifer et al. 2006). In such cases, the details of embodiment may take over some of the work that would otherwise need to be done by the brain or the neural network controller, an effect that Pfeifer and Bongard (2007, 100) aptly describe as "morphological computation."

The exploitation of passive-dynamic effects exemplifies one of several key characteristics of the embodied, embedded approach that we will encounter as the chapter progresses. This first characteristic has been called *nontrivial causal spread*. Nontrivial causal spread (see Clark 1998b; Wheeler and Clark 1999; Wheeler 2005) occurs whenever *something we might have expected to be achieved by a certain well-demarcated system turns out to involve the exploitation of more far-flung factors and forces.*[4] For the Mississippi alligator, the temperature of the rotting vegetation in which it lays its eggs determines the sex of its offspring. This is an example of nontrivial causal spread. When the passive dynamics of the actual legs and body take care of many of the demands that we

FIGURE 1.5 The Toddler robot, by Russ Tedrake, Teresa Zhang, and H. Sebastian Seung. The robot learns a control policy that exploits the passive dynamics of its own body. (Photo by Teresa Zhang, by permission)

might otherwise have ceded to an energy-hungry joint-angle control system, we likewise encounter nontrivial causal spread. One of the big lessons of contemporary robotics is that the coevolution of morphology (which can include sensor placement, body plan, and even the choice of basic building materials, etc.) and control yields a truly golden opportunity to spread the problem-solving load between brain, body, and world.[5] Robotics thus rediscovers many ideas explicit in the continuing tradition of J. J. Gibson and of "ecological psychology."[6] Thus, William Warren, commenting on a quote from Gibson (1979), suggests that

> biology capitalizes on the regularities of the entire system as a means of ordering behavior. Specifically, the structure and physics of the environment, the biomechanics of the body, perceptual information about the state of the agent-environment system, and the demands of the task all serve to constrain the behavioral outcome. (2006, 358)

Such causal spread may be wholly evolved or engineered, wholly learned, or some combination of the two. For example, some control systems are able to actively learn strategies that make the most of passive-dynamic opportunities. An example is the Toddler robot, a walking robot that learns (using so-called actor-critic reinforcement learning) a control policy that exploits the passive dynamics of the body (fig. 1.5). The Toddler robot, which features among the pack of passive-dynamics-based robots described in Collins et al. (2005), can learn to change speeds, go forward and backward, and adapt on the go to different terrains, including bricks, wooden tiles, carpet, and even a variable speed treadmill. And as you'd expect, the use of passive dynamics cuts power consumption to about one-tenth that of a standard robot like Asimo. The passive-dynamics-based robot described in Collins and Ruina (2005) similarly achieved a specific cost of transport of around 0.20, again around an order of magnitude lower than Asimo and quite comparable to the human case. The discrepancy here is thought not to be significantly reducible by further technological advance using Asimo-style control strategies (i.e., ones that do not exploit passive-dynamic effects). An apt comparison, Collins and Ruina suggest, is with the energy consumption of a helicopter versus airplane or glider. The helicopter, however well designed it may be, will still consume vastly more energy per unit distance traveled.

1.2   Inhabited Interaction

Let's switch gears, briefly, to ask what it might be like to be an agent embodied according to these very different sets of principles. What would it feel like to be an intelligent, conscious version of Asimo and, contrariwise, to be an intelligent, conscious version of a fully trained Toddler robot? In the latter case, might it not feel (all other things being equal) as if, with little effort and a simple act of will, directed bodily motion is achieved? In the former, the efforts are large and the body may perhaps be encountered as a complex, resistant object in need of much ongoing energetic micromanagement. Over time, per-haps, control can be streamlined, though energy consumption (as in the case of the helicopter) will still remain high. Nonetheless, the suc-cessful exploitation of passive-dynamic effects may well be a major contributing element to what Dourish (2001) nicely calls "inhabited interaction," a way of being in the world that is contrasted with "dis-connected control." Here is how Dourish describes the difference, using present-day (i.e., still fairly clunky) virtual-reality systems as a point of comparison:

> Even in an immersive virtual-reality environment, users are disconnected observers of a world they do not inhabit directly. They peer out at it, figure out what's going on, decide on some course of action, and enact it through the narrow interface of the keyboard or the data-glove, carefully monitoring the result to see if it turns out the way they expected. Our experience in the everyday world is not of that sort. There is no homunculus sitting inside our heads, staring out at the world through our eyes, enacting some plan of action by manipulating our hands,

and checking carefully to make sure we don't overshoot when reaching for the coffee cup. We inhabit our bodies and they in turn inhabit the world, with seamless connections back and forth. (2001, 102)

It seems unlikely that immersive virtual reality (VR) is *by its very nature* disconnected in this sense. Rather, it is just one more domain in which a skilled agent may act and perceive. But skill matters, and most of us are as yet unskilled in such situations. Moreover, the modes of sensing and interaction supported by current technologies often remain limited and clumsy, and this turns the user experience into that of a kind of alert game player rather than that of an agent genuinely located *inside* the virtual world.

It is worth noticing, however, that to the young human infant, the physical body itself may often share some of this problematic character. The infant, like the VR-exploring adult, must learn how to use initially unresponsive hands, arms, and legs to obtain its goals (for some detailed studies, see Thelen and Smith 1994). In so doing, the infant, like the Toddler robot, learns to make the most of the complex evolved morphology and passive dynamics of its own body. These have been selected so as to dramatically reduce the "gap" that needs to be bridged by the addition of energy and the imposition of control.

With time and practice, enough bodily fluency is achieved to make the wider world itself directly available as a kind of unmediated arena for embodied action. At this point, the extrabodily world becomes poised to present itself to the user not just as a problem space (though it is clearly that) but also as a problem-solving resource. For (as we'll see in more detail in chap. 2–4) the world, especially when encountered via inhabited interaction, is a place in which we can act fluently in ways that simplify or transform the problems that we want to solve. At such moments, the body has become "transparent equipment" (Heidegger 1927/1961): equipment (the classic example is the hammer in the hands of the skilled carpenter) that is not the focus of attention in use. Instead, the user "sees through" the equipment to the task in hand. When you sign your name, the pen is not normally your focus (unless it is out of ink etc.). The pen in use is no more the focus of your attention than is the hand that grips it. Both are transparent equipment.[7]

Doubtless, transparency of this kind may be achieved, with practice, without the large-scale exploitation of passive-dynamic effects.[8] But one way in which evolved agents truly inhabit, rather than simply

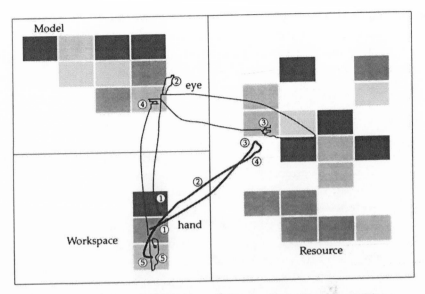

FIGURE 1.6 Copying a single block within the task. The eye-position trace is shown by the cross and the dotted line. The cursor trace is shown by the arrow and the dark line. The numbers indicate corresponding points in time for the eye and hand traces. (From Ballard et al. 2001, by permission)

control, their bodies may be usefully understood in terms of a pro-found fit between morphology and control. The kind of fit is exhib-ited by the wild walking systems devised by biological evolution and, in compelling microcosm, by autonomous, passive-dynamics-based walking robots.

1.3 Active Sensing

Suppose you were asked to solve the puzzle shown in figure 1.6. In this task (Ballard et al. 1997), you are given a model pattern of colored blocks that you are asked to copy by moving similar blocks from a reserve area to a new workspace. Using the spare blocks in the reserve area, your task is to re-create the pattern by moving one block at a time from the reserve to the new version you are busy creating. The task is performed using mouse clicks and drags on a computer screen. As you perform, eye-tracker technology is monitoring exactly where and when you are looking at different bits of the puzzle.

What problem-solving strategy do you think you would use? One neat strategy might be to look at the target, decide on the color and position of the next block to be added, and then execute the plan by moving a block from the reserve area. This is, for example, pretty much the kind of strategy you'd expect of a classical artificial intelligence planning system (e.g., STRIPS—the Stanford Research Institute Problem Solver) as used by the early mobile robot Shakey; see Nilsson (1984) for a thorough retrospective review.

When asked how we would solve the problem, many of us pay lip service to this neat and simple strategy. But the lips tell one story while the hands and eyes tell another. For this is emphatically not the strategy used by most human subjects. What Ballard et al. found was that repeated rapid saccades (spontaneous scanning eye movements) to the model were used in the performance of the task, and many more than you might expect. For example, the model is consulted *both before and after* picking up a block, suggesting that when glancing at the model, the subject stores only one piece of information: either the color or the position of the next block to be copied.

To test this hypothesis, Ballard et al. used a computer program to alter the color of a block while the subject was looking elsewhere. For most of these interventions, subjects did not notice the changes even for blocks and locations that had been visited many times before or that were the focus of the current action. This confirmed that when glancing at the model, the subject stores only one piece of information: either the color or the position of the next block to be copied (not both). In other words, even when repeated saccades are made to the same site, very minimal information is retained. Instead, repeated fixations provide specific items of information "just in time" for use. The experimenters conclude that

> in the block-copying paradigm…fixation appears to be tightly linked to the underlying processes by marking the location at which information (e.g., color, relative location) is to be acquired, or the location that specifies the target of the hand movement (picking up, putting down). Thus fixation can be seen as binding the value of the variable currently relevant for the task. (Ballard et al. 1997, 734)

Two morals matter for the story at hand. The first is that visual fixation is here playing an identifiable computational role. As Ballard et al. (1997) comment, "Changing gaze is analogous to changing the memory reference in a silicon computer" (725). (These uses of fixation are thus described using the term "deictic pointers.") The second is that repeated saccades to the physical model thus allow the subject to deploy what Ballard et al. dub "minimal memory strategies" to solve the problem. The idea is that the brain creates its programs so as to minimize the amount of working memory that is required and that eye motions are here recruited to place a new piece of information into memory. Indeed, by altering the task demands, Ballard et al. were also able to systematically alter the particular mixes of biological memory and active, embodied retrieval recruited to solve different versions of the problem. They conclude that, in this kind of task at least, "eye movements, head movements, and memory load trade off against each other in a flexible way" (732).

This is our first example of another important characteristic of embodied, embedded cognition, one that may be called the Principle of Ecological Assembly (PEA). According to the PEA, *the canny cognizer tends to recruit, on the spot, whatever mix of problem-solving resources will yield an acceptable result with a minimum of effort*. The PEA deliberately echoes Pfeifer and Scheier's Principle of Ecological Balance (see sec. 1.1). Pfeifer and Scheier are, however, most interested in the slowly evolved match among sensory, motor, and neural capabilities and hence between the organismic bundle and its ecological niche. The PEA, by contrast, tracks a kind of near-instantaneous version of such overall balance: the balanced use of a set of potentially highly heterogeneous resources assembled on the spot to solve a given problem. Ecological balance of this latter kind is what a flexible ecological control system seeks to achieve (sec. 1.1).

It is important that, according to the PEA, the recruitment process marks no special distinction among neural, bodily, and environmental resources except insofar as these somehow affect the total effort involved. Though the principle itself seems obvious enough, it is actually far from obvious how best to unpack the notion of effort so as to make sense of the idea of trading off one kind of effort (e.g., recall from biological memory) against another very different kind of effort, such as the production of a head or eye motion that (let's assume) retrieves the very same information. As our discussion progresses, we will encounter various attempts (see especially chap. 7 and 9) to make quantitative sense of this important but elusive notion of trade-offs among multiple heterogeneous sources of information and order.

1.4   Distributed Functional Decomposition

The Ballard et al. model is also our first example of an explanatory strategy that may usefully be called *distributed functional decomposition* (DFD). Distributed functional decomposition is a way of understanding the capacities of supersized mechanisms (ones created by the interactions of biological brains with bodies and aspects of the local environment) in terms of the flow and transformation of energy, information, control, and where applicable, representations.[9] The use of the term *functional* in distributed functional decomposition is meant to remind us that even in these larger systems, it is the *roles* played by various elements, and not the specific ways those elements are realized, that do the explanatory work. (This should not be contentious: Even in the case of Puppy's aluminum legs, it is not the material itself that matters as much as the slippage and give that it provides; sec. 1.1.) The goal, familiar enough from traditional internalist approaches, is thus to display some target performance as the outcome of an interacting multitude of unintelligent ("mechanical") interactions and effects but to do so relative to a larger organizational whole. (Imagine, to take a maximally simple case, an algorithm for addition that uses the agent's actual finger positions as a temporary storage buffer for key intermediate results.) Such approaches recognize the important contributions that embodiment and environmental embedding can make to the solution of a problem and then seek to understand those contributions by identifying the role of specific operations (perhaps some gross bodily, some environment involving, and some neural) in real-time performance of the task.

Ballard et al. explicitly recognize this element in their approach, commenting that their model "strongly suggests a functional view of visual computation where different operations are applied at different stages during a complex task" (1997, 735). As a result, a Ballard-style approach is able

> to combine the concept that looking is a form of doing with the claim that vision is computation [integrating the two points by] introducing the idea that eye movements constitute a form of deictic coding...that allow perceivers to exploit the world as a kind of external storage device. (Wilson 2004, 176–177)

Bodily actions here appear as among the means by which certain (in this case, quite familiar) computational and representational operations are implemented. The difference is just that the operations are realized not in the neural system alone but in the whole embodied system located in the world.

Ballard et al. (1997) suggest using the term "the embodiment level" to indicate the level at which functionally critical operations occur at timescales of around one-third second. This corresponds, nonaccidentally, to the observed frequency of saccades and is, the authors claim, the timescale at which "the natural sequentiality of body movements can be matched to the natural computational economies of sequential decision systems through a system of implicit reference (called *deictic*) in which pointing movements are used to bind objects in the world to cognitive programs" (723). Although this time frame is doubtlessly important, especially for the specific kinds of tasks the authors investigate, I here avoid the identification of (what's computationally crucial about) embodiment with any specific temporal or spatial window. As we shall see later in the text, body and world play varied and crucial roles at many (often interacting) timescales.

1.5   Sensing for Coupling

Finally, it is worth pausing to reflect on the role of sensing in the Ballard et al. block-copying scenario. For sensing here plays an importantly different role to the one associated with classical planning and reasoning. In the classical model, the role of sensing is to get as much information into the system as is needed to solve the problem. For example, a planning agent might scan the environment to build up a problem-sufficient model of what's out there and where it is located, at which point the reasoning engine can effectively throw away the world and operate instead upon the inner model, planning and then executing a response (perhaps checking now and then during execution to be sure that nothing has changed). In the block-copying scenario, by contrast, the agent does not use sensing to build up a rich inner model sufficient to solve the problem. Rather, sensing is used repeatedly, with the external scene functioning as an information store to be called upon just in time for the task fragment at hand. During all this, the external, screen-based model acts as "its own best model" (to adapt the famous usage from roboticist Rodney Brooks; see, e.g., Brooks 1991). Sensing here acts as a constantly available channel that productively couples agent and environment rather than as a kind of "veil of transduction" whereby world-originating signals must be converted into a persisting inner model of the external scene.

For an even more dramatic illustration of this possibility, consider the now-classic example of running to catch a fly ball in baseball. Giving perception its standard role, we might assume that the job of the visual system is to transduce information about the current position of the ball so as to allow a reasoning system to project its future trajectory. Here, too, however, nature looks to have found a more elegant and efficient solution: You simply run so that the optical image of the ball appears to present a straight-line constant speed trajectory against the visual background (McBeath, Shaffer, and Kaiser 1995). This solution (the so-called LOT, for Linear Optical Trajectory, model) exploits a powerful invariant in the optic flow, discussed in Lee and Reddish (1981). There is, however, now some debate concerning the precise nature of the simple invariant we lock onto in solving this kind of problem.[10] Thus, McLeod, Reed, and Dienes (2001, 2002) reported data that conflict with the predictions of the simple LOT model and that seem better predicted by an Optical Acceleration Cancellation (OAC) model first suggested by Chapman (1968). Shaffer et al. (2003) offer a mixed model combining uses of both strategies. For present purposes, however, the point is simply that the canny use of data available in the optic flow enables the catcher to sidestep the need to create a rich inner model to calculate the forward trajectory of the ball. In more recent work, multiple uses of the LOT approach seem to offer a better account of how dogs catch Frisbees, a more demanding task due to occasional dramatic fluctuations in the flight path (see Shaffer et al. 2004).

Important for present purposes, such strategies suggest (see also Maturana 1980) a very different role for the perceptual coupling itself. Instead of using sensing to get enough information inside, past the visual bottleneck, so as to allow the reasoning system to "throw away the world" and solve the problem wholly internally, they use the sensor as *an open conduit allowing environmental magnitudes to exert a constant influence on behavior.* Sensing is here depicted as the opening of a channel, with successful whole-system behavior emerging when activity in this channel is kept within a certain range. What is created is thus a kind of new, task-specific agent-world circuit. In such cases, as Randall Beer puts it, "the focus shifts from accurately representing an environment to continuously engaging that environment with a body so as to stabilize appropriate co-ordinated patterns of behavior" (2000, 97).

Interestingly, human subjects are typically unaware of their own deployment of such strategies. Shaffer and McBeath (2005) show that most people, including expert baseball fielders, think that they accurately perceive where the ball is located in physical space at each point in the unfolding trajectory, whereas the strategy actually used is unable, under most conditions, to reveal accurate ball-position information of this kind. That is, "observers seem to confuse or substitute their reasonably accurate semantic knowledge of the physical flight of the ball with the information that is optically available during projectile tracking tasks" (Shaffer and McBeath 2005, 1500).

Summing up the present section, we seem to confront what is really a whole spectrum of cases, ranging from the *classical extreme* (the use of perception to create a rich inner model sufficient to solve the problem) to many intermediate cases (e.g., the blocks-copying task where perception and ongoing bodily engagement are used repeatedly to retrieve and bind fragments of information just in time for use) to the (subjectively unobvious) *nonclassical extreme* (where perception opens a channel such that minimizing energetic variation within some fixed range can directly solve a problem). A third (partially overlapping) characteristic of embodied cognition can thus be added to our list: *The embodied agent is empowered to use active sensing and perceptual coupling in ways that simplify neural problem solving by making the most of environmental opportunities and information freely available in the optic array.*

1.6   Information Self-structuring

Embodied agents are also able to act on their worlds in ways that actively generate cognitively and computationally potent time-locked patterns of sensory stimulation. In this vein, Fitzpatrick et al. (2003; see also Metta and Fitzpatrick 2003), using both the COG and BABYBOT (fig. 1.7) platforms, show how active object manipulation (pushing and touching objects in view) can help generate information about object boundaries. The robot learns about the boundaries by poking and shoving. It uses motion detection to see its own hand–arm moving, but when the hand encounters and pushes an object, there is a sudden spread of motion activity. This cheap signature picks out the object from the rest of the environment.

In human infants, grasping, poking, pulling, sucking, and shoving create a rich flow of time-locked *multimodal* sensory stimulation. Such multimodal input streams have been shown (Lungarella, Sporns, and Kuniyoshi 2008; Lungarella and Sporns 2005) to aid category learning and concept formation. The key to such capabilities is the robot's or infant's capacity to maintain coordinated sensorimotor engagement with its environment. Self-generated motor activity, such work suggests, acts as a "complement to neural information-processing" in that

> the agent's control architecture (e.g. nervous system) attends to and processes streams of sensory stimulation, and ultimately generates sequences of motor actions which in turn guide the further production and selection of sensory information. [In this way] "information structuring" by motor activity and "information processing" by the neural system are continuously

FIGURE 1.7 BABYBOT learns about object properties and affordances by poking and shoving. (From Metta and Fitzpatrick 2003, by permission)

linked to each other through sensorimotor loops. (Lungarella and Sporns 2005, 25)

An important implication of this focus on the active self-structuring of information flows is that timing (and especially, the time-locked unfolding of multimodal data streams) plays a major functional role in supporting learning and adaptive response. In work implemented on the famous COG robot (Brooks et al. 1999), Fitzpatrick and Arsenio (2004) show that the cross-modal binding of incoming signals that display common rhythmic signatures can aid a robot in learning about objects and, by including proprioception as a modality, about the nature of its own body. The robot first detects rhythmic patterns in the individual modalities (sight, hearing, and proprioception) and then deploys a binding algorithm to associate signals that display the same kind of periodicity. Courtesy of such bindings, COG can learn about its own body parts by binding visual, auditory, and proprioceptive signals. COG's arm is noisy in action, unlike our own, so when a human grabs and moves the robot's arm out of its field of vision it can bind sound and proprioceptive information. With the arm in view binding occurs across three modalities. Thus equipped, COG can even learn to identify

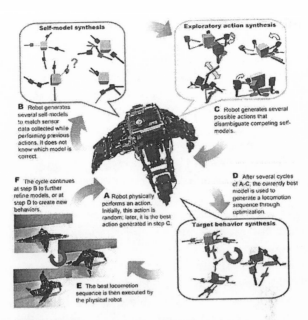

FIGURE 1.8   Outline of the algorithm. (From Josh Bongard, by permission)

its own arm with the moving image seen in a mirror. Summarizing this work, the authors write that

> our work is an attempt to build a perceptual system which, from the ground up, focuses on timing just as much as content. This is powerful because timing is truly cross-modal, and leaves its mark on all the robot's senses no matter how they are processed and transformed. (Fitzpatrick and Arsenio 2004, 65)

Here, then, is a nice example of an approach that combines a bedrock computational and information-processing perspective with a potent functional role for timing and environmentally coupled action. We will meet this combination repeatedly in the chapters that follow. Such work depicts intelligent response as grounded in processes of information extraction, transformation, and use, while recognizing the key roles, *in those very processes*, played by timing, action, and coupled unfolding.

Information self-structuring may also play a key role in continuous self-modeling of the kind necessary to regain behavioral competence following bodily injury or change. Bongard, Zykov, and Lipson (2006) describe an algorithm (fig. 1.8) by which a robot continuously learns about its own bodily structure (morphology) by the ongoing generation of competing internal models that are tested by self-generated actions. In brief, as the robot acts, it records the resulting sensory data and then generates a set (15, in the test case of a four-legged physical robot) of candidate models of its own morphology—models that would be broadly consistent with those data. It next (and this is the important part) finds an action (actuation pattern) that, when executed, will yield the greatest disagreement across the projected sensory consequences of the 15 candidate models. It then performs this action as part of an iterated cycle in which the robot learns about the possibly changing nature of its own body—for example, adapting to damage such as the loss of a limb or change such as the grasping of a tool (for more on this, see chap. 2). The key element in this process is, of course, the robot's ability to actively produce the kinds of action that will yield the greatest information: a clear case of information self-structuring.

Finally, the active structuring of an information flow is also a potent *between-agent* tool, as demonstrated in striking studies by Yu, Ballard, and Aslin (2005). In these studies, a subject, fitted with eye tracker, head-mounted camera, microphone, and hand and body trackers describes, as if to a child (slowly, with clear enunciations) their current actions (see fig. 1.9). The verbal descriptions, along with the time-locked stream of multimodal training data recorded by the eye, head, hand, and body trackers, are fed to an artificial neural network. The task of the network is to learn visually grounded "meanings" for words for some actions solely by exposure to the time-locked stream of multimodal training data created by the active "caregiver." In the presence of this critical active structuring, the net can learn image–sound associations using "raw" visual and auditory data (an unsegmented sound stream and an un-preprocessed video stream) and without the benefit of any inbuilt "language model." The demonstration is compelling to watch as, from this raw but correlated data, the net learns generalizable image–sound pairings (e.g., it learns to produce phonetic strings such as "sta-pling" when shown new video recordings of the same action type). The net has simultaneously learned speech segmentation into meaningful units and "visually grounded meanings" for the units themselves. Key to this success is the information carried by the caregivers "embodied intentions"—that is, their use of eye and body movement to track and isolate salient aspects of the scene (the ones currently being verbally described) from the mass of co-occurring visual data. The added informational punch created by this active structuring of the training data transforms a daunting learning problem into one that is visibly tractable without massive prestructuring or much in the way of prior knowledge.

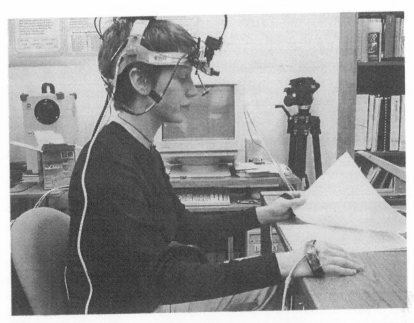

FIGURE 1.9   The associate training the computational model is wearing ASL eye tracker, CCD camera, microphone, and position sensors. The computational model thus shares multisensory information like a human language learner. This allows the association of coincident signals in different modalities. (From Yu, Ballard, and Aslin 2005, by permission)

In many ways, this is simply the flip side of the work on deictic pointing discussed in the previous section. Deictic pointing allows an agent to exploit the world as external storage. This work allows the learner to exploit another agent's use of deictic pointers (by tracking those very same eye fixations) as a kind of "gating mechanism that determines whether co-occurring data are relevant or not" (Yu, Ballard, and Aslin 2005, 994). As a result, social knowledge transmission is here supported by the very same kinds of embodied strategy (deictic uses of eye, head and body motions, and the active generation of time-locked data flows) that allow the individual learner to simplify her own problem solving and to learn about the world.

Here, then, is another way embodiment seems to matter to human cognition. It matters because *the presence of an active, self-controlled, sensing body allows an agent to create or elicit appropriate inputs, generating good data (for oneself and for others) by actively conjuring flows of multimodal, correlated, time-locked stimulation.* This trick promotes learning, bodily self-modeling, and categorization and may even (deep breath) hold out hope for grounded knowledge acquisition.

1.7   Perceptual Experience and Sensorimotor Dependencies

The appeal to action and to active sensing also lies at the heart of a recent, ambitious, and highly influential attempt to give an account of perception and of perceptual experience that centers upon what the agent (implicitly) knows about how sensory stimulation will vary as a result of change or movement.[11] This is in terms of our (implicit, nonconscious) knowledge or expectations concerning the many complex ways perceptual stimulations will morph and alter as we move our eyes, heads, and bodies. Such knowledge is dubbed (O'Regan and Noë 2001) "knowledge of sensorimotor dependencies" or of "sensorimotor contingencies": It is knowledge of the relations between movement or change and resulting patterns of sensory stimulation.

Though superficially similar, this story about perception and perceptual experience goes (as we shall see in much more detail in chap. 8) well beyond the claims made by Ballard et al. (1997) or by most other proponents of so-called active perception (e.g., Churchland, Ramachandran, and Sejnowski 1994). For where the latter depict the active use of bodily motion and just-in-time retrieval as ploys that productively reconfigure the tasks to be performed by the brain and central nervous system, Noë (along with Hurley in press, and others) depicts the sensorimotor-expectation laden cycles as strongly constitutive of the perceptual experiences themselves. By strongly constitutive, I mean they assert a kind of identity such that sameness of active bodies of sensorimotor knowledge (knowledge of sensorimotor dependencies) is required for sameness of perceptual experience.

The central claim is thus that differences in what we perceptually experience correspond to differences in sensorimotor signatures (patterns of association between movements and the sensory effects of movement). If two things look different, they do so because, as we engage them in space and time, we bring to bear (rightly or wrongly) different sets of sensorimotor expectations. As our encounter proceeds, these expectations may or may not be validated. Crucially, it is this whole cycle of (implicit) expecting and subsequent sensory stimulation that is said to determine the content and character of any given perceptual experience. The expectations we have must differ as between, for example, a soccer ball and a rugby ball or an American football. Such differences underwrite the difference in experienced look. But despite such differences, for all *visually* presented objects, there will be some parts of the sensorimotor signatures in common. It is these commonalities that are said to make the experiences visual rather than, say, auditory. For example, vision (unlike audition or touch) only samples the front or facing sides of objects and so on. The visual attributes of sensed objects are thus that subset of the signature sensorimotor contingencies that pertain to the distinctive ways that the visual sense can sample the real properties of objects. Thus, the very same real property (e.g., size) may be apprehended by vision or sometimes (for small objects) by touch. But the mode of sampling varies dramatically and with it the associated sensorimotor contingencies.

To visually perceive a square object, then, is to bring to bear a body of diverse practical knowledge concerning how movement of the eyes, head, or body would produce sensory change (new sensory inputs) as we inspect or interact with the object. An example is the way a leftward saccade would bring a certain (left-facing) shape of corner into central vision, while a rightward saccade would bring a different (right-facing) shape of corner into central vision. A rich body of such knowledge is said to constitute our visual perception of the square object. One upshot of all this, or so it is claimed, is that "what determines phenomenology is not neural activity set up by stimulation as such, but the way the neural activity is embedded in a sensorimotor dynamic" (Noë 2004, 227). For it is arguably the shape of a whole batch of sensorimotor loops that now determines the nature of the visual experience.

We can now formulate the next feature of recent work that I want to highlight: *attention to the possibility that the substrate (the "vehicles") of specific perceptual experiences may involve whole cycles of world-engaging activity.*

1.8   Time and Mind

Approaches that foreground embodiment, active sensing, and temporally coupled unfoldings are sometimes rather starkly contrasted with (any or all of) functional, computational, information-processing, and information-theoretic approaches to the study of mind and cognition.[12] The proper explanatory tools, when confronted with apparently intrinsically embodied and richly temporal phenomena, are instead said to be the geometric constructs and differential equations of Dynamical Systems Theory (DST). This polarization (among dynamical and computational and information-theoretic approaches) is, I think, one of the less happy fruits of recent attempts to put brain, body, and world together again. I shall largely refrain (but see chap. 9) in the treatment that follows from re-rehearsing my rather liberal views on the notions of representation, computation, and dynamical explanation. These views are quite well represented in previous work (especially Clark 1997a, 1997b, and 2001a). Instead, in a more positive vein, the various demonstrations, examples, and thought experiments that populate this book aim to reveal *computational, representational, information-theoretic, and dynamical approaches as deeply complementary elements in a mature science of the mind*. This emerging complementarity is the final feature of recent work that I want to highlight. But to very briefly motivate this more accommodating perspective, it may be worth just pausing to say a few words concerning time, dynamics, and computation (for a much more detailed treatment of these issues, see Clark 1997b).

One challenge that temporal considerations seem to pose to traditional forms of explanation and analysis is to account for cases of what I elsewhere (Clark 1997b) term continuous reciprocal causation. Continuous reciprocal causation (CRC) occurs when some system S is both continuously affecting and simultaneously being affected by activity in some other system O. Internally, we may well confront such causal complexity in the brain since many neural areas are linked by both feedback and feedforward pathways (e.g., Van Essen and Gallant 1994). On a larger canvass, we often find processes of CRC that crisscross brain, body, and local environment. Think of a dancer, whose bodily orientation is continuously affecting and being affected by her neural states, and whose movements are also influencing those of her partner, to whom she is continuously responding! Or imagine playing improvised jazz in a small combo. Each musician's playing is influencing and being influenced by everyone else. CRC looks, in fact, to pervade the field of natural adaptive intelligence. The delicate dance of predator and prey or of mating animals exhibits the same complex causal structure.

Enter Dynamical Systems Theory. DST is a powerful framework for describing and understanding the temporal evolution of complex systems.[13] In a typical explanation, the theorist specifies a set of parameters whose collective evolution is governed by a set of differential equations. Such equations always involve a temporal element, and in this way, timing is factored into the heart of the approach. Moreover, such explanations are easily able to span organism and environment. In such cases, the two components are treated as a coupled system in a specific technical sense; that is, the equation describing the evolution of each component contains a term that factors in the other system's current state (technically, the state variables of the first system are also the parameters of the second, and vice versa).

Thus, consider two wall-mounted pendulums placed in close proximity on a single wall. The two pendulums will tend (courtesy of vibrations running along the wall) to become swing synchronized over time. This process admits of an elegant dynamical explanation in which the two pendulums are analyzed as a single coupled system with the motion equation for each one including a term representing the influence of the other's current state (see Salzman and Newsome 1994). A useful way to think of this is by imagining two coevolving state spaces. Each pendulum traces a course through a space of spatial and temporal configurations. But the shape of this space is determined, in part, by the ongoing activity of the other pendulum, which is itself behaving in ways continuously modified by the action of its neighbor.

The crucial upshot of the emphasis on constant mutual interaction is a corresponding emphasis on what Van Gelder and Port (1995, 14) usefully term *total state*. Because we assume that there is widespread and complex interanimation among multiple systemic factors (x influences y and z, and x is itself influenced by y, which also influences z, etc.), the dynamicist chooses to focus on changes in total system state over time. The various geometric devices used to put intuitive flesh on the models (trajectories through state spaces populated by attractors, repellors, etc.; see Clark 2001a, chap. 7, for a brief introduction) thus reflect motion in a space of possible overall system states, with routes and distances defined relative to points each of which assigns a value to all the systemic variables and parameters. This emphasis on total state marks one of the deepest contrasts between (the purest of) dynamical and standard computationalist approaches, and it is both a boon and a burden. It is a boon insofar as it allows the dynamicist to respect the burgeoning complexity of causal webs in which everything (both inner and outer) is continuously influencing everything else. Relative to such cases, the mathematics of a system of interlocking differential equations can (at least in simple cases) accurately capture the way two or more systems engage in a continuous, real-time, and effectively instantaneous dance of mutual codetermining interaction.[14] But it is a burden insofar as it threatens to obscure the specifically intelligence-based route to evolutionary success. That route involves the ability to become apprised of information concerning our surroundings and to use that information as a guide to present and future action. As soon as we embrace the notion of the brain as the principal (though not the *only*) seat of information-processing activity, we are already seeing it as fundamentally different from, say, the flow of a river or the activity of a volcano. And this difference needs to be reflected in our scientific analysis—a difference that typically is reflected when we pursue the kind of information-processing model associated with computational approaches, but which threatens to be lost if we treat the brain, or any other systemic element engaged in information-based problem-solving activity, in exactly the same terms as the beating of a heart or the unfolding of a basic chemical reaction.[15]

The question, in short, is how to do justice to the idea that there is a principled distinction between knowledge-based and merely physical-causal systems. It does not seem likely that the dynamicist will deny that there is a difference (though hints of such a denial are occasionally found).[16] But rather than responding by embracing a different vocabulary for the understanding and analysis of brain events (at least as they pertain to cognition), the dynamicist recasts the issue as the explanation of distinctive kinds of behavioral flexibility and hopes to explain that flexibility using the very same apparatus that works for other physical systems. Such an apparatus, however, may not be intrinsically well suited to explaining the particular way certain neural, and sometimes bodily and extrabodily, processes contribute to behavioral flexibility. This is because (a) it is unclear how it can do justice to the fundamental idea of information-guided choice, and (b) the emphasis on total state may obscure the kinds of rich structural variation especially characteristic of information-guided control systems.

Total state explanations do not fare well as a means of understanding systems in which complex information flow plays a key role. This is because such systems, as Sloman points out, typically depend on multiple, "independently variable, causally interacting sub-states" (1993, 80).[17] Such systems support great behavioral flexibility by being able cheaply to alter the inner flow of information in a wide variety of ways. To understand the operation of a standard computational device, for example, we may appeal to multiple databases, procedures, and operations. The real power of the device consists in its ability to rapidly and cheaply reconfigure the way these components interact. Information-based control systems thus tend to exhibit a kind of complex articulation in which what matters most is the extent to which component processes may be rapidly decoupled and reorganized. This kind of articulation has been depicted as a pervasive and powerful feature of real neural processing.[18] The fundamental idea is that large amounts of neural machinery are devoted not to the direct control of action but to the trafficking and routing of information within the brain. The point, for present purposes, is that to the extent that neural control systems exhibit such complex and information-based articulation (into multiple independently variable information-sensitive subsystems), the *sole* use of total state explanations would tend to obscure explanatorily important details, such as the various ways in which substate x may vary independently of substate y and so on.

1.9   Dynamics and "Soft" Computation

The dynamicist should, at this point, reply that the dynamical framework really leaves plenty of room for the understanding of such variability. After all, any location in state space can be specified as a vector comprising multiple elements, and we may then observe how some elements change while others remain fixed and so on. This is true. But notice the difference between this kind of dynamical approach and the radical, total state vision introduced in section 1.8. If the dynamicist is forced (a) to give an information-based reading of various systemic substates and processes and (b) to attend as much to the details of the inner flow of information as to the evolution of total state over time, then it is unclear that we still confront a radical *alternative* to the computational story. Instead, what we seem to end up with is a very powerful and interesting hybrid: a kind of "dynamical computationalism" in which the details of the flow of information are every bit as important as the larger scale dynamics and in which some dynamical features lead a double life as elements in an information-processing economy. Indeed, we have already met one such case. The Ballard et al. model of the role of deictic pointing in the blocks-copying task story analyzed a cognitive task in part by using recognizable computational and information-processing concepts. But it also made coupling and fine temporal coordination crucial and thus applied those familiar computational and information-processing concepts to a larger, essentially embodied dynamic whole.[19] Such work aims to display the *specific contributions* that embodiment and environmental embedding make by identifying what might be termed the *dynamic functional role* of specific bodily and worldly operations in the real-time performance of some task.[20]

This kind of dynamical "soft" computationalism is surely attractive.[21] Indeed, it is already the norm in many treatments that combine the use of dynamical tools with notions of internal representation and/or of neural computation (see, e.g., Spencer and Schöner 2003; Elman 1995, 2005). Thus, consider once again those complex loops of reciprocal causal influence. Let us assume for now that some such loop is fully internal and involves some relation of continuous reciprocal causal influence binding the activity of two elements. From this, it does not follow that we could not assign representational and (more broadly) information-processing roles either to the elements or to their coupled unfolding. It might be, for example, that the two elements are still best understood as trading in different kinds of encoding or information, kinds that nonetheless mutually and continuously modify each other in some useful manner. We shall explore a concrete example of this involving a neural-bodily loop in chapter 6. There we examine a recent account of the role of physical gesture in the unfolding of thought and reason. According to that account, gesture and verbal thinking differ quite radically in the kinds of information they encode, but the gestural and verbal systems are nonetheless depicted as coupled in precisely the manner described earlier.[22] In such cases, we need to understand *both* the distinctive individual contributions of the various coupled elements *and* the powerful effects that flow from their coupled unfolding.

It should be admitted, however, that the issues concerning continuous reciprocal causation, and the potential threat it poses to representationalist and computationalist modes of understanding, are complex ones. For *some* forms of CRC may indeed threaten such understandings. This will be so where the nature of the contributions being made by the "parts" is *itself* changing radically over time as a result of the multiple influences from elsewhere in the system.[23] At the extreme limit, such variability may undermine attempts to gloss stable types of systemic events as the bearers or vehicles of specific contents. It is an empirical question where, on this continuum of possibilities, biological information-processing lies (for some discussion, see Clark 1997a, 1997b; Wheeler 2005).

Short of this extreme limit, however, considerations concerning the importance of time and continuous reciprocal causation mandate not an outright rejection of the computational/representational vision[24] but rather the addition of a potent and irreducibly dynamical dimension. Such a dimension may manifest itself in several ways, including the use of dynamical tools to recover potential information-bearing states and processes from highly complex (and sometimes bodily and environmentally extended) webs of causal exchange; the recognition that intrinsically dynamical and temporal features may sometimes themselves play identifiable representational and/or computational roles; the (consequent) extension of standard computational ideas to include analog systems that change continuously in time and that exploit continuous state; and the recognition (sec. 1.6) of the importance of information self-structuring (e.g., via the active creation of time-locked flows of multimodal input) in learning and reasoning.

1.10   Out from the Bedrock

We have now scouted some of the most fundamental ways in which appeals to the body, to the environment, and to embodied action may inform our vision and understanding of mind. Firm bedrock is provided by the wide suite of benefits enabled by the coevolution of morphology, materials, and control. Moving into the time frame of lifetime learning, we glimpsed related strategies of "ecological assembly" in which embodied agents exploit the opportunities provided by dynamic loops, active sensing, and iterated bouts of environmental exploitation and intervention. The next three chapters ramp up the complexity, exploring first the surprising lability and negotiability of human sensing and embodiment, then the transformative potential of material artifacts, language, and symbolic culture, and leading finally to the suggestion that *mind itself* leaches into body and world.

2

The Negotiable Body

2.1   Fear and Loathing

In a short article in the May 2004 edition of *WIRED* magazine (revealingly subtitled "Fear and Loathing on the Human–Machine Frontier"), the futurist and science fiction writer Bruce Sterling sounds an increasingly familiar alarm. After warning us of the imminent dangers of "brain augmentation," he adds:

> Another troubling frontier is physical, as opposed to mental, augmentation. Japan has a rapidly growing elderly population and a serious shortage of caretakers. So Japanese roboticists...envision walking wheelchairs and mobile arms that manipulate and fetch.
>
> But there's ethical hell at the interfaces. The peripherals may be dizzyingly clever gizmos...but the CPU is a human being: old, weak, vulnerable, pitifully limited, possibly senile. (116)

But such fears are rooted in a fundamentally misconceived vision of our own humanity: a vision that depicts us as "locked-in agents"— as beings whose minds and physical abilities are fixed quantities, apt (at best) for mere support and scaffolding by their best tools and technologies. In contrast to this view, I believe that human minds and bodies are essentially open to episodes of deep and transformative restructuring in which new equipment (both physical and "mental") can become quite literally incorporated into the thinking and acting systems that we identify as our minds and bodies (see, e.g., Clark 1997a, 2001b, 2003). In this chapter, I pursue this theme with special attention to the negotiability of our own embodiment.

It helps to start with the commonplace. Sensing and moving are the spots where the rubber of embodied agency meets the road of the wider world—the world outside the agent's organismic boundaries. The typical human agent, circa 2008, feels herself to be a bounded physical entity in contact with the world through a variety of standard sensory channels, including touch, vision, smell, and hearing. It is a common observation, however, that the use of simple tools can lead to alterations in that local sense of embodiment. Fluently using a stick, we feel as if we are touching the world at the end of the stick, not (once we are indeed fluent in our use) as if we are touching the stick with our hand. The stick, it has sometimes been suggested, is in some way incorporated, and the overall effect seems more like bringing a temporary whole new agent-world circuit into being rather than simply exploiting the stick as a helpful prop or tool (see Merleau-Ponty 1945/1962 and Gibson 1979; for some more recent explorations of this theme, see Burton 1993; Reed 1996; Peck et al. 1996; Smitsman 1997; Hirose 2002; Maravita and Iriki 2004; Wheeler 2005).

In thinking about the case of stick-augmented perception, there would seem to be two key interfaces at play: the place where the stick meets the hand and the place where the extended system "biological agent + stick" meets the rest of the world. When we read about new forms of human–machine interface, we are again confronted by a similar duality and an accompanying tension. What makes such interfaces *appropriate* as mechanisms for human enhancement is, it seems, precisely their potential role in creating *whole new agent-world circuits*. But insofar as they succeed at this task, the new agent-tool interface itself fades from view, and the proper picture is one of an extended or enhanced agent confronting the (wider) world.

A good place to start, then, is with the notion of an interface itself.

2.2   What's in an Interface?

Haugeland (1998) is, in part, an extended philosophical meditation on the very idea of an interface. The goal is to uncover the underlying principles "for dividing systems into distinct subsystems along nonarbitrary lines" (211). According to Haugeland, the notions of component, system, and interface are all interdefined and interdefining. Components are those parts of a larger whole that interact through interfaces. Systems are "relatively independent and self-contained" composites of such interfaced components. And an interface itself is "a point of interactive 'contact' between components such that the relevant interactions are well-defined, reliable and relatively simple" (Haugeland 1998, 213).

Haugeland is right to point to the nature of interactions as the key to the location of an interface. We discern an interface where we discern a kind of regimented, often deliberately designed, point of contact between two or more independently tunable or replaceable parts. It does not seem correct, however, to insist that flow across the interface be simple. The idea here seems to be that we find genuine interfaces only where we find energetic or informational bottlenecks, as if an interface must be a narrow channel yielding what Haugeland describes as "low bandwidth" coupling. This is important for Haugeland's argumentative purpose because he means to show that human sensing typically yields very task-variable, high-bandwidth forms of agent-environment coupling and thus to argue that no genuine interface or interfaces separate agent and world. Instead (and see also the longer version of this claim already presented in the Introduction), there is said to be "intimate intermingling of mind, body and world" (Haugeland 1998, 224).

But although agreeing with Haugeland that sensing is at least sometimes best understood in terms of direct agent-environment couplings (as we saw in the previous chapter), his own conclusion that no genuine interfaces then link agent and world seems premature. Haugeland depicts these kinds of "open-channel" solutions as involving "tightly coupled high-bandwidth interaction" (223) and hence as inimical to the very idea of an agent-world interface.[1] But it seems intuitive that there can be genuine interfaces that support extremely high-bandwidth forms of coupling. Think, for example, of multiple computers linked into a network by means of superfast, very high-bandwidth "grid technologies."[2] There is really no doubt that we here confront a web of distinct intercommunicating component machines. Yet that web, in action, can sometimes function as a single unified resource. Nonetheless, we still think of it as a web of distinct but interfaced devices. And we do so not because the point of each machine's contact with the grid is narrow (it isn't) but because there exist, for each machine on the grid, very well-defined points of potential detachment and reengagement. We discern interfaces at the points at which one machine can be easily disengaged and another engaged instead, allowing the first to join another grid or to operate in a stand-alone fashion. Grush (2003, 79) calls this the "plug points criterion" according to which "components are entities that can be plugged into, or unplugged from, other components and/or the system at large."

An interface, I conclude, is indeed a point of contact between two items across which the types of performance-relevant interaction are reliable and well defined. But there is no requirement that such interfaces be narrow-bandwidth bottlenecks. The way to argue for cognitive extensions and blurrings of the mind-world boundary is not by casting doubt on the presence of genuine interfaces (there are plenty of these within the brain, too, and that doesn't stop us from distinguishing parts and roles) but by displaying special features of the flow of information across those interfaces and by stressing the novel properties of the new systemic wholes that result. It is to these tasks that we now turn.

2.3   New Systemic Wholes

Biological systems, from lampreys to primates, display remarkable powers of bodily and sensory adaptability (see Mussa-Ivaldi and Miller 2003; Bach y Rita and Kercel 2003; Clark 2003). The Australian performance artist Stelarc routinely deploys a "third hand," a mechanical actuator controlled by Stelarc's brain through commands to muscle sites on his legs and abdomen.[3] Activity at these sites is monitored by electrodes that transmit signals (via a computer) to the artificial hand. Stelarc reports that, after some years of practice and performance, he no longer feels as if he has to actively control the third hand to achieve his goals. It has become "transparent equipment" (recall chap. 1), something through which Stelarc (the agent) can act on the world without first willing an action on anything else. In this respect, it now functions much as his biological hands and arms, serving his goals without (generally) being itself an object of conscious thought or effortful control.

Recent experimental work reveals more about the kinds of mechanisms that may be at work in such cases. A much publicized example is the work by Miguel Nicolelis and colleagues on a brain-machine interface (BMI) that allows a macaque monkey to use thought control to move a robot arm. In the most recent version of this work, Carmena et al. (2003) implanted 320 electrodes in the frontal and parietal lobes of a monkey. The electrodes allowed a monitoring computer to record neural activity across multiple cortical ensembles while the monkey learned to use a joystick to move a cursor across a computer screen for rewards. As in previous work, the computer was able to extract the neural activity patterns corresponding to different movements, including direction and grip. Next, the joystick is disconnected. But the monkey is still able to use its neural activity, interpreted through the intervening computer, to directly control the cursor for rewards, and it learns to do so. Finally, these commands are diverted to a robot arm whose actual motions are then translated into on-screen cursor movements, including an on-screen equivalent of forceful gripping. This closes the loop. Instead of the monkey merely moving an unseen robot arm by thought control alone, the movement of the distant unseen arm now yields visual feedback in the form of on-screen cursor motion.

When the robot arm was inserted into the control loop, the monkey displayed a striking degradation of behavior. It took two full days of practice to reestablish fluent thought control over the on-screen cursor. The reason was that the monkey's brain now had to learn to factor in the mechanical and temporal "friction" created by the new physical equipment: It had to factor in the mechanical and dynamical properties of the robot arm and the time delays (which were substantial, in the 60–90 millisecond range) caused by interposing the motion of the arm between neural command and on-screen feedback. By the time full fluency was achieved, it is reasonable to conjecture that these properties of the still unseen distant arm were in some sense incorporated into the monkey's own body schema. In support of this, the experimenters were able to track real long-term physiological changes in the response profiles of frontoparietal neurons following use of the BMI, leading them to comment that

> the dynamics of the robot arm (reflected by the cursor movements) become incorporated into multiple cortical representations...we propose that the gradual increase in behavioral performance...emerged as a consequence of a plastic reorganization whose main outcome was the assimilation of the dynamics of an artificial actuator into the physiological properties of fronto-parietal neurons. (Carmena et al. 2003, 205)

Creatures capable of this kind of deep incorporation of new bodily (and as we'll later see, also sensory and cognitive) structure are examples of what I shall call "profoundly embodied agents." Such agents are able constantly to negotiate and renegotiate the agent-world boundary itself.

Although our own capacity for such renegotiation is, I believe, vastly underappreciated, it really should come as no great surprise, given the facts of biological bodily growth and change. The human infant must learn (by self-exploration) which neural commands bring about which bodily effects and must then practice until skilled enough to issue those commands without conscious effort. This process has been dubbed "body babbling" (Meltzoff and Moore 1997) and continues until the infant body becomes transparent equipment (see 1.6). Because bodily growth and change continue, it is simply good design not to permanently lock in knowledge of any particular configuration but instead to deploy plastic neural resources and an ongoing regime of monitoring and recalibration (for some excellent discussion, see Ramachandran and Blakeslee 1998).

2.4   Substitutes

As a second class of examples of recalibration and renegotiation, consider the plasticity revealed by work in sensory substitution. Pioneered in the '60s and '70s by Paul Bach y Rita and colleagues, the earliest such systems were grids of blunt "nails" fitted to the backs of blind subjects and taking input from a head-mounted camera. In response to the camera input, specific regions of the grid became active, gently stimulating the skin under the grid. At first, subjects report only a vague tingling sensation. But after wearing the grid while engaged in various kinds of goal-driven activity (walking, eating, etc.), the reports change dramatically. Subjects stop feeling the tingling on the back and start to report rough, quasi-visual experiences of looming objects and so forth. After a while, a ball thrown at the head causes instinctive and appropriate ducking. The causal chain is "deviant": It runs via the systematic input to the back. But the nature of the information carried, and the way it supports the control of action, is suggestive of the visual modality. Performance using such devices can be quite impressive. In a recent article, Bach y Rita, Tyler, and Kaczmarek (2003) note that Tactile-Visual Substitution Systems (TVSS) have

> been sufficient to perform complex perception and "eye"-hand co-ordination tasks. These have included face recognition, accurate judgment of speed and direction of a rolling ball with over 95% accuracy in batting the ball as it rolls over a table edge, and complex inspection-assembly tasks. (287)

The key to such effective sensory substitution is goal-driven motor engagement. It is crucial that the head-mounted camera be under the subject's intentional motor control. This meant that the brain could, in effect, experiment through the motor system, giving commands that systematically varied the input so as to begin to form hypotheses about what information the tactile signals might be carrying. Such training yields quite a flexible new agent-world circuit. Once trained in the use of the head-mounted camera, the motor system operating the camera could be changed (e.g., to a hand-held camera) with no loss of acuity. The touch pad, too, could be moved to new bodily sites, and there was no tactile–visual confusion: An itch scratched under the grid caused no "visual" effects (for these results, see Bach y Rita and Kercel 2003).

Such technologies, though still experimental, are now increasingly advanced. The back-mounted grid is often replaced by a tongue-mounted coin-sized array and extensions in other sensory modalities. Bach y Rita and Kercel (2003) give the nice example of a touch-sensor-rich glove that allows leprosy patients to begin to feel again using their hands. The patient is fitted with the glove that transmits signals to a forehead-mounted tactile disc array and rapidly reports feeling sensations of touch *at the fingertips*. This is presumably because the motor control over the sensors runs via commands to the hand, so the sensation is subsequently projected to that site. (See also the discussion of the auditory visual-substitution system known as The Voice in sec. 8.3.)

As an aside, it is worth noticing that the line between these kinds of rehabilitative strategy and wholly new forms of bodily and sensory enhancement is already thin to the point of nonexistence. There is advanced work on night-vision versions of sensory substitution, and at the more dramatic end of this spectrum, it is possible to bypass the existing sensory peripheries, feeding all manner of signals (including commercial TV!) directly to the cortex (see Bach y Rita and Kercel 2003, and the discussion in Clark 2003, 125). Even without penetrating the existing surface of skin and skull, sensory enhancement and bodily extension are pervasive possibilities. One striking example (see Schrope 2001) is a U.S. Navy innovation known as a tactile flight suit. The suit (a kind of vest worn by the pilot) allows even inexperienced helicopter pilots to perform difficult tasks such as holding the helicopter in a stationary hover in the air. It works by generating bodily sensations (via safe puffs of air) inside the suit. If the craft is tilting to the right or left or forward or backward, the pilot feels a puff-induced vibrating sensation on that side of the body. The pilot's own responses (moving in the opposite direction to correct the vibrations) can even be monitored by the suit to control the helicopter. The suit is so good at transmitting and delivering information in a natural and easy way that military pilots can use it to fly blindfolded. While the pilot wears the suit, the helicopter behaves very much like an extended body for the pilot: It rapidly links the pilot to the aircraft in the same kind of closed-loop interaction that linked Stelarc and the third hand, the monkey and the robot arm, or the blind person and the TVSS system. What matters, in each case, is the provision of closed-loop signaling so that motor commands affect sensory input. What varies is the amount of training (and hence the extent of deeper neural changes) required to fully exploit the new agent-world circuits thus created.

It is important, in all these cases, that the new agent-world circuits be trained and calibrated in the context of a whole agent engaged in world-directed (goal-driven) activity. One sign of successful calibration is, as we noted earlier, that once fluency is achieved, the specific details of the (old or new) circuitry by which the world is engaged fall "transparent" in use. The conscious agent is then aware of the oncoming ball, not (usually) of *seeing* the ball or (by the same token) of using *a tactile substitution channel* to detect the ball. In just this way, the tactile-vest-wearing pilot becomes aware of the aircraft's tilt and slant, not of *the puffs of air*.

In all these diverse ways, humans and other primates are revealed as constantly negotiable bodily platforms of sense, experience, and (as we'll see in later chapters) reasoning, too. Such platforms are biologically primed so as to fluidly incorporate new bodily and sensory kit, creating brand new systemic wholes. This is just what one would expect of creatures built to engage in what we earlier (sec. 1.1) called "ecological control": systems evolved so as to constantly search for opportunities to make the most of the reliable properties and dynamic potentialities of body and world.

2.5   Incorporation Versus Use

A very natural doubt to raise, at about this point, would be the following:

> Critic: "You are making quite a song and a dance out of this, what with talk of brand new systemic wholes and so on. But we all know we can use tools and that we can learn to use them fluently and transparently. Why talk here of new systemic wholes, of extended bodies and reconfigured users, rather than just the same old user in command of a new tool?"

This is the right question to ask. We have already begun to see a hint of the answer in the quoted comments of Carmena et al. concerning the "assimilation of the dynamics of an artificial actuator into the physiological properties of fronto-parietal neurons." To bring the key idea into focus, it helps next to consider a closely related body of research on tool use by primates.

Recent years have seen the discovery, in primate brains, of a variety of so-called bimodal neurons. These are "pre-motor, parietal and putaminal neurons that respond both to somatosensory information from a given body region (i.e., the somatosensory Receptive Field; sRF) and to visual information from the space (visual Receptive Field; vRF) adjacent to it" (Maravita and Iriki 2004, 79).

For example, some neurons respond to somatosensory stimuli (light touches) at the hand *and* to visually presented stimuli near the hand so as to yield an action-relevant coding of visual space. In a series of experiments, recordings were taken from bimodal neurons in the intraparietal cortex of Japanese macaques while the macaques learned to reach for food using a rake. The experimenters found that after just five minutes of rake use, the responses of some bimodal neurons whose original vRFs picked out stimuli near the hand had expanded to include the entire length of the tool, "as if the rake was part of the arm and forearm" (Maravita and Iriki 2004, 79). Similarly, other bimodal neurons, which previously responded to visual stimuli within the space reachable by the arm, now had vRFs that covered the space accessible by the arm-rake combination.[4] After surveying a number of other related findings, including some fascinating work in which similar effects are observed after experience of reaching with a virtual arm in an on-screen display, Maravita and Iriki conclude: "Such vRF expansions may constitute the neural substrate of use-dependent assimilation of the tool into the body-schema, suggested by classical neurology" (2004, 80).

In human subjects suffering from unilateral neglect (in which stimuli from within a certain region of egocentrically coded space are selectively ignored), it has been shown that the use of a stick as a tool for reaching actually extends the area of visual neglect to encompass the space now reachable using the tool (see Berti and Frassinetti 2000). Berti and Frassinetti conclude that

> the brain makes a distinction between "far space" (the space beyond reaching distance) and "near space" (the space within reaching distance) [and that]...simply holding a stick causes a remapping of far space to near space. In effect the brain, at least for some purposes, treats the stick as though it were a part of the body. (2000, 415)

The plastic neural changes reported by Carmena et al., and now further emphasized by Maravita and Iriki and by Berti and Frassinetti, suggest a real (philosophically important and scientifically well-grounded) distinction between true incorporation into the body schema and mere use. The body schema, it is important to note, is not the same as the body image, though the two can sometimes be related. As I shall use the terms (see Gallagher 1998), the body image is a conscious construct able to inform thought and reasoning about the body. The body schema, by contrast, names a suite of neural settings that implicitly (and nonconsciously) define a body in terms of its capabilities for action, for example, by defining the extent of "near space" for action programs.[5]

We can certainly *imagine* tool users (perhaps even fluent tool users?) whose brains were not engineered so as to adapt the body schema in these ways. Such beings would *always* use tools the way we typically *begin* to use them: by roughly representing the tool and its features and powers (e.g., its length) and calculating effective uses accordingly. We can probably even imagine beings who were so fast and good at these calculations as to deploy the tools with the same skill and efficacy as an expert human agent. The contrast that would remain, even in the latter kind of case, would be between (a) the skilled agent's first explicitly representing the shape, dimensions, and powers of the tool and then inferring (consciously or otherwise) that she can now reach such and such and do such and such and (b) agents whose brains were so constituted that experience with the tool results in, for example, a suite of altered vRFs such that objects within tool-augmented reaching range are now *automatically* treated as falling within near space. These are surely distinct strategies. The latter strategy might be especially recommended for beings whose bodies (like our own) are naturally subject to growth and change, as it seems designed to support genuine episodes of integration across change: cases that can now be defined as cases in which plastic neural resources become recalibrated (in the context of goal-directed whole agent activity) so as to automatically take account of new bodily and sensory opportunities. In this way, to paraphrase Varela, Thompson, and Rosch (1991), our own embodied activity *enacts or brings forth new systemic wholes.*

2.6   Toward Cognitive Extension

Could anything like this notion of incorporation (rather than mere use) and the consequent emergence of new systemic wholes get a grip in the more ethereal domain of mind and cognition? Could human *minds* be genuinely extended and augmented by cultural and technological tweaks, or is it (as many evolutionary psychologists, such as Pinker 1997, would have us believe) just the same old mind with a shiny new tool?

Here, the story is murkier by far. My own view, as will become increasingly clear, is that external and nonbiological information-processing resources are *also* apt for temporary or long-term recruitment and incorporation rather than simply knowledge-based use (see Clark 1997a, 2003; Clark and Chalmers 1998). To whatever extent this holds, we are not just bodily and sensorily but also *cognitively* permeable agents. But whereas we can now begin to point, in the case of basic tool use, to the distinctive kinds of visible neural changes that accompany the genuine assimilation of tools or of new bodily structure, it is harder to know just what to look for in the case of mental and cognitive routines. For the present, we may look for some preliminary hints from the more basic case of physical and sensory augmentation and incorporation.

It may be helpful first to display the bare logical possibility of such cognitive extension. For even the bare possibility, some might feel, is ruled out by a simple argument to the effect that, as an anonymous journal referee once put it, "cognitive enhancement requires that the cognitive operations of the resource be intelligible to the agent." If this were so, cognitive enhancement would always be in some clear sense superficial: It would provide tools while leaving the user fundamentally untouched. But the argument is flawed because the cognitive operations of much of my own brain (even those elements that mature later during development) are not thus intelligible to me, the conscious agent. Yet those operations surely help make me the cognitive agent I am. It also helps to reflect that biological brains must sometimes change and evolve by coordinating old activities and processes with new ones made available (e.g., by maturation and growth) courtesy of new or subtly altered structures. To insist that such change requires the literal intelligibility of the operations of the new by the old, rather than simply the emergence of appropriate integration and coordination, is to miss the potential for new wholes that are then *themselves* the determiners of what is and is not intelligible to the agent. It must thus be possible, at least in principle, for new *nonbiological* tools and structures to likewise become sufficiently well integrated into our problem-solving activity as to yield new agent-constituting wholes. What might such integration (genuine cognitive incorporation) require?

Consider the case when some existing neural system or systems learn a complex problem-solving routine that makes a variety of deep implicit commitments to the robust bioexternal availability of certain operations and/or bodies of information. This is the cognitive equivalent, I suggest, of the implicit commitments to details of bodily shape and potentials for action made (in the case of the rake) by rapidly retuning the receptive fields of key bimodal neurons and (in the case of the robot arm) by retuning key cortical representations (specifically, populations of frontoparietal neurons).

A quick (though frequently misused; see the critical discussion in sec. 7.3) illustration is provided by recent work on so-called change blindness. In this work (see Simons and Rensink 2005, for a balanced review), simple experimental manipulations, involving the masking of motion transients while various changes are made to a visually presented scene, reveal the surprising sparseness of the change-specifying information easily available to conscious reflection. Subjects seldom spot quite large and important changes, even when the changes are made in focal vision. Subjects are frequently amazed when they realize just how much has changed without their noticing it. How should we reconcile the limitations of such conscious change spotting with our strong sense of rich visual contact with our surroundings? Part of the answer (and see chap. 7 and 8 for more discussion) may be that the strong feeling of rich visual contact is really a reflection of something implicit in the larger overall problem-solving organization in which moment-by-moment vision merely participates. That larger organization "assumes" the (ecologically normal) ability to retrieve, via saccades or head and body movements, more detailed information as and when needed. Given such "availability on demand," we feel (correctly, in an important sense) that we (qua agents engaged in knowledge-based interactions with the world) are fully in command of the detail (for this idea, see O'Regan and Nöe 2001; Clark 2002).

Or recall the use of visual fixation for binding in the block-copying task described in section 1.3. Here, the brain deploys a problem-solving routine that directly factors in the availability of certain types of information by certain types of embodied action. It is in just this way that nonbiological informational resources can become—either temporarily or more or less permanently—deeply incorporated into a subpersonally defined problem-solving whole. In such cases, a problem-solving routine is delicately geared to automatically exploit, on pretty much an equal footing, both internal and (bio)external forms of information storage.[6] Rather than drawing a firm line around the inner encodings, we thus expand the relevant forms of storage and retrieval to include inner biological resources, environmental structure, and the data (and operations) made available by cognitive artifacts such as notebooks and laptops. As we move toward an era of wearable computing and ubiquitous information access, the robust, reliable information fields to which our brains delicately adapt their inner cognitive routines will surely become increasingly dense and powerful, perhaps further blurring the boundaries between the cognitive agent and his or her best tools, props and artifacts.[7]

2.7   Three Grades of Embodiment

We can now distinguish three grades of embodiment. Let's call them (simply if unimaginatively) mere embodiment, basic embodiment, and profound embodiment. A merely embodied creature or robot is one equipped with a body and sensors, able to engage in closed-loop inter-actions with its world, but for whom the body is nothing but a highly controllable means to implement practical solutions arrived at by pure reason. A basically embodied creature or robot would then be one (we saw several in chap. 1) for whom the body is not just another problem space, requiring constant micromanaged control, but is rather a resource whose own features and dynamics (of sensor placement, of linked ten-dons and muscle groups, etc.) could be actively exploited allowing for increasingly fluent forms of action selection and control. Much (though by no means all) work in contemporary robotics has explored this mid-dle ground of modest embodiment. Such systems are, however, con-genitally unable to learn new kinds of body-exploiting solution "on the fly," in response to damage, growth, or change. By contrast, as we have seen, biological systems (and especially we primates) seem to be spe-cifically designed to constantly search for opportunities to make the most of body and world, checking for what is available, and then (at various timescales and with varying degrees of difficulty) integrating new resources very deeply, creating whole new agent-world circuits in the process. A profoundly embodied creature or robot is thus one that is highly engineered to be able to learn to make maximal problem-simplifying use of an open-ended variety of internal, bodily, or external sources of order.

Why describe this as profound embodiment rather than as a return to the outdated (or so many of us believe; see Clark 1997a, for a review) image of mind as a truly disembodied organ of control? The answer is that these kinds of minds are not in the least disembodied. Rather, they are *promiscuously* body-and-world exploiting. They are forever testing and exploring the possibilities for incorporating new resources and struc-tures deep into their embodied acting and problem-solving regimes. They are, to use the jargon of Clark (2003), the minds of "natural-born cyborgs"—of systems continuously renegotiating their own limits, com-ponents, data stores, and interfaces. On this account, the body is both critically important and constantly negotiable. It is critically important as a key player on the problem-solving stage. It is not simply the point at which processes of transduction pass the real problems (now rendered in rich internal representational formats) to an inner engine of disem-bodied reason. Instead, much of our successful performance depends on constant and subtle trade-offs among morphology, real-world action and opportunities, and neural control strategies. But this empowering body is constantly negotiable, constructed moment by moment from the flux of willed action and resulting sensory stimulation.

Those first waves of fear and loathing now give way to something more rewarding. Sterling (sec. 2.1) saw frightening scenes of a merely *superficially augmented* agent within whom "the CPU is a human being: old, weak, vulnerable, pitifully limited, possibly senile." Such fears play upon a deeply misguided image of who and what we *already* are. They play upon an image of the human agent as doubly locked in: as a fixed mind (one constituted solely by a given biological brain) and as a fixed bodily presence in a wider world. Fortunately for us, human minds are not old-fashioned CPUs trapped in immutable and increasingly feeble corporeal shells. Instead, they are the surprisingly plastic minds of *profoundly* embodied agents: agents whose boundaries and components are forever negotiable and for whom body, sensing, thinking, and reasoning are all woven flexibly and repeatedly from the accommodating weave of situated, intentional action.

3

Material Symbols

3.1 Language as Scaffolding

Where does language fit into our emerging picture of the plastic, environmentally exploitative, ecologically efficient agent? One useful way to approach this question is to consider language itself as a form of mind-transforming cognitive scaffolding: a persisting, though never stationary, symbolic edifice whose critical role in promoting thought and reason remains surprisingly ill understood.

In this chapter, I examine three distinct but interlocking benefits of the linguistic scaffold. First, the simple act of labeling the world opens up a variety of new computational opportunities and supports the discovery of increasingly abstract patterns in nature. Second, encountering or recalling structured sentences supports the development of otherwise unattainable kinds of expertise. And third, linguistic structures contribute to some of the most important yet conceptually complex of all human capacities: our ability to reflect on our own thoughts and characters and our limited but genuine capacity to control and guide the shape and contents of our own thinking.

3.2   *Augmenting Reality*

Consider the case of Sheba and the treats as recounted in Boysen et al. (1996). Sheba (an adult female chimpanzee) has had symbol and numeral training: She knows about numerals. Sheba sits with Sarah (another chimp), and two plates of treats are shown. What Sheba points to, Sarah gets. Sheba always points to the greater pile, thus getting less. She visibly hates this result but can't seem to improve. However, when the treats arrive in containers with a cover bearing numerals on top, the spell is broken, and Sheba points to the smaller number, thus gaining *more* treats.

What seems to be going on here, according to Boysen, is that the material symbols, by being simple and stripped of most treat-signifying physical cues, allow the chimps to sidestep the capture of their own behavior by ecologically specific, fast-and-frugal subroutines. The material symbol here acts as a manipulable and, in some sense, a merely "shallowly interpreted" (Clowes 2007) stand-in, able to loosen the bonds between perception and action. Importantly, the presence of the material symbol impacts behavior not in virtue of being the key to a rich inner mental representation (though it may be this also) but rather by itself, qua material symbol, providing a new target for selective attention and a new fulcrum for the control of action. Such effects, as Clowes (2007) argues, do of course depend on the presence of something akin to a system of interpretation. But it is their ability to provide simple, affect-reduced, perceptual targets that (I want to suggest) explains much of their cognitive potency.

In much the same way, the act of labeling creates a new realm of perceptible objects upon which to target basic capacities of statistical and associative learning. The act of labeling thus alters the computational burdens imposed by certain kinds of problems. I have written quite a bit on this elsewhere, so I'll keep this brief. My favorite example (Clark 1998b) begins with the use, by otherwise language-naive chimpanzees, of concrete tags (simple and distinct plastic shapes) for relations such as sameness and difference. Thus, a pair such as cup–cup might be associated with a red triangle (sameness) and cup–shoe with a blue circle (difference). This is not in itself surprising. What is more interesting is that after this training, the tag-trained chimps (and only tag-trained chimps) prove able to learn about the abstract properties of higher order sameness; that is, they are able to learn to judge of two presented pairs (e.g., cup–cup and cup–shoe) that the relationship between the relations is one of higher order difference (or better, lack of higher order sameness) because the first pair exhibits the sameness relation and the second pair shows the difference relation (Thompson, Oden, and Boysen 1997). The reason the tag-trained chimps can perform this surprising feat is, so the authors suggest, because by mentally recalling the tags, the chimps can reduce the higher order problem to a lower order one: All they have to do is spot that the relation of difference describes the pairing of the two recalled tags (red triangle and blue circle).

This is a nice concrete example of what may well be a very general effect (see Clark 1998b and Dennett 1993). Once fluent in the use of tags, complex properties and relations in the perceptual array are, in effect, artificially reconstituted as simple inspectable wholes. The effect is to reduce the descriptive complexity of the scene. Kirsh (1995b), as we shall see in more detail in chapter 4, describes the intelligent use of space in just these terms. When, for example, you group your groceries in one bag and mine in another, or when the cook places washed vegetables in one location and unwashed ones in another, the effect is to use spatial organization to simplify problem solving by using spatial proximity to reduce descriptive complexity. It is intuitive that once descriptive complexity is thus reduced, processes of selective attention, and of action control, can operate on elements of a scene that were previously too "unmarked" to define such operations over. Experience with tags and labels may be a cheap way of achieving a similar result. Spatial organization reduces descriptive complexity by means of physical groupings that channel perception and action toward functional or appearance-based equivalence classes. Labels allow us to focus attention on all and only the items belonging to equivalence classes (the red shoes, the green apples, etc.). In this way, both linguistic and physical groupings allow selective attention to dwell on all and only the items belonging to the class. And the two resources are seen to work in close cooperation. Spatial groupings are used in teaching children the meanings of words, and mentally rehearsed words may be used to control activities of spatial grouping.

Simple labeling thus functions as a kind of augmented reality trick by means of which we cheaply and open-endedly project new groupings and structures onto a perceived scene.[1] Labeling is cheap because it avoids the physical effort of putting things into piles. And it is open-ended insofar as it can group in ways that defeat simple spatial display—for example, by allowing us to selectively attend to the four corners of a tabletop, an exercise that clearly cannot be performed by physical reorganization! Linguistic labels, on this view, are tools for grouping and in this sense act much like real spatial reorganization. But in addition (and unlike mere physical groupings), they effectively and open-endedly add new "virtual" items (the recalled labels themselves) to the scene. In this way, experience with tags and labels warps and reconfigures the problem spaces for the cognitive engine.

A related effect may also be observed in recent work on language learning. Thus, in a recent review, Smith and Gasser (2005) ask a very nice question. Why, given that human beings are such experts at grounded, concrete, sensorimotor driven forms of learning, do the symbol systems of public language take the special and rather rarified forms that they do?

> One might expect that a multimodal, grounded, sensorimotor sort of learning would favor a more iconic, pantomime-like language in which symbols were similar to referents. But language is decidedly not like this...there is no intrinsic similarity between the sounds of most words and their referents: the form of the word *dog* gives us no hints about the kind of thing to which it refers. And nothing in the similarity of the forms of *dig* and *dog* conveys a similarity in meaning. (Smith and Gasser 2005, 22)

The question, in short, is: "Why in a so profoundly multimodal sensorimotor agent such as ourselves is language an arbitrary symbol system?" (24).

One possible answer, of course, is that language is like that because (biologically basic) *thought* is like that, and the forms and structures of language reflect this fact. But another answer says just the opposite. Language is like that, it might be suggested, because thought (or rather, biologically basic thought) is *not* like that. The computational value of a public system of essentially context-free, arbitrary symbols, lies, according to this opposing view, in the way such a system can push, pull, tweak, cajole, and eventually cooperate with various nonarbitrary, modality-rich, context-sensitive forms of biologically basic encoding.[2]

3.3   Sculpting Attention

The role of structured language as a tool for scaffolding action has been explored in a variety of literatures, ranging from Vygotskyian developmental psychology to cognitive anthropology (see, e.g., Berk 1994; Hutchins 1995; Donald 2001). Mundane examples of such scaffolding abound and range from memorized instructions for tying one's shoelaces to mentally rehearsed mantras for crossing the road, such as " look right, look left, look right again, and if all is clear, cross with caution" (that's for UK-style left-hand-drive roads; don't try that in the United States, folks!). In such cases, the language-using agent is able (once the instructions are memorized or, in the written case, visually accessed) to engage in a simple kind of behavioral self-scaffolding, using the phonetic or spatial sequence of symbolic encodings to stand proxy for the temporal sequence of acts. Frequent practice then enables the agent to develop genuine expertise and to dispense with the rehearsal of the helpful mantra.

More interesting than all this, however, is the role of linguistic rehearsal in expert performance itself. In previous work (Clark 1996), I discussed some ways in which linguaform rehearsal enables experts to temporarily alter their own focus of attention, thus fine-tuning the patterns of inputs that are to be processed by fast, fluent, highly trained subpersonal resources. Experts, I argued, are doubly expert. They are expert at the task in hand but also expert at using well-chosen linguistic prompts and reminders to maintain performance in the face of adversity. Sometimes, inner rehearsal here plays a distinctly affective role, as the expert encourages herself to perform at her peak.[3] But in addition to the important cognitive-affective role of inner dialogue, there may also be cases in which verbal rehearsal supports a kind of perceptual restructuring via the controlled disposition of attention (for a nice example, see the discussion of linguistic rehearsal by expert Tetris players in Kirsh and Maglio 1992). The key idea, once again, is that the linguistic tools enable us to deliberately and systematically sculpt and modify our own processes of selective attention. In this regard, Sutton (2007) describes in some detail the value of "instructional nudges" (small strings of words, simple maxims). Such nudges, Sutton argues, are often best employed not by the novice but by the expert, who can use them to tune and modulate highly learned forms of embodied performance.[4]

Direct cognitive benefits from linguaform encodings are also suggested in work by Hermer-Vazquez, Spelke, and Katsnelson (1999). In this study, prelinguistic infants were shown the location of a toy or food in a room and then were spun around or otherwise disoriented and required to try to find the desired item. The location was uniquely determinable only by remembering conjoined cues concerning the color of the wall and its geometry (e.g., the toy might be hidden in the corner between the long wall and the short blue wall). The rooms were designed so that the geometric or color cues were individually insufficient and would yield an unambiguous result only when combined. Prelinguistic infants, though perfectly able to detect and use both kinds of cue, were shown to exploit only the geometric information, searching randomly in each of the two geometrically indistinguishable sites. Yet adults and older children were easily capable of combining the geometric and nongeometric cues to solve the problem. Importantly, success at combining the cues was not predicted by any measure of the children's intelligence or developmental stage except for the child's use of language. Only children who were able to spontaneously conjoin spatial and color terms in their speech (e.g., who would describe something as, say, to the right of the long green wall) were able to solve the problem. Hermer-Vazquez, Spelke, and Katsnelson (1999) then probed the role of language in this task by asking subjects to solve problems requiring the integration of geometric and nongeometric information while performing one of two other tasks. The first task involved shadowing (repeating back) speech played over headphones. The other involved shadowing (with their hands) a rhythm played over the headphones. The working memory demands of the latter task were at least as heavy as those of the former. Yet subjects engaged in speech shadowing were unable to solve the integration-demanding problem, while those shadowing rhythm were unaffected. Agents' linguistic abilities, the researchers concluded, are indeed actively involved in their ability to solve problems requiring the integration of geometric and nongeometric information.

The precise nature of this linguistic involvement is, however, still in dispute. Hermer-Vazquez, Spelke, and Katsnelson (1999), and following them Carruthers (2002), interpret the results as suggesting that public language provides (or perhaps better, engenders) a unique internal representational medium for the cross-modular integration of information.[5] The linguaform templates of encoded sentences provide, according to Carruthers, special representational vehicles that allow information from otherwise encapsulated resources to interact. This is an attractive and challenging story, and one that I cannot pretend to do justice to here. But it is one that presupposes a specific (and quite contentious; see Fodor 2001) view of the mind as massively (not merely peripherally) modular, requiring linguaform templates to bring multiple knowledge bases into fruitful contact.

Suppose we abandon this presupposition of massive modularity? We may still account, or so I suggest, for the role of language in enabling complex multicued problem solving by depicting the linguistic structures as providing essential scaffolding for the distribution of selective attention to complex (in this case, color–geometry conjunctive) aspects of the scene. According to this alternative account, linguistic resources enable us better to control the disposition of selective attention to ever more complex feature combinations.[6] Attention to a complex conjoined cue, I suggest, requires the (possibly unconscious) retrieval of at least some of the relevant lexical items. This explains the shadowing result.

And it fits nicely with the earlier account of the cognitive impact of simple labels insofar as linguistic activity (in this case, more structured activity) again allows us to target our attentional resources on complex, conjunctive, or otherwise elusive elements of the encountered scene. The idea that language enables new forms of selective attention by, in effect, providing new objects for old (i.e., not specifically linguistic) attentive processes can be further illustrated by the case of arithmetical thought and reason, to which we now turn.

3.4   Hybrid Thoughts?

What is going on when you have the thought that 98 is one more than 97? According to a familiar model, you must have succeeded (if you managed to think the thought at all) in translating the English sentence into something else. The something else might be a sentence of mentalese (e.g., Fodor 1987) or a point in some exotic state space (e.g., Churchland 1989).

But consider a recent account due to Stanislas Dehaene and colleagues (see Dehaene 1997; Dehaene et al. 1999). Dehaene depicts this kind of precise mathematical thought as emerging at the productive intersection of three distinct cognitive contributions. The first involves a basic biological capacity to individuate small quantities: 1-ness, 2-ness, 3-ness, and more-than-that-ness, to take the standard set. The second involves another biologically basic capacity, this time for approximate reasoning concerning magnitudes (discriminating, say, arrays of 8 dots from arrays of 16 but not from more closely matched arrays). The third, not biologically basic but arguably transformative, is the learned capacity to use the specific number words of a language and the eventual appreciation that each such number word names a distinct quantity. Notice that this is not the same as appreciating, in at least one important sense, just what that quantity is. Most of us can't form any clear image of, for example, 98-ness (unlike, say, 2-ness). But we appreciate nonetheless that the number word 98 names a unique quantity between 97 and 99.

When we add the use of number words to the more basic biological nexus, Dehaene argues, we acquire an evolutionarily novel capacity to think about an unlimited set of exact quantities.[7] We gain this capacity not because we now have a mental encoding of 98-ness just like our encoding of 2-ness. Rather, the new thoughts depend directly, but not exhaustively, on our tokening the numerical expressions themselves as symbol strings of our own public language. The actual numerical thought, on this model, occurs courtesy of the *combination* of this token-ing (of the symbol string of a given language) and the appropriate acti-vation of the more biologically basic resources mentioned earlier.

Here is some of the evidence for this view, as presented in Dehaene et al. (1999). First, there are the results of studies of Russian-English bilinguals. In these studies, Russian-English bilinguals were trained quite extensively on 12 cases involving exact and approximate sums of the same pairs of two-digit numbers presented as words in one or other language. For example, in English, subjects might be trained on the problem "Four + Five" and asked to select their answer from "Nine" and "Seven." This is called the exact condition, as it requires exact reasoning because the two candidate numbers are close to each other. By contrast, a problem like "Four + Five" with the choices "Eight" and "Three" belongs to the approximate condition, as it requires only rough reasoning because the candidates are now quite far apart.

After extensive training on the pairs, subjects were later tested on the very same sums in either the original or the other (nontrained) lan-guage. After training, performance in the approximation condition was shown to be unaffected by switching the language, whereas in the exact condition, language switching resulted in asymmetric performance, with subjects responding much faster if the test language corresponded to the training language. Crucially, then, there were no switching costs at all for trained approximate sums. Performance was the same regard-less of language switching. Training-based speed-up is thus nonlan-guage switchable for the exact sums and fully switchable for the inexact sums. Such studies, Dehaene et al. (1999) concluded, provide

> evidence that the arithmetic knowledge acquired during train-ing with exact problems was stored in a language-specific format.... For approximate addition, in contrast, performance was equivalent in the two languages providing evidence that the knowledge was stored in a language-independent form. (973)

A second line of evidence draws on lesion studies in which (to take one example) a patient with severe left-hemisphere damage cannot determine whether 2 + 2 equals 3 or 4 but reliably chooses 3 or 4 over 9, indicating a sparing of the approximation system.

Finally, Dehaene et al. (1999) present neuroimaging data from subjects engaged in exact and approximate numerical tasks. The exact tasks show significant activity in the speech-related areas of the left frontal lobe, while the approximate tasks recruit bilateral areas of the parietal lobes implicated in visuospatial reasoning. These results are presented as a demonstration "that exact calculation is language dependent, whereas approximation relies on nonverbal visuo-spatial cerebral networks" (970) and that "even within the small domain of elementary arithmetic, multiple mental representations are used for different tasks" (973).

Dehaene (1997) also makes some nice points about the need to somehow establish links between the linguistic labels and our innate sense of simple quantities. At first, it seems, children learn language-based numerical facts *without* such appreciation. According to Dehaene (1997), "for a whole year, children realize that the word 'three' is a number without knowing the precise value it refers to" (107). But once the label gets attached to the simple innate number line, the door is open to understanding that *all* numbers refer to precise quantities, even when we lack the intuitive sense of what the quantity is (e.g., my own intuitive sense of 53-ness is not distinct from my intuitive sense of 52-ness, though all such results are variable according to the level of mathematical expertise of the subject).

Typical human mathematical competence, all this suggests, is plausibly seen as a kind of hybrid, whose elements include:

1. images or encodings of actual words in a specific language,
2. an appreciation of the fact that each distinct number word names a specific and distinct quantity, and
3. a rough appreciation of where that quantity lies on a kind of approximate, analog number line (e.g., 98 is just less than halfway between 1 and 200).

Many of our mathematical thoughts rely, if this is correct, on the coordinated action of various resources. On this view, there is (at least) an internal representation of the numeral, of the word form, and of the phonetics, along with other resources (e.g., the analog number line) to which these become (with learning) roughly keyed via some sense of relative location. What matters for present purposes is that there may be no need to posit (for the average agent[8]), in addition to this coordinated medley, any further content-matching internal representation of, say, 98-ness. Instead, the presence of actual number words in a public code (and of internal representations *of those very public items*) is itself part of the coordinated representational medley that constitutes many kinds of arithmetical knowing.

Consider the thought that there are 98 toys on the table. According to the standard models, to think the thought that there are 98 toys on the table you must have succeeded in translating the English sentence into *a fully content-providing something else*. The something else might be an atom or sentence of mentalese (for Fodor) or a point in some exotic state space (for Churchland). By contrast, according to this quite radical alternative, the thought that there are 98 toys on the table is (for most of us) dependent on the presence of a hybrid representational vehicle. This is a vehicle that includes, as expected, the activation of a variety of content-relevant internal representations (in neuralese or mentalese, let's assume). But it also includes as a co-opted proper part, a token (let's think of it as an image, very broadly construed) of a conventional public language encoding ("ninety-eight") appropriately linked to various other resources (e.g., some rough position on an analog number line).[9]

3.5 From Translation to Coordination

What general model of language and its relation to thought do these various illustrations suggest? A good place to begin is with the conception of language as complementary to more basic forms of neural processing (for my own explorations of the theme, see Clark 1996, 1998b, 2000b, 2000c, 2006). According to this conception, language works its magic not (or not solely) by means of translation into appropriate expressions of neuralese or the language of thought but also by something more like coordination dynamics. Encounters with words and with structured linguistic encodings act to anchor and discipline intrinsically fluid and context-sensitive modes of thought and reason.

This notion of anchoring is best appreciated in the light of connectionist or artificial neural network models of memory, storage, and processing (for basic overviews, see Clark 1989, 1993; for something closer to the state of the art, see O'Reilly and Munakata 2000). For present purposes, what matters is that such models posit a fundamentally fluid system in which the fine details of recent context color and nuance recall and representation in quite fundamental ways. For systems such as these, the problem of *stabilization* becomes pressing. On the one hand, it is a virtue of these systems that new information automatically impacts similar items that are already "stored" and that information retrieval is highly context sensitive. On the other hand, advanced thought and reason plausibly require the ability to reliably follow trajectories in representational space and to reliably lead others through certain trajectories. All this requires some means to discipline our own, and others', mental spaces in ways that tame (though never eradicate) those biologically more "natural" processes of merging and change. Words and linguistic strings are among the most powerful and basic tools we use to discipline and stabilize dynamic processes of reason and recall. The shift is thus from seeing words and sentences as items apt only for translation into an inner code to seeing them as inputs (whether externally or internally generated) that drive, sculpt, and discipline the internal representational regime.

Elman (2004) suggests:

Rather than putting word knowledge into a passive storage (which then entails mechanisms by which that knowledge can be "accessed," "retrieved," "integrated" etc.) words might be thought of in the same way that one thinks of other kinds of sensory stimuli: they act directly on mental states. (301)

"Words," Elman goes on to argue, "do not have meaning, they are cues to meaning" (306).[10] Linguistic inputs, on this model, are quite literally modes of systematic neural manipulation and operate in similar ways both between and within human individuals. Words and sentences act as artificial input signals, often (as in self-directed speech) entirely self-generated, that nudge fluid natural systems of encoding and representation along reliable and useful trajectories. This remarkable display of virtuosic artificial self-manipulation allows language-laden minds to sculpt and guide their own processes of learning, of recall, of representation, and of selective attention (for more on this important theme, see Barsalou 2003). In this way, the symbolic environment (very broadly construed) can impact thought and learning both by selectively activating other internal representational resources (the usual suspects) and by allowing the material symbols themselves, or shallow imagelike internal representations of them, to act as additional fulcrums of attention, memory, and control. In the maximum strength version, these shallow symbolic objects can even appear as elements in representationally hybrid thoughts.

For quite a few years, I thought this was a radical idea that fans of (to take the most extreme example) the Language of Thought Hypothesis would surely reject out of hand. Their idea, I believed, was that words mean what they do entirely by virtue of being paired with expressively parallel snippets of mentalese and that thinking was all done in mentalese. Imagine my surprise, then, when I found this little snippet hidden away in that review of Carruthers by Fodor (1998):

I don't think that there are decisive arguments for the theory that all thought is in Mentalese. In fact, I don't think it's even true, in any detail...I wouldn't be in the least surprised, for example, if it turned out that some arithmetic thinking is carried out by executing previously memorized algorithms that are defined *over public language symbols for numbers* ("now carry the '2'" and so forth). It's quite likely that Mentalese co-opts bits of natural language in all sorts of ways; quite likely the story about how it does so will be very complicated indeed by the time that the psychologists get finished telling it. (72, emphasis in original)

Fodor here gestures, it seems to me, at an incredibly potent mechanism of cognitive expansion. Pretty clearly, though, Fodor (1998) himself attaches little importance to the concession, quickly adding that: "For all our philosophical purposes (e.g., for purposes of understanding what thought content is, and what concept possession is, and so forth) *nothing essential is lost* if you assume that all thought is in Mentalese" (72, emphasis added).

By contrast, I am inclined to see the potential for representational hybridity as massively important to understanding the nature and power of much distinctively human cognition. There are, I think, two issues that make the difference between Fodor's assessment of the situation and my own.

First, Fodor has the LOT (Language of Thought) already in place, so the basic biological engine, on his account, comes factory primed with innovations favoring structure, generality, and compositionality.

But what if your vision of the basic biological engine is not one that echoes the properties and features of sentences and propositional attitudes? What if, for example, it is closer to Churchland's vision of a complex but thoroughly connectionist device or to Barsalou's (1999) vision of a "perceptual symbol system"? What if, in short, you don't have what Dennett once called the "walking encyclopedia" view of the basic innards? In such a case, the potential cognitive impact of a little hybridity and co-opting may be much greater than Fodor concedes. It may be essential to such a system's ability to think rather a wide variety of thoughts that the inner goings-on involve, as genuinely constitutive elements, something like images or traces of the public language symbols (words) themselves. Words and sentences, on this view, may be potent real-world structures (material symbols), many of whose features and properties (arbitrary amodal nature, extreme compactness and abstraction, compositional structure, etc.) simply complement, without full replication, the contributions of basic biological cognition. In such a case, it is not clear to me that it would be right to treat the co-opting strategies as marginal for the understanding of thought and concepts.

Second, much of Fodor's insistence upon a deflationary reading of the hybrid option flows directly from his (in)famous views concerning concept learning. For given those views, the meaning of hybrid representational forms cannot be learned unless the learner already had the resources to represent that very meaning using more biologically basic (indeed, innate) resources.[11] This is not the time or place to engage in this important discussion. But it may be noted that Fodor's skepticism depends (as he himself is the first to admit; see, e.g., Fodor 2004) on detaching our ideas about meaning from any essential (i.e., meaning-constituting) links to action or use. The view I embrace (see Prinz and Clark 2004) is quite different and makes grasp of meaning a function of the range of ways an encoding (ultimately, a mere syntactic structure) poises us to act (where acts include but are not exhausted by acts of thinking and inferring) in the world. On such a view (which is the unremarked norm in much cognitive science) there is, even on Fodor's own account, no need to suppose true (radical, expansive) concept learning impossible. Pretty clearly, such a view leaves room for hybrid representational forms to poise a system to act in new ways and thus to count as understanding brand new kinds of things. The case of mathematical understanding, as rehearsed earlier, looks to be one example of this.

This vision of mind expansion by the use of hybrid representational forms remains visibly close to that of Dennett (1991a, 1996). But Dennett depicts exposure to language as installing a new virtual serial machine in the neural wetware by affecting "myriad microsettings in the plasticity of the brain" (1991a, 219). He thus places most of his bets on the *radically internally transformative* power of our encounters with language and ends up with a story that seems more developmental than genuinely hybrid. On the artifact model, by contrast, words and sentences remain potent real-world structures encountered and used by a basically (though this is obviously too crude) pattern-completing brain. Admittedly, drawing these lines is a delicate task (see, e.g., Densmore and Dennett 1999). For even on this account, the brain sometimes represents these structures so myriad microsettings *must* alter. But perhaps the brain represents these potent real-world items in much the same way it represents anything else. In that case (see Churchland 1995, chap. 10), language need not reorganize neural coding routines in any way that is deeper or more profound than might occur, say, when we first learn to swim or play volleyball.

Wheeler (2004, in press-a) argues that there is an important disanalogy between the volleyball case and the language case. For in learning to represent the structures of volleyball, we do not thereby learn to represent a syntactically structured domain. To represent linguistic structures just is, Wheeler claims, to install brand new modes of representation and processing: It is to install at least a kind of virtual syntactic engine. I don't think this can be quiet right because, as I argue in Clark (2004), it must be possible to represent syntactically structured language without using syntactically structured representations to do so (just as it is possible to represent green objects without using green representations to do so). But Wheeler's real point (see Wheeler in press-a) is that language presents a very special kind of domain and that experience with language may thus have much more profound effects (from a cognitive point of view) than experience with other domains. I agree with that. It does not follow, though, that experience with language need install radically new forms of processing and encoding and, still less (and here Wheeler might agree), that those forms of encoding and processing would amount to the implementation of a language of thought. Wheeler and I thus agree that minds like ours are transformed by the web of material symbols and epistemic artifacts. But that transformation, at least on the version I favor, may neither require nor result in the installation of brand new internal representational forms. Instead, there may be much underexplored merit in the canny use of the external forms (and internal images of those very forms) themselves. Such forms may help sculpt and modify processes of selective attention and act as elements within hybrid representational wholes.

One immediate merit of such a view is a more nuanced attitude to the vexing question of evolutionary cognitive continuity. Jesse Prinz (2004) makes the point well:

> Researchers who presume that we think in amodal symbols face a dilemma. If they argue that nonhuman animals lack such amodal symbols, they must postulate a radical leap in evolution. If they suppose that animals have amodal thoughts, they must explain why human thought is so much more powerful. Empiricism [Prinz's favorite, though not obligatory in the present context!] when coupled with the assumption that we can think in public language, explains the discrepancy in cognitive capacities without postulating a major discontinuity in evolution. (427)

Needless to say, this radical story leaves many questions unanswered. It would be good to have a clear account of just what attention—that crucial variable that linguistic scaffolding seems so potently to adjust—actually *is*. It would be good to have much more in the way of genuine, implementable, fully mechanistic models of the various ways that internalized language might enhance thought. And it would be good to know just what it is about human brains and/or human history that has enabled structured public language to get such a comprehensive grip on minds like ours. But shortfalls aside, I hope to have at least brought the strong material symbol model into clearer view and to have shown why it might be attractive to anyone who thinks that language makes a truly *deep* contribution to human thought and reason.

3.6   Second-order Cognitive Dynamics

The augmentation of biological brains with linguaform resources may also shed some light on our ability to display second-order cognitive dynamics (Clark 1998a; and see further discussion in Bermudez 2003). By second-order cognitive dynamics, I mean a cluster of powerful capacities involving reflection on our own thoughts and thought processes. It has recently been suggested, for example, that our capacities for flexible reasoning about others' beliefs depend directly on the linguistic externalization of beliefs using the grammatical structures of embedded complements (de Villiers and de Villiers 2003). Consider also the cluster of powerful capacities that include systematic attempts to train our skills and repair our faults, as well as practices that engender critical self-reflection. Further cases include recognizing a flaw in our own plan or argument and dedicating further cognitive efforts to fixing it, or reflecting on the unreliability of our own initial judgments in certain types of situations and proceeding with special caution as a result. Moving to a kind of meta-meta level, consider the act of thinking about the conditions under which we think best and trying to bring them about. The list could be continued, but the pattern should be clear. In all these cases, we are effectively thinking about our own cognitive profiles or about specific thoughts.

Rather amazingly, we are animals who can think about any aspect of our own thinking and can thus devise cognitive strategies (which may be more or less indirect and baroque) aimed to modify, alter, or control aspects of our own psychology.

All this "thinking about thinking" is a good candidate for a distinctively human capacity and one that may depend on language for its very existence. For (to rehearse a line pursued at length in Clark 1998a) as soon as we formulate a thought in words or on paper, it becomes an object for both ourselves and for others. As an object, it is the kind of thing we can have thoughts about. In creating the object, we need have no thoughts about thoughts, but once it is there, the opportunity immediately exists to attend to it as an object in its own right. The process of linguistic formulation thus creates the stable attendable structure to which subsequent thinkings can attach. Just such a view concerning the potential role of the inner rehearsal of sentences appears in Jackendoff (1996), who suggests that the mental rehearsal of sentences may be the primary means by which our own thoughts are able to become objects of further attention and reflection.

Linguaform reason, if this is correct, is not just a tool for the novice (e.g., as suggested by Dreyfus and Dreyfus 2000). Instead, it emerges as a key cognitive tool by means of which we are able to objectify, reflect upon, and hence knowingly engage with our own thoughts, trains of reasoning, and cognitive and personal characters. This positions language to act as a kind of cognitive superniche: a cognitive niche, one of whose greatest virtues is to allow us to construct ("with malice aforethought," as Fodor 1994, rather elegantly puts it) an open-ended sequence of new cognitive niches. These may include designer environments in which to think, reason, and perform as well as special training regimes to install (and to make habitual) the complex skills such environments demand.

3.7   Self-made Minds

Coming to grips with our own special cognitive nature demands that we take very seriously the material reality of language: its existence as an additional, actively created, and effortfully maintained structure in our internal and external environment. From sounds in the air to inscriptions on the printed page, the material structures of language both reflect, and then systematically transform, our thinking and reasoning about the world. As a result, our cognitive relation to our own words and language (both as individuals and as a species) defies any simple logic of inner versus outer. Linguistic forms and structures are first encountered as simply objects (additional structure) in our world. But they then form a potent overlay that effectively, and iteratively, reconfigures the space for biological reason and self-control.

The cumulative complexity here is genuinely quite staggering. We do not just self-engineer better worlds to think in. We self-engineer ourselves to think and perform better in the worlds we find ourselves in. We self-engineer worlds in which to build better worlds to think in. We build better tools to think with and use these very tools to discover still better tools to think with. We tune the way we use these tools by building educational practices to train ourselves to use our best cognitive tools better. We even tune the way we tune the way we use our best cognitive tools by devising environments that help build better environments for educating ourselves in the use of our own cognitive tools (e.g., environments geared toward teacher education and training). Our mature mental routines are not merely self-engineered: They are massively, overwhelmingly, almost *unimaginably* self-engineered. The linguistic scaffoldings that surround us, and that we ourselves create, are both cognition enhancing in their own right and help provide the tools we use to discover and build the myriad *other* props and scaffoldings whose cumulative effect is to press minds like ours from the biological flux.

4

World, Incorporated

4.1   Cognitive Niche Construction

Niche construction, as defined by Laland et al., refers to

> the activities, choices and metabolic processes of organisms,
> through which they define, choose, modify and partly create
> their own niches. For instance, to varying degrees, organisms
> choose their own habitats, mates, and resources and construct
> important components of their local environments such as
> nests, holes, burrows, paths, webs, dams, and chemical envi-
> ronments. (2000, 131)

Niche construction is a pervasive, though still widely underestimated, force in nature. All animals act on their environments and, in so
doing, alter those environments in ways that may sometimes change the
fitness landscape of the animal itself. A classic example is the spider's
web.[1] The existence of the web modifies the sources of natural selection
within the spider's selective niche, allowing subsequent selection for
web-based forms of camouflage and communication, for example.

Still further complexity is introduced when organisms collectively
build structures that persist beyond their own lifetime. A familiar
example is the communally constructed beaver's dam, whose physical

presence subsequently alters selection pressures on both the beaver and its progeny that inherit the dam and the altered river flows it has produced. Similar effects can be seen in the nest-building activities of many wasps and termites, where the presence of the nest introduced selection pressures for behaviors that regulate nest temperature, for example, by sealing entrances at night (Frisch 1975).

The cultural transmission of knowledge and practices resulting from individual lifetime learning, when combined with the physical persistence of artifacts, yields yet another source of potentially selection-impacting feedback. The classic example here (from Feldman and Cavalli-Sforza 1989) is the practice of domesticating cattle and dairying, which paved the way for selection for adult lactose tolerance in (and only in) those human populations engaging in such activities.

In all these cases, what ultimately matters, as Laland et al. (2000) stress, is the way niche-construction activity leads to new feedback cycles. In the standard cases, these feedback cycles run across evolutionary time. Animals change the world in ways that change the selective landscapes for biological evolution. Important for our purposes, however, this whole process has a direct analog within lifetime learning. Here, the feedback cycles alter and transform processes of individual and cultural reasoning and learning. For example, both educational practices and human-built structures (artifacts) are passed on from generation to generation in ways that dramatically alter the fitness landscape for individual lifetime learning. To adapt an example I have used elsewhere (Clark 2001a), the novice bartender inherits an array of differently shaped glassware and cocktail furniture and a practice of serving different drinks in different kinds of glasses. As a result, expert bartenders (see Beach 1988) learn to line up differently shaped glasses in a spatial sequence corresponding to the temporal sequence of drink orders. The problem of remembering which drink to prepare next is thus transformed, as a result of learning within this prestructured niche, into the problem of perceiving the different shapes and associating each shape with a kind of drink. The bartender, by creating persisting spatially arrayed stand-ins for the drink orders, actively structures the local environment to press more utility from basic modes of visually cued action and recall. In this way, the exploitation of the physical situation allows relatively lightweight cognitive strategies to reap large rewards.

This is a simple illustration of the power of "cognitive niche construction," defined as the process by which animals build physical structures that transform problem spaces in ways that aid (or sometimes impede) thinking and reasoning about some target domain or domains.[2] These physical structures combine with appropriate culturally transmitted practices to enhance problem solving and, in the most dramatic cases, to make possible whole new forms of thought and reason.

4.2   Cognition in the Globe: A Cameo

Elizabethan and Jacobean theatrical practice provides an unexpected illustration of the cognitive potency of a well-tailored environment. Early modern acting companies were required to perform "a staggering number of plays: six different plays a week, with relatively infrequent repetition, and with the additional demands of putting on a new play roughly every fortnight" (Tribble 2005, 135–136).

How could the actors learn their parts? One standard account depicted the parts of any one actor as all following a single kind of character (being "in a line"). This, alongside some very heavy doses of rote learning and some last-minute saves as the production lurches toward disaster, was meant to explain the (bare) viability of such a punishing schedule. But such devices fall dramatically short of explaining the documented robustness and success of early modern theater. In a groundbreaking article in *Shakespeare Quarterly*, Tribble (2005) suggests that the true explanation emerges only once we look outside the head of the individual actor and recognize the complex interplays between actor recall and the specially engineered spaces and social practices of the early modern theater.

Consider first the physical space of the theater itself. Such spaces varied tremendously from venue to venue, but two constant features were the playing platform and the multiplicity of stage doors for entrances and exits. Concerning the stage doors, Tribble suggests that "it would be difficult to overestimate their importance in structuring, organizing and simplifying the complex activity of the playing companies" (2005, 11) and quotes David Bradley's lovely (1992) description of the doors as "the systole and diastole of the great heart-beat of the Elizabethan stage as it fills and empties, fills and empties" (29).

The role of the stage doors may be inferred from key staging manuscripts, known as plots, that were created for each play. These plots were physically imposing, written on large sheets of about 12 to 16 inches in size, often with a hole on top for hanging on a wall. They paid maximum attention to character features, casting, entrances and exits, sound and music cues, and so on. Taken on their own, the plots look too thin and scanty to determine the stage play. Yet for the actors, they provided the only high-level map of the overall play. The key to understanding their action, Tribble argues, is their size and physical layout. They are designed to allow actors who have never seen the full text of the play to quickly grasp its general structure, content, and flow. Each actor was also provided with a kind of minimal personalized script: a "need-to-know" document containing only information about their own speeches, entrances, and exits. None of these resources, taken on their own, looks sufficient to do the job. But working together, using multiple physical cues in the physical space of the theater and guided by the overlearned practices and conventions of the day, they provided the minimal scaffolding needed. Taken in context, the puzzlingly scanty plots can thus be understood as "a two-dimensional map of the play designed to be grafted on to the three-dimensional space of the theatre and to be used in conjunction with the parts" (Tribble 2005, 146).

The solution to the puzzle of early modern theatre, it seems, is an object lesson in the power and scope of distributed and situated cognition:[3]

> The productive constraint of the stripped-down part reduces the need to filter signal (one's own part) from noise (everyone else's); the plot provides a schematic diagram of the shape of the play as a whole to supplement the part, the physical space of the theatre and the conventions of movement it supports enables the transition from the two-dimensional maps of plot and part to its three-dimensional embodiment on stage, and the structures and protocols of the theatrical company pass on its practices to new members. (Tribble 2005, 155)

Those prodigious performances of the past are thus explained in part by reference to the special features of their singular dramatic niche.

4.3   Thinking Space

A vast amount of contemporary human cognitive niche construction likewise involves the active exploitation of space. David Kirsh, in his classic treatment "The Intelligent Use of Space" (1995b), divides these uses into three broad and overlapping categories. The first is "spatial arrangements that simplify choice," such as laying out cooking ingredients in the order you will need them or putting your groceries in one bag and mine in another. The second is "spatial arrangements that simplify perception," such as putting the washed mushrooms on the right of the chopping board and the unwashed ones on the left or the color green dominated jigsaw puzzle pieces in one pile and the red dominated ones in another. The third is "spatial dynamics that simplify internal computation," such as repeatedly reordering the Scrabble pieces so as to prompt better recall of candidate words or the use of instruments such as slide rules, which transform arithmetical operations into perceptual alignment activities.

Kirsh's detailed analysis is concerned solely with the adult's expert use of space as a problem-solving resource. But it is worth asking how and when children begin to use active spatial reorganization in this kind of way. Is this something that we, as humans, are just naturally disposed to do, or is it something we must learn? A robot agent, though fully able to act on its world, will not ipso facto know to use space as a resource for this kind of cognitive niche construction! Indeed, it seems to me that no other animal on this planet is as adept as we are at the intelligent use of space: No other animal uses space as an open-ended cognitive resource, developing spatial offloadings for new problems on a day-by-day basis.

It is perhaps noteworthy, then, that the majority of these spatial arrangement ploys work, as Kirsh himself notes at the end of his long treatment, by *reducing the descriptive complexity of the environment*. Space is often used as a resource for grouping items into equivalence classes for some purpose (e.g., *washed* mushrooms, *red* jigsaw pieces, *my* groceries, etc.). It is intuitive that once descriptive complexity is thus reduced, processes of selective attention, and of action control, can operate on elements of a scene that were previously too "unmarked" to define such operations over. Human language is itself notable both for its open-ended expressive power and for its ability to reduce the descriptive complexity of the environment. Reduction of descriptive complexity, however achieved, makes new groupings available for thought and action. In this way, the intelligent use of space and the intelligent use of language form a mutually reinforcing pair, pursuing a common cognitive agenda.

Developmental investigations lend some substance to such a hypothesis. To take just one example, Namy, Smith, and Gershkoff-Stowe (1997) conducted a series of experiments involving children's use of space to represent similarity. Very briefly, what the experiments suggest is that spatial groupings of play objects (e.g., putting all the balls *here* and all the boxes *there*) are not mere spatially expressed reflections of fully achieved grasp of category membership but rather part and parcel of the process of coming to learn about categories and to discover the use of space as a means of representing category membership. The process the investigators document, in rich microgenetic detail, is one of bootstrapping that starts with early play experiences in which the child is interested in one kind of play object and hence ends up (as a side effect) with those objects grouped together in space. Such self-created groupings help the child to discover the possibility and value of spatial classification itself. Crucial to this discovery is the child's engagement in preferential play in which one type of object is preferred to another. This kind of play was shown to lead, over relatively short periods of developmental time, to the emergence of true exhaustive classification behavior in which spatial organization functions as a symbolic indicator of category membership.

This whole process is one of *incremental cognitive self-stimulation*. The perceptually available (grouped) products of the child's own activity form the new inputs that favor learning about exhaustive classification and, simultaneously, about the use of space as a means of representing category membership. The capacities of spontaneous spatial classification that this developmental bootstrapping helps create may then further scaffold the process of learning names and labels, while the acquisition of new names and labels in turn promotes the exploration of new and more sophisticated spatial groupings. Developmental investigations thus strongly suggest that space, classification, and language are made for each other, with spatial indexing of various forms (for some more of these, see Smith and Gasser 2005, and sec. 3.2) playing a major role in the learning of language, and language itself (as we shall later see) playing a cognitive role very similar to that of space.

4.4   Epistemic Engineers

To appreciate just how *powerful* a force cognitive niche construction may actually be in the evolution and development of human cognition, it helps to introduce the notion, due to Sterelny (2003), of *cumulative downstream epistemic engineering*. Sterelny, in a rich and detailed synthesis of work in biology, anthropology, and the study of primate minds, offers an account of human uniqueness that gives pride of place to our extraordinary capacities as "ecological engineers"—that is to say, as the active constructors of our own cognitive niches. Having earlier argued for group selection as a key force in human evolution, Sterelny notes that groups of humans engineer their own habitats and that these are transmitted to the next generation, who further modify the habitat. Importantly, some of these modifications are to the epistemic environment and affect the informational structures and opportunities presented to each subsequent generation. Although other animals clearly engage in niche construction, it is only in the human species, Sterelny argues, that we see this potent, cumulative, runaway (self-fueling) process of epistemic engineering.

Niche construction is depicted by Sterelny as a kind of additional inheritance mechanism, working alongside and interacting with genetic inheritance. One of the points of interaction concerns phenotypic plasticity. For rampant niche construction yields a rapid succession of selective environments and hence favors the biological evolution of phenotypic plasticity. Hominid minds, Sterelny suggests, are adapted not to the "statistical composite" of the Pleistocene (as some brands of evolutionary psychology suggest; see, e.g., Tooby and Cosmides 1990) but to the variability of environments and to the spread of variation itself. To cope with such variability, we are said to have evolved powerful forms of developmental plasticity. These allow early learning to induce persisting and stable forms of neural reorganization, impacting our range of automatic skills, affective responses, and generally reorganizing human cognition in deep and profound ways. The upshot, in direct opposition to much recent evolutionary psychological speculation, is that "we do not have essentially Pleistocene minds in our contemporary world" (Sterelny 2003, 166). Instead, "the same initial set of developmental resources can differentiate into quite different final cognitive products" (166). In this way, "transforming hominid developmental environments transformed hominid brains themselves. As hominids remade their own worlds, they indirectly remade themselves" (173).

We see this explanatory template in action in, for example, Sterelny's account of our capacity to interpret others as intentional agents. Instead of an innate "folk psychology" module, in the form of a domain-specific adaptation for "mind-reading," Sterelny offers a niche-construction-based account according to which

> selection for interpretative skills could lead to a different evolutionary trajectory: selection on parents (and via group selection on the band as a whole) for actions which scaffold the development of the interpretative capacities. Selection rebuilds the epistemic environment to scaffold the development of those capacities. (2003, 221)

Basic perceptual adaptations (e.g., for gaze monitoring etc.) are thus supposed to be bootstrapped up to a full-blown mind-reading ability via the predictable effects of intense social scaffolding: The child is surrounded by exemplars of mind-reading in action, she is nudged by cultural inventions such as the use of simplified narratives, prompted by parental rehearsal of her own intentions, and provided with a rich palate of linguistic tools such as words for mental states. Such "incremental environmental engineering" provides, according to Sterelny, a "wealth of the stimulus" argument against the innateness hypothesis (223).

Our theory of mind, according to this argument, is not wired in at birth but acquired by rich developmental immersion. Such immersion may itself have "architectural consequences" (225), but these are the upshot, not the precondition, of learning. This explanatory strategy thus depicts much of what is most distinctive in human cognition as rooted in the reliable effects, on developmentally plastic brains, of immersion in a well-engineered, cumulatively constructed cognitive niche.

Sterelny's emphasis is thus very much upon the direct neural consequences of the culturally and artifactually scaffolded training regimes applied to young human minds. But although such consequences are surely of the utmost importance, they do not yet exhaust the cognition-transforming effects of material artifacts and culture. For many of the new cognitive regimes supported by our best bouts of incremental epistemic engineering seem to resist full internalization. It is no use, as Ed Hutchins (personal communication) points out, trying to imagine a slide rule when you need to work out a log or cosine! Plastic human brains may nonetheless learn to factor the operation and information-bearing role of such external props and artifacts deep into their own problem-solving routines, creating hybrid cognitive circuits that are themselves the physical mechanisms underlying specific problem-solving performances. We thus come to what is arguably the most radical contemporary take on the potential cognitive role of nonbiological props, aids, and structures: the idea that, under certain conditions, such props and structures might count as *proper parts of extended cognitive processes.*

4.5   Exploitative Representation and Wide Computation

Recall once more the blocks-copying experiments (Ballard et al. 1997, and sec. 1.2). What this work seemed to show was that the brain uses repeated bouts of visual fixation to link a target location to a type of information (color or position of a target block), retrieving that information just in time for use. This was an instance of using embodied action so as to allow the external world to act as a kind of stable, cheap memory store. It was also our first example of what we there dubbed a "distributed functional decomposition," in which neural states and bodily actions together form the means by which certain computational and representational operations are implemented.

With this in mind, consider an accountant, Ada, who is extremely good at dealing with long tables of figures. Over the years, Ada has learned how to solve specific classes of accounting problems by rapidly scanning the columns, copying some numbers onto a paper scratchpad, and then looking to and from those numbers (carefully arrayed on the page) back to the columns of figures. This is all now second nature to Ada, who scribbles at lightning speed deploying a variety of "minimal memory strategies" (Ballard et al. 1997, and sec. 1.3). Instead of attempting to commit multiple complex numerical quantities and dependencies to biological short-term memory, Ada creates and follows trails through the scribbled numbers, relying on self-created external traces every time an intermediate result is obtained. These traces are visited and revisited on a just-in-time, need-to-know basis, briefly shunting specific items of information into and out of short-term biomemory in much the same way as a serial computer shifts information to and from the central registers in the course of carrying out some computation. This extended process may again be best analyzed in familiar terms as a set of problem-solving state transitions whose implementation happens to involve a distributed combination of biological memory, motor actions, external symbolic storage, and just-in-time perceptual access.

Robert Wilson's notions of "exploitative representation" and "wide computation" (1994, 2004) capture the key features of such an extended approach. Exploitative representation occurs when a subsystem gets by without explicitly encoding and deploying some piece of information by virtue of its ability to track that information in some other way. Wilson gives the example of an odometer that keeps track of how many miles a car has traveled not by first counting wheel rotations and then multiplying according to the assumption that each rotation equals x meters but by being built so as to record x meters every time a rotation occurs: "In the first case it encodes a representational assumption and uses this to compute its output. In the second it contains no such encoding but instead uses an existing relationship between its structure and the structure of the world" (2004, 163).

Wilson's descriptions and central examples can make it seem as if exploitative representation is all about achieving success without representations at all, at least in any robust sense of representation. But this need not be so. Another, very pertinent, range of cases would be those in which a subsystem does not contain within itself a persisting encoding of certain things but instead leaves that information in the world or leaves encoding it to some other subsystem to which it has access. Thus, Ada's biological brain does not create and maintain persistent internal encodings of every figure she generates and offloads onto the page, though it may very well create and maintain persistent encodings of several other key features (e.g., some kind of running approximation that acts to check for gross errors). In much the same way as Ballard's block puzzlers, Ada's biological brain may thus, via the crucial bridging capacities of available embodied action, key its own internal representational and internal computational strategies to the reliable presence of the external pen-and-paper buffer. Even robustly representational inner goings-on may thus count as exploitative insofar as they merely form one part of a larger, well-balanced process whose cumulative set of state transitions solves the problem. In this way, "explicit symbolic structures in a cognizer's environment...together with explicit symbolic structures in its head [may] constitute[4] the cognitive system relevant for performing some given task" (Wilson 2004, 184).

The use of various forms of exploitative representation immediately yields a vision of what Wilson dubs "wide computationalism," according to which "at least some of the computational systems that drive cognition reach beyond the limits of the organismic boundary" (165). Wide computationalism, stressing at it does the many interactive processes that span brain, body, and world, is also intrinsically dynamics friendly. Many of the internal representational states invoked will be fleeting, generated on the spot, and delicately, temporally keyed to making the most of other closely coupled internal and external resources. Extended systems may include coupled motor behaviors as processing devices (see sec. 6.7) and more static environmental structures as longer term storage and encoding devices. Bodily and worldly elements may thus emerge as genuine parts of extended cognitive regimes, apt for formal description in both dynamical and information-processing terms. The larger systems thus constituted are, Wilson insists, unified wholes such that "the resulting mind-world computational system itself, and not just the part of it inside the head, is genuinely cognitive" (2004, 167).

Extended systems theorists[5] thus reject the image of mind as a kind of input-output sandwich with cognition as the filling (for this picture and many more arguments for its rejection, see Hurley 1998; see also Clark 1997a). Instead, we confront an image of the local mechanisms of human cognition quite literally bleeding out into body and world.

4.6   Tetris: The Update

Kirsh and Maglio (1994) presented the classic discussion that gave to the cognitive scientific world the useful notion of an "epistemic action." And epistemic actions, I want to suggest, are paramount among the ways in which bodily activity yields transient but cognitively crucial extended functional organizations.[6]

Epistemic actions stand in contrast to pragmatic actions. The latter are actions designed to bring one physically closer to a goal. Walking to the fridge to fetch a beer is a pragmatic action. Epistemic actions may or may not yield such physical advance. Instead, they are designed to extract or uncover information. Looking inside the fridge to see what ingredients are available to cook tonight's dinner is a mild species of epistemic action. Epistemic actions are thus:

> Actions designed to change the input to an agent's information-processing system. They are ways an agent has of modifying the external environment to provide crucial bits of information just when they are needed most. (Kirsh and Maglio 1994, 38)

Or again:

> Epistemic actions—physical actions that make mental computation easier, faster or more reliable—are external actions that an agent performs to change its own computational state. (Kirsh and Maglio 1994, 3)

Epistemic actions, we were also told (1994, 4), might bring benefits by reducing the demands on internal memory, by reducing the number of steps to be taken by the biological engine, by reducing the probability of error in a computation, or by any of these in combination.

Kirsh and Maglio's (1994) claim was that epistemic actions are pervasive and their importance underestimated by the sciences of mind. Animating the original paper was an extended discussion of expert performance at the video game Tetris. In Tetris, variously shaped "zoids" rain down from the top of the screen and must be placed in neatly interlocking rows at the bottom. A fully filled row disappears. The less skillfully the filling is done, the more unfilled rows build up, clogging the screen, and the closer the player comes to the point of failure, when no new zoids can fall. This fate is exacerbated by the increasing speed of zoid-fall as ground is lost. During zoid-fall, a player may use a button to rotate the falling shape 90 degrees to fit it into a waiting slot. A player may also move it left and right.

Tetris is thus a fast, perception–action-loop dominated game, in which one might well expect all acts of physical zoid rotation and left–right movement to be directed at the merely pragmatic end of filling a row. Strikingly, Kirsh and Maglio showed this is not so. In many cases, players use rotation as a means of helping to identify the shape of a zoid and may also shove a zoid all the way to a side wall as a means of better ensuring correct placement for drop (i.e., correct identification of target column) during the now standardized return journey. The latter is an especially clear case of epistemic action because the move to the wall initially takes the zoid *farther* from its destination drop point, not closer to it. This act is usually undertaken when a player is about to drop a zoid from higher than usual on the screen, which would probably explain the need for an epistemic safety check (Kirsh and Maglio 1994, 37). Subsequent work (Maglio et al. 1999; Neth and Payne 2002) displays further evidence of epistemic action in detailed analyses of domains such as Scrabble and the Tower of Hanoi puzzle.

A natural way to think about epistemic actions is in terms of the Principle of Ecological Assembly (sec. 1.3). The costs (temporal and/or energetic) of adding nonpragmatic actions to the problem-solving mix are outweighed by the benefits conferred. In more recent Tetris-based work, Maglio and his colleagues have tried to show that this is indeed the case, using a sequence of ingenious measures and experiments. The goal is to quantify the net benefit of using epistemic actions by laying the time cost of the extra rotations against the resultant "increase in the player's mental capacity" (Maglio, Wenger, and Copeland 2003, 1). The first of these is not so hard to calculate. It takes two keystrokes to induce an on-screen action and then undo it, and the time costs for this were calculated for each player. The second quantity is obviously more elusive. But work by Townsend and Ashby (1978), Townsend and Nozawa (1995), and Wenger and Townsend (2000) provides a promising tool in the form of a measure known as the *hazard function* of the response time (RT) distribution during problem solving. Very informally, this is a measure of the instantaneous probability of completing a process in the next move. In engineering, this is also known as the intensity function. When the measure is high, there is a higher conditional probability of completion in the next instant than there would be for a process operating at a lower measure. The target process is, in that technical sense, then said to be operating at a high level of intensity. The hazard or intensity function is thus a conditional probability function that expresses the likelihood of imminent completion conditional on the process not yet having been completed (for further detail, see Maglio, Wenger, and Copeland 2003).

To turn this into a plausible measure of " increase in mental capacity" as a result of epistemic action taking, Maglio, Wenger, and Copeland compared the values of the hazard function for conditions in which extra rotations are used to provide additional zoid-identifying information ("previews," to use the authors' term) and conditions in which they are not.[7] The final measure, following some innocent data manipulations that I will not discuss here, then displays the percentage of change in the hazard function (itself a reflection of RT distribution) associated with the availability of previews.

Previews were shown to produce a clear increase in capacity, as measured by the change in value of the hazard function, and these benefits increased when memory load was greatest (i.e., with greater lags between preview and decision). This increase was found to substantially outweigh the added time costs of extra rotations, with the ratio of benefit to cost itself improving with increasing lag. Overall then, the recent work provides useful quantitative measures of the positive role of epistemic actions in task performance.

The Tetris story also illustrates the importance of what I'll call "active dovetailing." In the original paper, after presenting a detailed process model of expert play, Kirsh and Maglio (1994) comment: "Its chief novelty lies in allowing individual functional units inside the agent to be in closed-loop interaction with the outside world" (38). By this, they mean that the various "calls to epistemic action" can be instigated directly by individual internal procedures or components, yielding changes in the world that very robustly generate (just in time) the information required by that very subroutine. This means that the overall problem-solving activity will not properly decompose into a neat sphere of internally achieved computations surrounded by a well-behaved nimbus of calls to the world. In place of such a neat "inside–outside" boundary-respecting cycle, we confront (and this fits the model of cognitive incorporation introduced in sec. 2.6) a bunch of unfolding internal processes, each of which is directly issuing, at differing timescales, calls both to other inner processes and to outward-looping epistemic acts that result in cognitively crucial episodes of closed-loop interaction. As Kirsh more recently puts it,

> Once we conceive the agent environment relation to be a dynamic one where agents are causally coupled to their environments at different temporal frequencies with less or more conscious awareness of the nature of their active perceptual engagement, we are moving in a direction of seeing agents more as managers of their interaction, as coordinators locked in a system of action reaction, rather than as pure agents undertaking actions and awaiting consequences. (2004, 7)

In the most interesting class of cases, then, a tight yet promiscuous temporal dovetailing binds the inner and the outer at multiple timescales and levels of processing and organization. This invites understanding in terms of an extended functional organization in which the inner–outer boundary is both analytically unhelpful and computationally far less significant than one might have pretheoretically supposed.

4.7   The Swirl of Organization

Consider once more the question of how the inner and outer elements in some distributed problem-solving ensemble must interact if they are to form a sufficiently integrated cognitive whole (sec. 2.6). Intuitively, not every form of interaction, even when what is interacted *with* is a tool, medium, or device that makes a visible contribution to some episode of intelligent problem solving, looks set to yield a plausible case of extended or distributed cognitive circuitry. For example, imagine you are struggling to use a new piece of software to solve a problem. Phenomenologically, our experience in such cases is not at all suggestive of anything like tool-based cognitive extension.[8] Instead, you are likely to feel quite alienated from the tool in question. The software package dominates as the local problem space that you confront rather than as a piece of transparent equipment through which you confront a wider world.[9]

What kinds of information flow, by contrast, characterize fluent, integrated unfoldings? One key characteristic (first discussed in sec. 2.6) concerns the delicate temporal integration of multiple participating elements and processes (including, e.g., the emergence of automatic, subpersonally mediated calls to internal or external information stores). Such delicate tuning characterized the availability, by rapid saccade, of specific kinds of environmentally stored information in the blocks-copying task introduced in chapter 1. It also strongly characterized the epistemic use of the rotate operation by skilled Tetris players. In such cases, the brain is not required explicitly to represent the availability of such and such information from any given internal or external location. Instead, it simply deploys a problem-solving routine whose fine structure has been selected (by learning and practice) so as to *assume* the easy availability of such and such information from (for example) such and such a visual location via the performance of such and such a gross motor action. One may compare the situation here with the standard cognitivist observation that a successful algorithm for solving some problem may make various assumptions about the problem domain itself. The difference is just that in the cases we have been displaying, the assumptions have become built into whole perception-action loops. These loops then effectively assume the availability of such and such information from such and such location or by means of such and such actions.[10]

A useful way to think about the structuring of such resources may be in terms of what I shall call *implicit metacognitive commitments*.[11] When our brains detect a sudden flash and our eyes automatically saccade in that direction, the motor routine embodies a kind of hard-wired implicit metacognitive commitment to the effect that we may gain useful, perhaps lifesaving, information by such a rapid saccade. This fact about the possible availability of useful information need be nowhere represented in the brain. It is now fully implicit in the way evolution has wired a basic sense-act routine. Similarly, I am suggesting, the effect of extended problem-solving practice may often be to install a kind of motor-informational tuning such that repeated calls to epistemic actions become built into the very heart of many of our daily cognitive routines. Such calls do not then depend on (consciously or unconsciously) *representing* the fact that such and such information is available by such and such a motor act. Rather, that fact is simply implicit, for example, in the learned associations between certain types of game positions in Tetris and the initiation of such and such an epistemic action. Players need have neither conscious nor unconscious knowledge of the role of these important information-creating acts in their own problem solving. The same is true, I suspect, when we speak, scribble, or gesture in ways that, unbeknown to us, actively contribute to our thinking (an example we shall pursue in detail in chap. 6).

Deeply integrated, progressively automated, epistemic actions figure prominently in the construction of complex skill hierarchies. As Donald (2001) nicely argues, we humans are the agents most able to self-assemble complex skills:[12]

> Humans build skill upon skill, creating very complex contingent hierarchies, as in driving or piano playing. A driver must learn a whole range of somewhat independent actions for driving, such as starting, turning, backing-up, steering, accelerating, braking, checking the mirror, shifting gears, monitoring traffic, reading road signs, maintaining speed, keeping track of directions and street names, and so on. These sub-skills are usually self-taught, self-rehearsed, and self-evaluated with some overall guidance. The result is an amazingly complex chain of habit systems or demons, each with its own executive demands, which must eventually be integrated into a massive meta-system that coordinates all of them... no other primate can assemble hierarchies that are anything close to this complex. (146)

The human agent, one might say, is nature's expert at becoming expert. Those striking skill mountains, deliberately created and maintained, often include a wide variety of epistemic actions. Such actions are factored deep into the nested habit systems that enable the embodied embedded agent, in a swirl of active engagements with all manner of props, tools, and artifacts, to succeed at even the most cognitively demanding tasks.

4.8   Extending the Mind

The considerations concerning efficient processing (chap. 1), organizational plasticity (chap. 2), the potential role of material symbols in hybrid organizations (chap. 3), and cognitive scaffolding and distributed functional decomposition (sec. 1.4 and 4.5) all come together in ongoing debates concerning "the extended mind" (Clark and Chalmers 1998).[13] Proponents of the extended mind story hold that even quite familiar human mental states (e.g., states of believing that so and so) can be realized, in part, by structures and processes located outside the human head. Such claims go far beyond the important but far less challenging assertion that human cognizing leans heavily on various forms of external scaffolding and support. Instead, they paint mind itself (or better, the physical machinery that realizes some of our cognitive processes and mental states) as, under humanly attainable conditions, extending beyond the bounds of skin and skull. The machinery of mind, if this is correct, is not simply the biomachinery contained within the ancient skinbag. In this section, I briefly rehearse the main argument, reserving critical discussion and defense for subsequent chapters. The full original paper (Clark and Chalmers 1998) is here included as an appendix. Readers unfamiliar with that treatment may find it useful to refer to the appendix as well the rather summary version presented in this section.

It is important, in considering these issues, to respect the distinction between vehicles and contents. Possessing a contentful mental state is most plausibly a property of a whole active system, perhaps in some historical and/or environmental context. Within that system, certain enduring material aspects may play a special role in enabling the system to possess (whether occurrently or dispositionally) a given mental state. These material aspects are the vehicle of the content. The "extended mind" hypothesis is really a hypothesis about extended vehicles—vehicles that may be distributed across brain, body, and world. We conflate vehicles and contents, as Dennett (1991a) and Hurley (1998) stress, at our philosophical and scientific peril.

Clark and Chalmers's (1998) aim was to show that external traces (pencil marks in a notebook) may sensibly be considered, given the right additional circumstances, as among the physical vehicles of specific dispositional beliefs. This occurs if the traces become poised for the control of action in roughly (the "roughly" is important, as we shall later see) the same kind of way as internal memory traces, yielding an extended supervenience base for some of the agent's dispositional (i.e., genuine but not consciously occurrent) beliefs. The claim here was not, implausibly, that an external, passive encoding might somehow behave exactly like the fluid, automatically responsive resources of internal biological memory. Rather, it was that external encodings were, under certain circumstances, capable of becoming so deeply integrated into online strategies of reasoning and recall as to be only artificially distinguished from proper parts of the cognitive engine itself.

Two examples animated the original paper. The first involved a human agent playing (yes, it's that game again) the video game Tetris. The human player, recall, has the option of trying to identify the falling pieces (a) by mental rotation or (b) by the use of epistemic actions in which the on-screen button causes the falling zoid to rotate. The reader was then asked to imagine (c) a near future human agent with both standard imaginative rotation capacities and also a retinal display that can fast rotate the image on demand, just like using the rotate button. She was also to imagine that to initiate this latter action, the future human issues a thought command straight from motor cortex (aside: This is the same technology already used in many so-called thought control experiments; see chap. 2).

Case (a) looks, we argued, to be a simple case of mental rotation. Case (b) looks like a simple case of nonmental (merely external) rotation. Yet case (c) now looks hard to classify. By hypothesis, the main computational operations involved (motor command, fast-rotate effect fed back into low-level perceptual system at the next time step) are the same as in case (b). Yet our intuitions seem far less clear. But now consider a Martian player (case d) whose natural cognitive equipment includes (for obscure ecological reasons) just the kind of biotechnological fast-rotate machinery imagined in case (c). In the Martian case, we would surely have no hesitation in classifying the on-board fast-rotate circuitry as an element of Martian mental processing.

With this thought experiment as a springboard, we offered a Parity Principle as a rule of thumb, namely:

> Parity Principle. If, as we confront some task, a part of the world functions as a process which, were it to go on in the head, we would have no hesitation in accepting as part of the cognitive process, then that part of the world is (for that time) part of the cognitive process. (Clark and Chalmers 1998, 8)

In other words, for the purposes of identifying the material vehicles of cognitive states and processes, we should (normatively speaking) ignore the old metabolic boundaries of skin and skull and attend to the computational and functional organization of the problem-solving whole. The Parity Principle thus provided a "veil of ignorance" style test meant to help avoid biochauvinistic prejudice. Applied to the case at hand, it invites us, or so we argued, to treat the standard players' epistemic use of the external rotate button, the near future agent's use of a cyberpunk implant, and the Martian player's use of native endowment as all on a cognitive par.

Of course, there are differences. Most strikingly, in case (b), the fast-rotate circuitry is located outside the head, and the results are read in by perception, whereas in cases (c) and (d), the circuitry is all bounded by skin and skull, and the results are read off by introspection. I return to these issues later. Nonetheless, there remained, we argued, at least a prima facie case for parity of treatment based on the significant commonalities rather than simple prejudices about skin and skull, inner and outer. The most important difference, we felt, concerned not the arbitrary barriers of skin and skull, or the delicate (and potentially question-begging) call between perception and introspection, but the more basic functional issues of portability and general availability for use. The standard player's use of the fast-rotate button is limited by the availability of the Tetris console, whereas the cyberpunk and Martian players exploit a resource that is part of the general equipment with which they confront the world.

Taking the argument one step further, we then considered a second example, one designed to address the portability issue and to extend the treatment to the more central case of an agent's beliefs about the world. This was the now-infamous case of Otto and Inga. Inga hears of an intriguing exhibition at the Museum of Modern Art (MOMA) in New York. She thinks, recalls it's on 53rd Street and sets off. Otto suffers from a mild form of Alzheimer's, and as a result, he always carries a thick notebook. When Otto learns useful new information, he always writes it in the notebook. He hears of the exhibition at the MOMA, retrieves the address from his trusty notebook, and sets off. Just like Inga, we claimed, Otto walked to 53rd Street because he *wanted* to go to the museum and *believed* (*even before consulting his notebook*) that it was on 53rd Street. The functional poise of the stored information was, in each case, sufficiently similar (we argued) to warrant similarity of treatment. Otto's long-term beliefs just weren't all in his head.

In the paper, we showed (in some detail; see the appendix) why all this was orthogonal to the more familiar Putnam–Burge style externalism. The key point here is that such traditional forms of externalism (see, e.g., Putnam 1975a, 1975b; Burge 1979, 1986) focus on distal and historical features claimed to impact the contents of beliefs without necessarily impacting what might be thought of as their local physical vehicles. Thus, in the classic cases concerning beliefs about water and twin-earth water, the difference in belief between, say, Andy and twin-Andy are traceable to features that are in an obvious sense currently causally inert. If I happen to be surrounded by XYZ right now (having been abruptly teleported to Twin Earth while typing this sentence), my beliefs still concern standard water, courtesy of my history. The external features that matter are, in these cases, visibly *passive* and play no role in driving the cognitive process in the here and now. In the cases described by Clark and Chalmers, by contrast, the relevant external features are *active*. They are part of the local equipment that plays a causal role in the generation of action. Subtract the notebook encoding and Otto does not go to 53rd Street. Replace it with an encoding that mistakenly indicates 56th Street, and Otto ends up there instead. Here, then, the causally active physical organization that yields the target behavior seems to be smeared across the biological organism and the world. Such active externalism was quite different, we claimed, from any form of passive, reference-based externalism.

Finally, we allowed that (at least as far as our own argument was concerned) conscious mental states might well turn out to supervene only on local processes *inside the head*. But insofar as the scope of the mental is held to outrun that of conscious, occurrent contents (to include, e.g., long-term dispositional beliefs as well as numerous ongoing yet unconscious activities), there was no reason to restrict the physical vehicles of such nonconscious mental states to states of the brain or central nervous system.

In response to the concerns about availability and portability, we then offered a rough-and-ready set of additional criteria to be met by nonbiological candidates for inclusion into an individual's cognitive system. They were

1. That the resource be reliably available and typically invoked. (Otto always carries the notebook and won't answer that he "doesn't know" until after he has consulted it.)
2. That any information thus retrieved be more or less automatically endorsed. It should not usually be subject to critical scrutiny (e.g., unlike the opinions of other people). It should be deemed about as trustworthy as something retrieved clearly from biological memory.
3. That information contained in the resource should be easily accessible as and when required.
4. That the information in the notebook has been consciously endorsed at some point in the past and indeed is there as a consequence of this endorsement.

The status of the fourth feature as a criterion for belief was presented, in the original treatment, as uncertain. Perhaps one can acquire beliefs through subliminal perception or through memory tampering. If so, the "past conscious endorsement" criterion looks too strong. On the other hand, to drop this requirement opens the floodgates to what many would regard as an unwelcome explosion of potential dispositional beliefs (an issue we shall return to in subsequent chapters).

Applying the four criteria yielded, we claimed, a modestly intuitive set of results for putative individual cognitive extensions. A book in my home library would not count. The cyberpunk implant would. Mobile access to Google would not (it would fail conditions 2 and 4). Otto's notebook would. Other people typically would not (but could in rare cases) and so on.

There is only one reply among the many that we considered in the paper that I choose to repeat here, just because it is still the most common response to our story. I call it the Otto 2-step and it goes like this: "All Otto actually believes (in advance) is that the address is in the notebook. That's the belief (step 1) that leads to the looking (step 2) that then leads to the (new) belief about the actual street address."

Despite its initial plausibility, we did not (and do not) think this can work. Suppose we now ask why we do not depict Inga in similar terms. Why don't we say that Inga's only antecedent belief was that the information was stored in her memory and depict her retrieval as an Inga 2-step? Intuitively, the reason seems to be that in the case of Inga, the 2-step model adds spurious complexity: "Inga wanted to go to MOMA. She believed that her memory held the address. Her memory yielded 53rd Street." What's more, it seems likely that in the normal course of events, Inga relies on no beliefs about her memory as such. She just uses it, transparently, as it were. But *ditto* (we may suppose) for Otto: Otto is so accustomed to using the book that he accesses it automatically when biomemory fails. Calls to the notebook are as deeply and subpersonally integrated into his problem-solving routines as calls to external rotation for the expert Tetris players. The notebook has become transparent equipment for Otto, just as biological memory is for Inga. And in each case, doesn't it add needless and psychologically unreal complexity to introduce additional beliefs about the book or biological memory into the explanatory equations?

Overall, then, our claim was that Inga's biological memory systems, working together, govern *her* behaviors in the ways distinctive of believing and that Otto's smeared-out biotechnological matrix (the organism and the notebook) governs his behavior in the same sort of way. So the explanatory apparatus of mental state ascription gets an equal grip in each case, and what looks at first like Otto's action (looking up the notebook) emerges as part of Otto's thought. The gap between deeply integrated calls to epistemic action and true cognitive extension, if this is correct, is slim to vanishing. (Whether this *is* correct, and if so, what it means for the sciences of mind, will occupy us extensively in chap. 5–9.)

4.9   BRAINBOUND Versus EXTENDED: The Case So Far

We have highlighted in chapters 1 to 4 some key ways in which body and world come to share the problem-solving load with the biological brain. These include:

- The complex interplay between morphology and control and the value of "ecological control systems" in which goals are not achieved by micro managing every detail of the desired action or response but by making the most of robust, reliable sources of relevant order in the bodily or worldly environment of the controller (sec. 1.1).
- The use of "deictic pointers" and active sensing routines that retrieve information from worldly sources just in time for problem-solving use (sec. 1.2) and the possible role of whole sensorimotor cycles in the construction of phenomenal experience (sec. 1.3 and 1.4).
- The use of open perceptual channels as a means of stabilizing an ongoing organism–environment relation rather than as transducers leading to internal recapitulations of the external scene (sec. 1.2).
- Our propensity to incorporate bodily and tool-based extensions (sec. 2.3) and substitute sensory strategies (sec. 2.4) deep into our problem-solving routines.
- The use of material symbols to augment our mental powers by adding problem-simplifying structure to our external and internal environments (sec. 3.3 and 3.4).
- The repeated and nested use of space (sec. 4.3), environmental structuring (sec. 4.2 and 4.8), and epistemic actions (sec. 4.7) in online problem solving.
- The potential role of nonbiological media as support for an agent's dispositional beliefs (sec. 4.9).

Such ploys and stratagems all conform to a Principle of Ecological Assembly (sec. 1.3) according to which the canny cognizer often recruits, on the spot, whatever mix of problem-solving resources will yield an acceptable result with a minimum of effort.[14] This recruitment process looks to be systematically insensitive to the nature and location of the resources concerned, which may include just about any mix of calls to neural resources (including biological memory) external resources (including external encodings), and real-world actions and operations. Such heterogeneous mixes, actively dovetailed in time and space, together constitute (or so I have claimed) the physical underpinnings of many of the most characteristic cases of human cognizing.

Such reflections begin to make a case for the view of mind that (way back in the Introduction) we dubbed EXTENDED. Whereas BRAINBOUND locates all our mental machinery firmly in the head and central nervous system, EXTENDED allows at least some aspects of human cognition to be realized by the ongoing work of the body and/or the extraorganismic environment. The physical mechanisms of mind, if this is correct, are not all in the head.

This conclusion must for the moment remain tentative. For perhaps there are compelling reasons, which we have not yet canvassed, to restrict the realm of the *truly cognitive* in the way BRAINBOUND (or its close cousin, ORGANISMBOUND) suggests. In the remaining chapters, I aim to clarify what is at issue here and to defend the claim that the cognitive and the mental are indeed (sometimes) best viewed through the more accommodating lens of EXTENDED.

II

BOUNDARY DISPUTES

5

Mind Re-bound?

5.1   EXTENDED Anxiety

The physical mechanisms of mind, EXTENDED suggests, are simply not all in the head. Is this correct? To raise this question is not necessarily to doubt that heterogeneous mixes of neural, bodily, and environmental elements support much human problem-solving behavior or that understanding such coalitions matters for understanding human thought and reason. It is certainly important, for example, that we appreciate and learn how to analyze the role of epistemic actions in Tetris, of deictic pointers in visual problem solving, and even perhaps of Otto's notebook in his decision making. But should we really count such actions and loops through nonbiological structure as genuine aspects of extended cognitive processes? In this chapter, I consider a range of worries whose starting points concern real or apparent *differences* between what the brain accomplishes and what the other elements in such problem-solving matrices provide.

5.2   Pencil Me In

Adams and Aizawa, in a series of recent and forthcoming papers (2001, in press-a, in press-b), seek to refute, or perhaps merely to terminally embarrass, the proponents of EXTENDED. One such paper begins with the following illustration:

Question: Why did the pencil think that 2 + 2 = 4?
Clark's Answer: Because it was coupled to the mathematician.
(Adams and Aizawa in press-a, 1)

"That," the authors continue, "about sums up what is wrong with Clark's extended mind hypothesis." The example of the pencil, they suggest, is just an especially egregious version of a fallacy said to pervade the literature on distributed cognition and the extended mind. This fallacy, which they usefully dub the "coupling-constitution fallacy," is attributed, in varying degrees and manners, to Van Gelder and Port (1995), Clark and Chalmers (1998), Haugeland (1998), Dennett (2000), Clark (2001a), Gibbs (2001), and Wilson (2002).[1] The fallacy is to move from the causal coupling of some object or process to some cognitive agent to the conclusion that the object or process is part of the cognitive agent or part of the agent's cognitive processing (see, e.g., Adams and Aizawa in press-a, 2).[2]

Proponents of the extended mind and related theses are said to be prone to this fallacy in part because they either ignore or fail to properly appreciate the importance of "the mark of the cognitive"—namely, the importance of an account of "what makes something a cognitive agent" (Adams and Aizawa in press-a). The positive part of Adams and Aizawa's critique then emerges as a combination of the assertion that this "mark of the cognitive"[3] involves the idea that "cognition is constituted by certain sorts of causal process that involve non-derived contents" (in press-a, 3) and that these processes look to be characterized by psychological laws that turn out to apply to many internal goings-on but not currently (as a matter of contingent empirical fact) to any processes that take place in nonbiological tools and artifacts. Let's take these matters in turn.

5.3   The Odd Coupling

Consider the following exchange, loosely modeled on Adams and Aizawa's attempted reductio:

Question: Why did the V4 neuron think that there was a spiral pattern in the stimulus?
Answer: Because it was coupled to the monkey.

Now clearly, there is something wrong here. But the absurdity lies not in the appeal to coupling but in the idea that a V4 neuron (or even a group of V4 neurons or even a whole parietal lobe) might *itself* be some kind of self-contained locus of thinking.[4] It is indeed crazy to think that a V4 neuron thinks, and it is (just as Adams and Aizawa imply) crazy to think that a pencil might think. Yet the thrust of Adams and Aizawa's rhetoric is mostly to draw attention to the evident absence of cognition *in the putative part* as a way of "showing" that coupling (even when properly understood; see later) cannot play the kind of role it plays in the standard arguments for cognitive extension. Thus, we read: "When Clark *makes an object cognitive* when it is connected to a cognitive agent, he is committing an instance of a 'coupling-constitution fallacy'" (Adams and Aizawa in press-a, 2, emphasis added).

But this talk of an object's being or failing to be "cognitive" seems almost unintelligible when applied to some putative *part or aspect* of a cognitive agent or of a cognitive system. What would it mean for the pencil *or* the neuron to be, as it were, brute factively "cognitive"? This is not, I think, merely an isolated stylistic infelicity on the part of Adams and Aizawa. For the same issue arose many times during personal exchanges concerning the vexing case of Otto and his notebook.[5] And it arises again, as we shall later see, in various parts of their more recent challenges concerning "the mark of the cognitive."

Let us first be clear, then, about the precise role of the appeal to coupling in the arguments for cognitive extension. The appeal to coupling is not intended to make any external object cognitive (insofar as this notion is even intelligible). Rather, it is intended to make some object, which in and of itself is not usefully (perhaps not even intelligibly) thought of as *either cognitive or noncognitive*, into a *proper part of some cognitive routine*. It is intended, that is to say, to ensure that the putative part is poised to play the kind of role that *itself* ensures its status as part of the *agent's* cognitive routines. Now, it is certainly true (and this, I think, is one important fact to which Adams and Aizawa's argument quite properly draws the reader's attention) that not just any old kind of coupling will achieve this result. But as far as I am aware, nobody in the literature has ever claimed otherwise. It is not the mere presence of a coupling that matters but the effect of the coupling—the way it poises (or fails to poise) information for a certain kind of use within a specific kind of problem-solving routine.

The question that needs to be addressed, then, is: When is some physical object or process acting as part of a larger cognitive routine? It is not the much murkier (probably unintelligible) question: When should we say of some such candidate part, such as a neuron or a notebook, that it is *itself* cognitive? In the case of Otto, Clark and Chalmers chose to be guided by a set of intuitions derived from reflection on the ordinary "common-sense" use of talk of nonoccurrent dispositional beliefs. In essence, we took these intuitions and systematically showed that the kinds of coarse-grained functional poise (poise to guide various forms of behavior and various conscious states) associated with such dispositional believings on the part of Otto might sometimes be partially supported by a highly nonstandard physical realization in which a mundane, nonmagical notebook acted as the physical medium of long-term storage.

Clark and Chalmers thus offered an argument (which one may accept or reject; that is, of course, another matter) concerning conditions (not of being cognitive) but for recognition as part of the physical substrate of a cognitive system. The key issues concerned coupling only indirectly; what *mattered* was the achieved functional poise of the stored information. In terms of the form of the argument, this is not even close to the commission of a coupling-constitution fallacy. It is better viewed as a simple argumentative extension of at least a subset (see discussion following) of what Braddon-Mitchell and Jackson (2007) describe, and endorse, as "commonsense functionalism" concerning mental states. According to such a view, normal human agents already command a rich (albeit largely implicit) theory of the coarse functional roles distinctive of various familiar mental states—states such as "believing that the MOMA is on 53rd Street." Knowledge of such roles involves knowledge "of the essentials of a certain complex and detailed story about situations, behavioral responses, and mental states" (Braddon-Mitchell and Jackson 2007, 63). This is to be distinguished from the kinds of "empirical functionalism" (Braddon-Mitchell and Jackson 2007, chap. 5) that would use the folk knowledge only as a kind of staging post, going on to identify mental states with further functional role properties as identified by scientific investigation.[6] (Note that Clark and Chalmers's argument concerned only a subset of the folk-identified mental states, since all it requires is a form of common-sense functionalism concerning nonconscious, dispositional states.[7] As such, the argument does not commit us to any sort of functionalism about conscious mental states.[8])

EXTENDED thus involves a kind of double appeal to the functional or systemic role. First, there is an appeal to the common-sense or coarse-grained role implicitly grasped by normal human agents: a broad pattern of flexible, informationally sensitive systemic behavior that underwrites the ascription of some mental state or cognitive activity (dispositional belief, in the case of Otto). Second, we may go on to seek a much more fine-grained description of the actual flow of processing and representation in the (possibly extended) physical array that *realizes* the coarse functional role itself. It is the coarse or common-sense functional role that, on this model (unlike that of empirical functionalism), displays what is essential to the mental state in question. By way of contrast, "distributed functional decompositions," in the sense introduced in section 1.4, are concerned with the second project—namely, the description of how specific systems (perhaps extending across brain, body, and world) realize the common-sense functional role. In laying out the details at this more refined (and cognitive scientifically interesting) level, we display only the *particular way* that a given physical system manages to realize the mental state or activity in question.

5.4   Cognitive Candidacy

Adams and Aizawa seem to suggest that some objects or processes, *in virtue of their own nature*, are, as I shall now put it, at least *candidate parts* for inclusion in a cognitive process. And they think that other objects or processes, still in virtue of their own nature, are not even candidates. Or such, I think, is the best way to give sense to that otherwise baffling question "is some X cognitive?" when asked of some putative part of the realizing apparatus. Thus, they ask "if the fact that an object or process X is coupled to a cognitive agent does not entail that X is part of the cognitive agent's cognitive apparatus, what does? *The nature of X of course.* One needs a theory of what makes a process a cognitive process. One needs a theory of the 'mark of the cognitive.'" (Adams and Aizawa in press-a, 3, emphasis added).

What is the mark of the cognitive? The question is nontrivial and has, as Adams and Aizawa (somewhat reluctantly) admit, no well-established answer either within cognitive science or philosophy of mind. Nonetheless, they tie their colors to what they depict as "a rather orthodox theory of the nature of the cognitive" (Adams and Aizawa 2001, 52). According to this theory, "cognition involves particular kinds of processes involving non-derived representations" (53). This is the line also pursued in Adams and Aizawa (in press-a and in press-b). It comprises two distinct elements—namely, an appeal to "non-derived representations" and an appeal to "particular kinds of process."

Despite its prominence in their account, Adams and Aizawa tell us very little about what the first of these (nonderived representations) might amount be. We learn that they are representations whose content is in some sense intrinsic (2001, 48). We learn that this is to be *contrasted* with, for example, the way a public language symbol gets its content by "conventional association" (48). And we are told, in the same place, that Dretske, Fodor, Millikan, and others are sometimes in search of an adequate theory of such content and that the combination of a language of thought with some kind of causal–historical account is a hot contender for such an account.

Of course, we are not *required* to think of Otto's notebook as contravening some plausible story about intrinsic content. A plausible response would be to argue that what makes *any* symbol or representation (internal or external) mean what it does is just something about its behavior-supporting role (and maybe its causal history) within some larger system. We might then hold that when we understand enough about that role (and perhaps, history), we will see that the encodings in Otto's notebook are in fact on a par with those in his biological memory. In other words, just because the symbols in the notebook happen to look like English words and require some degree of interpretative activity when retrieved and used, that need not rule out the possibility that they have also come to satisfy the demands on being, in virtue of their role within the larger system, among the physical vehicles of various forms of intrinsic content.[9]

Recall that Adams and Aizawa insist that "whatever is responsible for non-derived representations seems to find a place only in brains" (2001, 63). I am not convinced this is true. It seems quite possible, for example, to ascribe representational contents, in ways that are not obviously conventional or derivative, to the states and processes of artificially evolved creatures (see Pfeifer and Scheier 1999, chap. 8). Or if simple artificial creatures do not move you, take any inner neural structure deemed (by whatever nonquestion-begging criteria Adams and Aizawa choose) to be the vehicle of some intrinsic content X. Can we not imagine replacing part or all of that structure with a functionally equivalent silicon part? (As a matter of fact, this kind of replacement has already been done, albeit only with one artificial neuron that functions successfully within a group of 14 biological neurons in a Californian spiny lobster; see Szucs et al. 2000). Unless we question-beggingly assert that only neural stuff can be the bearer of intrinsic content, then surely we should allow that the siliconized vehicle, or at least the hybrid circuit that now includes it, is as capable of supporting intrinsic content as was its biological predecessor. For these kinds of reason, I do not believe that there is any nonquestion-begging notion of intrinsic content that picks out all and only the neural in any clear and useful fashion.

But since Adams and Aizawa stress that they are defending only a contingent, humans-as-currently-constituted, form of cognitive intracranialism, I suspect that they will concede this general point without much argument. The force of Adams and Aizawa's worry does not lie in any simple (and surely naive) identification of the neural and the cognitive. Rather, the real worry is that the inscriptions in Otto's notebook (unlike, say, the hybrid neural and silicon-based activity that now underlies control of the oscillatory rhythms in the stomatogastric ganglion in the Californian spiny lobster) are out-and-out conventional. They are passive representations that are parasitic, for their meaning, on public practices of coordinated use.

Let us agree that there is something quite compelling about the idea that the notebook encodings are all conventional and derivative. Let us agree also, at least for the sake of argument, that some parts of any genuinely cognitive system need to trade in representations that are not thus conventional and derivative. To accept all this, however, is not to give up on the extended mind claim for Otto, unless one *also* accepts (what seems to me an independent and far less plausible assertion) that *no proper part* of a properly cognitive system can afford, at any time, to trade solely in conventional representations.

In Clark (2005b), I offered a thought experiment meant to show that such an additional requirement was too strong and should be rejected. The thought experiment concerned Martians endowed with an extra biological routine that allowed them to store *bitmapped images* of important chunks of visually encountered text. Later on, at will, they could access (and then interpret) this stored text. Surely, I argued, we would have no hesitation in embracing that kind of bitmapped storage, even prior to an act of retrieval, as part and parcel of the Martian cognitive equipment. But what is stored is just a bitmapped image of a fully conventional form of external representation. Upon retrieval, that image, too, would need to be interpreted to yield useful effects. If, courtesy of our common-sense psychological intuitions, we accept this aspect of Martian memory into the cognitive fold, surely only skin-and-skull-based prejudice stops us from extending the same courtesy to Otto. To do so is simply to abide by the Parity Principle as it was meant to be deployed. Thus, even if we demand the involvement, in any cognitive process, of *at least some* items that bear their contents intrinsically, it is quite unclear how we should distribute this requirement across time and space. The Martian encodings are poised, here and now, to participate in processes that invoke intrinsic contents. So are those in Otto's notebook. Since it is arguably poise that matters, at least where dispositional believing is concerned, it seems that any reasonably plausible form of the requirement involving intrinsic content can, with a little imagination, be met. From the requirement, if it is a requirement, that every truly cognitive agent trade in states that bear intrinsic contents, it cannot follow that every proper part of the cognitive system of an agent must trade (and trade solely) in such contents.

5.5   The Mark of the Cognitive?

Consider now the other major part of Adams and Aizawa's challenge. Recall that their suggestion concerning the "mark of the cognitive" was that "cognition involves particular kinds of processes involving non-derived representations" (Adams and Aizawa 2001, 53). We have, I think, just said all that needs to be said concerning the appeal to non-derived representation. But what about the other part of the clause, the appeal to "particular kinds of process" involving such representations? It is at this point that a new kind of consideration comes into play. This concerns the possible existence of a *characteristic set of causal processes* found, by painstaking empirical investigation, to pervade the internal, biologically supported aspects of human cognitive architecture. The operation of these signature causal processes, the authors claim, gives rise to a number of laws and regularities that seem to apply to these known cognitive processes but that do not apply elsewhere (e.g., to Otto's notebook). In the light of this, Adams and Aizawa ask, shouldn't we judge that the notebook falls outside the class of the cognitive? We should indeed do so, they claim, because "the cognitive must be discriminated on the basis of underlying causal processes" (Adams and Aizawa 2001, 52).

The kinds of law and regularity the authors have in mind here include the pervasiveness in human biological memory systems of effects of chunking, priming, recency, and so forth (Adams and Aizawa 2001, 61) and in human perceptual systems of various psychophysical laws (e.g., Weber's law, according to which the change in a stimulus that will be "just noticeable" is a constant ratio of the original stimulus). Given that science has uncovered these undeniably important and interesting regularities, what does this imply concerning the nature of cognition? Adams and Aizawa's argument seems to go like this. Empirical investigations have turned up a number of features (e.g., priming effects in the case of memory) that reflect the detailed operation of processes internal to the brain. Since these clearly pertain to some of our paradigm cases of terrestrial cognition, we should (defeasibly) believe that these kinds of causal process are essential to the "cognitive" status (I use this notion with great discomfort for the reasons mentioned earlier in sec. 5.3) of the neural goings-on.

But this is something we should surely deny. Do Adams and Aizawa really believe that the cognitive status of some target process requires that process to exhibit all the idiosyncratic features of terrestrial neural activity? To insist that some alien mode of storage and retrieval was not cognitive just because it failed to exhibit features such as recency, priming, and crosstalk would be simultaneously to scale new heights of anthropocentrism and neurocentrism, inflating properties of the human neural realizers of certain brainbound cognitive process into requirements that must be met before any process is properly deemed cognitive. Such inflation is both undesirable in itself and question begging in the context of arguments for the extended mind.

One might also reflect that, for all we know, the fine details of the causal role of, say, stored beliefs differ from person to person or (within one person) from hour to hour.[10] This point is merely dramatized by those alien beings whose recall is not subject to recency effects, crosstalk, or error. Do such differences make a difference? Is the mutant human whose recall is fractionally slower, fractionally faster, or much less prone to loss and damage also to be banned from the ranks of true believers and rememberers? To demand identity of fine-grained causal role is surely to set the cognitive bar too high and way too close to home.

5.6   Kinds and Minds

In their 2001 paper, Adams and Aizawa also raise a different (though related) kind of worry. This concerns the nature and feasibility of the scientific enterprise implied by taking so-called transcranialism seriously. The worry, in its simplest form, is that "science tries to carve nature at its joints" (51). But they argue that the various types of neural and extraneural goings-on that the transcranialist lumps together as cognitive seem to have little or nothing in common by way of underlying causal processes.

To make this concrete, we are invited to consider once again (see sec. 4.8) the process that physically rotates the image on the Tetris screen. This, they correctly note, is nothing like any neural process. It involves firing electrons at a cathode ray tube! It requires muscular activity to operate the button. Similarly, "Otto's extended 'memory recall' involves cognitive-motor processing not found in Inga's memory recall" (Adams and Aizawa 2001, 55). More generally, they suggest, just look at the range of human memory augmenting technologies (photo albums, Rolodexes, Palm Pilots, notepads, etc.): "what are the chances of there being interesting regularities that cover humans interacting with all these sorts of things? Slim to none, we speculate" (61).

By contrast, biological memory systems, as noted previously, are said to "display a number of what appear to be law-like regularities, including primacy effects, recency effects, chunking effects and others" (61). And unlike the biological memory processes, "transcranial [extended] processes are not likely to give rise to interesting scientific regularities. There are no laws covering humans and their tool-use over and above the laws of intercranial [inner] human cognition and the laws of the physical tools" (61).

The first thing to say in response to all this is that it is probably unwise to judge, from the armchair, the chances of finding "interesting scientific regularities" in any domain, be it ever so superficially diverse. Consider, for example, the recent successes of complexity theory in unearthing unifying principles that apply across massive differences of scale, physical type, and temporality. There are power laws, it now seems, that compactly explain aspects of the emergent behavior of systems ranging from ant colonies to the World Wide Web. In a similar vein, it is quite possible that despite the bottom-level physical diversity of the processes that write to and read from Otto's notebook, and those that write to and read from Otto's biological memory, there is a level of description of these systems that treats them in a single unified framework (e.g., how about a framework of information storage, transformation, and retrieval?). The mere fact that Adams and Aizawa can find *one* kind of systemic description at which the underlying processes look wildly different says very little, really, about the eventual prospects for an integrated scientific treatment. It is rather as if an opponent of rule and symbol models of mental processing were simply to cite the deep physical differences between brains and von Neumann computers as proof that there could be no proper science that treated processes occurring in each medium in a unified way. Or to take a different kind of case, as if one were to conclude from the fact that chemistry and geology employ distinct vocabularies and techniques, that the burgeoning study of geochemistry is doomed from the outset. But neither of these, I presume, are conclusions that Adams and Aizawa would wish to endorse.

The bedrock problem thus lies with the bald assertion that "the cognitive must be discriminated on the basis of underlying causal processes" (Adams and Aizawa 2001, 52). For it is part of the *job* of a special science to establish a framework in which superficially different phenomena can be brought under a unifying explanatory umbrella. To simply cite radical differences in some base-level physical story goes no way at all toward showing that this cannot be done. Moreover, it is by no means clear that acceptable forms of unification require that all the systemic elements behave according to the same laws. As long as there is an intelligible domain of convergence, there may be many subregularities of many different kinds involved. Think, for example, of the multiple kinds of factor and force studied by those interested in creating better home audio systems. Even if "home audio" is rejected as any kind of unified science, it certainly names a coherent and proper topic of investigation. The study of mind might, likewise, need to embrace a variety of different explanatory paradigms whose point of convergence lies in the production of intelligent behavior.

Moreover, it seems quite possible that the *inner* goings-on that Adams and Aizawa take to be paradigmatically cognitive themselves will turn out to be a motley crew as far as detailed causal mechanisms go, with not even a family resemblance (at the level of actual mechanism) to hold them together. It is arguable, for example, that conscious seeing and nonconscious uses of visual input to guide fine-grained action involve radically different kinds of computational operation and representational form (see, e.g., Milner and Goodale 1995; Goodale and Milner 2004). And Adams and Aizawa to the contrary, some kinds of mental rehearsal (e.g., watching sports or imagining typing a sentence) do seem to reinvoke distinct motor elements, whereas others (e.g., imagining a lake) do not (see Decety and Grezes 1999). Some aspects of biological visual routines may even use a form of table lookup (Churchland and Sejnowski 1992). In addition, the inner mechanisms of mind seem to include both conscious, controlled, slow processes and fast, automatic, uncontrolled ones, with each of these sets of processes displaying its own characteristic sets of regularities (see Shiffrin and Schneider 1977; and for more recent discussions, Wegner 2005; Bargh and Chartrand 1999). Among such regularities, we may count the finding that controlled processes tend to degrade rapidly under cognitive load, whereas automatic processes do not; that controlled processes are apt for conscious interruption, whereas automatic ones are not; that controlled processes are slow, whereas automatic ones are relatively fast; and so on. With such findings in mind, Levy (in press) concludes that "if it is true that causal regularities pick out natural kinds, then the mind is not a natural kind: it is a compound entity comprised of at least two (and probably many) natural kinds."

In the light of all this, my own suspicion is that the differences between external-looping (putatively cognitive) processes and purely inner ones will be *no greater than those between the inner ones themselves.* But insofar as they all form parts of a flexible and information-sensitive control system for a being capable of reasoning, of feeling, and of experiencing the world (a "sentient informavore" if you will), the motley crew of mechanisms has something important in common. It may be far less than we would require of any natural or scientific kind. But so what?

The argument from scientific kinds is thus doubly flawed. It is flawed by virtue of its rather limited conception of what makes for a proper scientific or explanatory enterprise. And it is flawed in its assessment of the potential for some form of higher level unification despite mechanistic dissimilarities. It is, above all else, a matter of empirical discovery, not armchair speculation, whether there can be a fully fledged science of the extended mind.

It is also perhaps worth noting that nascent forms of just such a science have been around for quite some time. The field of human-computer interaction (HCI) and its more recent cousins human-centered computing (HCC) and human-centered technologies (HCT) are ongoing attempts to discover unified scientific frameworks in which to treat processes occurring in and between biological and nonbiological information-processing media (see, e.g., Scaife and Rogers 1996; Norman 1999; Dourish 2001).

Adams and Aizawa next attempt to parlay the misconceived appeal to scientific kinds into a kind of dilemma. Either, the argument goes, Clark and Chalmers are radically mistaken about the causal facts, or more likely, they are closet behaviorists. On the one hand, if our claim is that "the active causal processes that extend into the environment are just like the ones found in intracranial cognition" (Adams and Aizawa 2001, 56), we are just plain wrong. On the other hand, if we don't care about that and claim only that "Inga and Otto use distinct sets of capacities in order to produce similar behavior" (56), then we are behaviorists.

This is surely a false dilemma. To repeat, our claim was not that the processes in Otto and Inga are identical, or even similar, in terms of their detailed implementation. It is simply that, with respect to the role that the long-term encodings play in guiding current response, both modes of storage can be seen as supporting dispositional beliefs. It is the way the information is poised to guide reasoning (e.g., conscious inferences that nonetheless result in no overt actions) and behavior that counts. This is not behaviorism but (extended) common-sense functionalism. It is coarse systemic role that matters, not brute similarities in public behavior (though the two are of course related). Perhaps Adams and Aizawa believe that common-sense functionalism just *is* a species of behaviorism. That seems wrong, however, because common-sense functionalism is quite compatible with the assertion that there are *some* internal constraints on being a cognizer. Thus, Braddon-Mitchell and Jackson (2007, chap. 5 and 7) argue that a creature all of whose actions were generated by table lookup would not count, even by the standards of common-sense functionalism, as a thinker. Such coarse architectural requirements flow, they believe, from ordinary intuitions about mind and reason. The issue between the common-sense functionalist and the empirical functionalist is thus not whether there are any internal constraints on being a thinker but "whether it is right to let the *particular* way that we handle the informational problems set by the world dictate what is to count as having a mind" (94). To this question they, and the common-sense functionalist, give a firmly negative response.

A related concern was raised by Terry Dartnall (personal communication). Dartnall worried that the plausibility of the Otto scenario depends on an outmoded image of biological memory itself: the image of biological memory as a kind of static store of information awaiting retrieval and use. This image, Dartnall claimed, cannot do justice to the active nature of real memory. It is somewhat ironic, Dartnall argued, that the present author (in particular) should succumb to this temptation, given his long history of interest in, and support for, the connectionist alternative to classical (text- and rule-based) models of neural processing. By way of illustration (though the illustration may actually raise other issues, too, as we shall see), he offered the following example: Suppose I have a chip in my head that gives me access to a treatise on nuclear physics. That doesn't make it true that *I know* about nuclear physics. In fact, the text might even be in a language I don't understand. "Sterile text," Dartnall concluded, cannot support cognition (properly understood). In a sense, then, the claim once again is that text-based storage is so unlike biological memory that any claim of role parity must fail.

This is an interesting line of objection but one that ultimately fails for reasons closely related to the discussion of intrinsic content in section 5.2. Certainly, biological memory is an active process. And retrieval is to a large extent reconstructive rather than literal: What we recall is influenced by our current mood, by our current goals, and by information stored after the time of the original experience. It is possible, in fact, that biological memory is such an active process as to blur the line between memory systems and reasoning systems. All this I happily accept. But to repeat, the claim is that in the special context of the rest of Otto's information-processing economy, the notebook is co-opted into playing a real cognitive role. And the informal test for this is, just supposing some inner system provided the functionality that Otto derives from the reliable presence of the notebook, would we hesitate to classify that inner system as part of Otto's cognitive apparatus?

Readers must here rely on their own intuitions. But according to Clark and Chalmers, there would be no such hesitation. To cement the intuition, recall once more (sec. 5.2) the Martians with their additional bitmapped memories or humans with quasi-photographic recall. Or consider the familiar act of rote learning. When we learn a long text by rote, we create a memory object that is in many ways unlike the standard case. For example, to recall the sixth line of the text, we may have to first rehearse the others. Moreover, we can rote learn a text we do not even understand (e.g., a Latin text). Assuming that we count rote learning as the acquisition of some kind of knowledge (even in the case of the Latin text), it seems that we should not be bothered by the consequences that Dartnall unearths. The genuine differences that exist between the notebook-based storage and standard cases of biological memory do not matter because our claim was not one of identity in the first place.

The deeper question is thus how to balance the Parity Principle (which makes no claims about process-level identity at all) against the somewhat stronger claim of "sufficient functional similarity" that underpins treating Otto's notebook as a contributor to Otto's long-term store of dispositional beliefs. Part of the answer emerges as soon as we focus on the role the retrieved information will play in guiding current behavior. It is at that point (and there, of course, all kinds of active and occurrent processing come into play as well) that the common-sense functional similarity becomes apparent. True, that which is stored in Otto's notebook won't shift and alter while stored away. It won't participate in the ongoing underground reorganizations, interpolations, and creative mergers that characterize much of biological memory. But *when called upon*, its immediate contributions to Otto's behavior still fit the profile of a stored belief. Information retrieved from the notebook will guide Otto's reasoning and behavior in the same way as information retrieved from biological memory. The fact that *what* is retrieved may be different is unimportant here. Thus, had Otto stored the information about the color of the car in the auto accident in biological memory, he may be manipulated into a false memory situation by a clever experimenter. The notebook storage is sufficiently different to be immune to that manipulation (though others will be possible). But the information recalled (veridical in one case but not the other) will nonetheless guide Otto's behavior (the way he answers questions and the further beliefs he forms etc.) in exactly the same kind of way. Or simply reflect that for many years the classical "text- and rule-based" image of human cognition was widely accepted. During that time, nobody (to my knowledge) thought that an implication of this was that humans were not cognizers! It might have turned out that all our memory systems operated as sterile storage and that false memory cases and so on were all artifacts of retrieval processes. This shows, again, that there is nothing intuitively noncognitive about less active forms of storage.

Does the stress on similarity of coarse-grained functional role commit us to a merely prosthetic use of nonbiological props and aids? That is, does it commit us to the nonbiological structures merely standing in (as in the case of Otto) for what is normally provided by fully internal means? The many examples sketched in earlier chapters suggest it does not. We should instead be impressed by our remarkable capacity to form extended, densely integrated systems that factor in a variety of distinctive contributions, some of which have no clear internal analogs (a simple example might be an architect whose fluent problem depends in part on the functioning of a fancy software package).[11] Given sufficient complementarity and integration, I want to say, we may sometimes confront hybrid systems displaying novel cognitive profiles that supervene on more than the biological components alone.[12]

Some remain wary of the appeal to complementarity in the non-pathological case. Thus, Michael Wheeler (personal communication) suggests that all the truly persuasive arguments for EXTENDED depend on displaying coarse-grained functional similarities to standard internal cases (e.g., to standing beliefs, as in the case of Otto). Such cases play a key argumentative role but should not be taken as limning the space of extended cognitive circuitry. Rather, they provide the essential first means by which to begin to break the stranglehold of vehicle-internalist intuitions concerning cognition. Once the possibility of vehicle externalism, in humanly possible worlds, is thus established (once, as it were, the hegemony of skin and skull is finally broken), we are free to recognize, as genuinely cognitive and as owned by the human agent, all kinds of process that have no fully biological analog.[13]

5.7 Perception and Development

Another common worry, at least about the rather specific test case of Otto (though similar considerations will apply to all manner of actual mind-expanding media and apparatus) is that the role of perception, in "reading in" the information from the notebook, marks a sufficient disanalogy to discount the notebook as part of Otto's cognitive apparatus. We made a few brief comments on this issue in the original paper, noting that whether the reading in counts as genuinely perceptual or introspective depends, to a large extent, on how one classifies the overall case. From our perspective, the systemic act is more like an act of introspection than one of perception. As a result, each side is here in danger of begging the question against the other.

Thus, Keith Butler complains that

in the world-involving cases, the subjects have to *act* in a way that demands of them that they perceive their environment [whereas Inga just introspects]... the very fact that the results are achieved in such remarkably different ways suggests that the explanation for one should be quite different from the explanation for the other

and that

Otto has to look at his notebook while Inga has to look at nothing. (both quotes from Butler 1998, 211)

But from the EXTENDED point of view, Otto's inner processes and the notebook constitute a single cognitive system. Relative to *this* system, the flow of information is wholly internal and functionally akin to introspection (for more on this, see sec. 5.8).

One way to try to push the argument is to seek an independent criterion for the perceptual. With this in mind, Martin Davies (personal communication) has suggested that it is revealing that Otto could misread his own notebook. This opening for error may, Davies suggests, make the notebook seem more like a perceived part of the external world than an aspect of the agent. But parity still prevails: Inga may misremember an event not due to an error in her memory store but because of some disturbance during the act of retrieval. The opening for error does not yet establish that the error is, properly speaking, perceptual. It only establishes that it occurs during retrieval.

A slight variant, again suggested by Davies, is that perception (unlike introspection) targets a potentially public domain. Notebooks and databases are things to which other agents could in principle have access. But, the worry goes, my beliefs are essentially the beliefs to which *I* have a special kind of access unavailable to others.

Notice first that there is, in any case, something special about Otto's relation to the information in the notebook. For as we commented in the original paper, Otto more or less automatically endorses the contents of the notebook. Others, depending on their views of Otto, are less likely to share this perspective. But this is not a special kind of access as much as a special kind of cognitive relationship. But why then suppose that uniqueness of access is anything more than a contingent fact about standard biological recall? If, in the future, science devised a way for you to occasionally tap into my stored memories, would that make them any less *mine* or part of my cognitive apparatus? Imagine, for that matter, a form of multiple personality disorder (MPD) in which two personalities have equal access to some early childhood memories. Here we have, at least arguably, a case where two distinct persons share access to the same memories. Of course, one may harbor all kinds of reasonable doubts about the proper way to conceptualize MPD in general. But the point is simply that it seems to be at most a contingent fact that I and I alone have a certain kind of access to my own biologically stored memories and beliefs.

Before leaving this topic, I want to briefly mention a very interesting worry raised by Ron Chrisley (personal communication). Chrisley notes that, as children, we do not begin by experiencing our biological memory as any kind of object or resource. This is because we do not encounter our own memory perceptually. Instead, it is just part of the apparatus through which we relate to and experience the world. Might it be this special developmental role that decides what is to count as part of the agent and what is to count as part of the wider world?

Certainly, Otto first experiences notebooks, and even his own special notebook, as objects in his world. But I am doubtful that this genuine point of disanalogy can bear the enormous weight that Chrisley's argument requires. First of all, consider the child's own bodily parts. It is quite possible, it seems to me, that these are first experienced (or at least simultaneously experienced) as objects in the child's world. The child sees its own hand. It may even want to grab a toy and be unable to control the hand well enough to do so. The relation here seems relatively "external," yet the hand is (and is from the start) a proper part of the child.

Perhaps you doubt that there is any moment at which the child's own hand is really experienced, or at any rate conceptualized, as an object for the child. But in that case, we can surely imagine future nonbiological (putatively cognitive) resources being developmentally incorporated in just the same way. Such resources would be provided so early that they, too, are not first conceptualized as objects (perhaps spectacles are like this for some of us already). Contrariwise, as Chrisley himself helpfully points out, we can imagine beings who from a young age are taught to experience even their own *inner* cognitive faculties as objects, courtesy of being plugged into biofeedback controllers and trained to monitor and control their own alpha rhythms and so on.

The developmental issue, though interesting, is thus not conceptu-ally crucial. It points only to a complex of contingent facts about human cognition. What counts in the end is the resource's current role in guid-ing reasoning and behavior, not its historical positioning in a develop-mental nexus.

5.8 Deception and Contested Space

In a most interesting and constructive critique of the Extended Mind Thesis, Kim Sterelny (2004) worries that Clark and Chalmers underplay the importance of the fact that our "epistemic artifacts" (our diaries, Filofaxes, compasses, and sextants) operate in a "common and often contested" space. By this, he means a shared space apt for sabotage and deception by other agents. As a result, when we store and retrieve information from this space, we often deploy strategies meant to guard against such deception and subversion. More generally still, the devel-opment and functional poise of perceptual systems are, for this very reason, radically different from the development and functional poise of biologically internal routes of information flow. The intrusion of acts of perception into Otto's information retrieval routine thus introduces a new set of concerns that justify us in not treating the notebook (or whatever) as a genuine part of Otto's cognitive economy.

Sterelny does not mean to deny the importance of epistemic artifacts (as he calls them; see sec. 4.4) in turbo-charging human thought and reason. Indeed, he offers a novel and attractive coevolutionary account in which our ability to use such artifacts both depends on and further drives a progressive enrichment of our internal representational capaci-ties. In this way, "Our use of epistemic artifacts explains the elaboration of mental representation in our lineage and this elaboration explains our ability to use epistemic artifacts" (Sterelny 2004, 239).

What he does mean to deny, however, is that the use of such arti-facts reduces the load on the naked brain and that the brain and the artifacts can coalesce into a single cognitive system. Instead, he sees increased load and a firm boundary between the biological integrated system and the array of props, tools, and storage devices suspended in public space. I tend to differ on both counts but will here restrict my comments to the point about the boundary between the agent and the public space.

Within the biological sheath, Sterelny argues, information flow occurs between a "community of co-operative and co-adaptive parts [that are] under selection for reliability." Over both evolutionary and developmental time, the signals within the sheath should become clearer, less noisy, and less and less in need of constant vetting for reliability and veridicality. As soon as you reach the edge of the sheath, however, things change dramatically. Perceptual systems may be highly optimized for their jobs. But it is still the case that the signals they deliver have their origins in a public space populated in part by organisms under pressure to hide their presence, to present a false appearance, or to otherwise trick and manipulate the unwary so as to increase their own fitness at the other's expense. Unlike internal monitoring, Sterelny (2004, 239) says, "perception operates in an environment of active sabotage by other agents [and] often delivers signals that are noisy, somewhat unreliable and functionally ambiguous."

One result of all this is that we are forced to develop strategies to safeguard against such deceptions and manipulations. The cat moves gingerly across the lawn and may stop and look very hard before trusting even the clear appearance of a safe passage to the other side. While at a higher level by far, we may even deploy the tools of folk logic and consistency checking (here, Sterelny cites Sperber 2001).

The point about vulnerability to malicious manipulation is well taken. Many forms of perceptual input are indeed subject, for that very reason, to much vetting and double-checking. I do not think, however, that we treat all our perceptual inputs in this highly cautious way. Moreover, *as soon as we do not do so*, the issue about extended cognitive systems seems to open up (see below). As a result, I am inclined to think that Sterelny has indeed hit on something important here but something that may in the end be helpful, rather than harmful, to the EXTENDED account.

Take the well-known work on magic tricks and so-called change blindness (for a review, see Simons and Rensink 2005, and further discussion in sec. 7.3). In a typical example of such work, you might be shown a short film clip in which major alterations to the scene occur while you are attending to other matters. Often, these alterations are simply not noticed. Once they are drawn to your attention, however, it seems quite amazing that you ever missed them. The art of the stage magician, it is often remarked, depends on precisely such manipulations. We are, it seems, remarkably vulnerable to certain kinds of deception. But this, I want to suggest, may be grist to the extended mind mill. For on a day-to-day basis, the chances of these kinds of espionage are sufficiently low that they may be traded against the efficiency gains of (for some cognitive purposes) leaving some information "out in the world" and relying on just-in-time access. We may, under certain circumstances, treat a perception-involving loop to the environment as if it were an inner, relatively safe, and noise-free channel, thus allowing us (with some important qualification; see sec. 7.3) to use the world as a form of "external memory" (O'Regan 1992; O'Regan and Noe 2001).

It is important, in our story about Otto, that he, too, treats the notebook as a typically safe and reliable storage device. He must not feel compelled to check and double-check retrieved information. If this should change (perhaps someone does begin to interfere with his external stored knowledge base) and Otto should notice the change and become cautious, the notebook would at that point cease to unproblematically count as a proper part of his individual cognitive economy. Of course, Otto might wrongly become thus suspicious. This would parallel the case of a person who begins to suspect that aliens are inserting thoughts into his or her head. In these latter cases, we begin to treat biologically internal information flow in the cautious way distinctive of (some) perception. What emerges from the considerations concerning espionage and vigilance is thus not so much an argument *against* the extended mind as a way of further justifying our claim that in some contexts signals routed via perceptual systems are treated *in the way more typical of internal channels* (and vice versa in the case of feared thought insertion). To decide, in any given case, whether the channel is acting more like one of perception or more like one of internal information flow, we must look to the larger functional economy of conscious vigilance and active defenses against deception. The lower the vigilance and defenses, the closer we approximate to the functionality of a typical internal flow.

Sterelny might reply to this by shifting the emphasis from the extent to which agents actually do guard against deception and manipulation to the extent to which they are, as a matter of fact, vulnerable to it. Thus, the fact that we are vulnerable to the magician's art may be said to count for more than the fact that in being thus vulnerable we treat (as I tried to argue) the perceptual route as a quasi-internal one. But this seems unprincipled because, given the right "magician" (say, an alien able to directly affect the flow of energy between my synapses), all routes seem about equally vulnerable. Recall also that false beliefs can (as noted earlier) be generated in biological memory by quite simple psychological manipulations. Or for that matter, consider the many ways in which biological memory and reason can be systematically impaired (e.g., the patients whose memories, like their ongoing experience, exhibit hemispatial neglect; Bisiach and Luzzatti 1978; Cooney and Gazzaniga 2003). What seems to count is not vulnerability as such but rather something like our "ecologically normal" level of vulnerability. And our actual practices of defense and vetting are, I claim, rather a good guide to this. If Otto doesn't worry about tricksters copying his writing and adding false entries, maybe that is because the channel is *as secure as it needs to be.*

5.9 Folk Intuition and Cognitive Extension

Consider the following challenge to the story currently under consideration:

> You invoke our implicit grasp of a common-sense model of mind as part of the case for thinking that (the physical machinery underlying some) mental states and processes extends out into the world. But that latter picture is itself so radically opposed to what common sense believes as to belie the premise. How can our intuitive pretheoretic grip on the notion of mind yield such counterintuitive fruit?

The first point to note is that all the argument requires is an appeal to some notion of the coarse (i.e., unscientifically visible) role associated with some mental state. Given *just that much grip on the mind,* so the argument goes, we can be brought to see (as in the case of Otto) that bioexternal stuff may sometimes help to realize that role. If that comes as something of a surprise, it in no way undermines the form of argument.

Nonetheless, I am also inclined (though nothing in the present treatment depends on this) to dispute the claim that the Extended Mind Model runs so wildly contrary to common sense. For it is only counterintuitive, it seems to me, if we are already in the grip of a form of theoretically loaded neurocentrism. If we subtract the loaded neurocentric intuitions, it is by no means clear that the common-sense grip on mind has any fixed opinion concerning the location of the machinery of mind. Indeed, insofar as one can discern any leanings at all, they may even contain traces of the extended model. For example, ordinary talk about one another's plans and intentions seems already to allow that external media (and often other agents, too) can play the role of physical vehicles for various contents. As Houghton (1997) convincingly argues, it is perfectly in keeping with standard ways of thinking to say that *my* plans for a week's vacation have detailed contents that I never hold, all at once, in my head, let alone before conscious inspection. Similarly, the architect may properly be said to have complex standing intentions, vehicled in drawings and drafts, regarding the shape and structure of a building even though she may never hold, or even have held, the full sequence and combination of features (the ones that together form the content of those very intentions) in her head or before conscious inspection. To insist that the architect's real intentions are something less (perhaps merely to build whatever the plans she has drafted happen to describe) is surely to do her a serious injustice. The folk grip on mind and mental states, it seems to me, is surprisingly liberal when it comes to just about everything concerning machinery, location, and architecture.

5.10 Asymmetry and Lopsidedness

Such liberality is notably absent from Adams and Aizawa's account. The general form of their argument has as a consequence a claim that we may now dub the Dogma of Intrinsic Unsuitability. It goes like this:

Dogma of Intrinsic Unsuitability

Certain kinds of encoding or processing are intrinsically unsuitable to act as parts of the computational substrate of any genuinely cognitive state or process.

In Adams and Aizawa (2001), the dogma emerged as the claim that certain human neural states, and no extraneural goings-ons, exhibit "intrinsic intentionality," conjoined with the assertion that no proper part of a truly cognitive process can trade solely in representations lacking such intrinsic content (e.g., the conventionally couched encodings in Otto's notebook). The dogma was also at work in their later suggestion that cognitive psychology, in discovering pervasive features of inner biological systems of memory and perception, is uncovering the essential signatures of the kinds of causal process required of all possible forms of cognition.

The Dogma of Intrinsic Unsuitability is, however, just that: a dogma. Moreover, it is one that is ultimately in some tension with a cognitive scientific commonplace that might be dubbed the Tenet of Computational Promiscuity—namely, the idea that pretty much any kind of processing or encoding can form part of an information-based system for flexible adaptive response, just as long as it is properly located in some larger ongoing web of activity. When computational promiscuity meets intrinsic unsuitability, something surely has to give. I think what has to give is pretty clearly the notion of intrinsic unsuitability.

Part of the problem here is that the Dogma of Intrinsic Unsuitability is superficially similar to a quite different and rather more plausible claim—namely:

Claim of Intrinsic Suitability

Certain kinds of processing and encoding are intrinsically suited to act as the computational substrate of the kinds of fluent, pattern-sensitive engagement characteristic of, and perhaps even essential to, the behavior of intelligent organisms.

Such a claim may well be true. It may, for example, be the case that the action of some kind of interpolating statistical sponge (e.g., a connectionist-style associative learning device) provides the only computationally viable means of supporting some of the basic skills of perceiving and learning that we share with many other earthly animals. At the heart of this skill set lie the rich abilities of subtle pattern recognition that we share with many other animals and that allow us to learn about important regularities in our environment by exposure to repeated exemplars. In combination with affective and motivational systems, this kind of potent, slow, pattern-based learning enables many animals, ourselves included, to learn to deal with highly complex situations in a remarkably nuanced and efficient manner. Since these features are plausibly crucial to the kinds of fluent, adaptable, real-world responses we demand of intelligent beings, it may turn out (purely as a matter of empirical fact) that cognizing systems always incorporate some, very loosely speaking, connectionist kinds of computational underpinning.

Even if this is true, however, it does not follow that, *once such core systems are in place*, other kinds of representational and computational resources may not come to act, either temporarily or permanently, as proper parts of more complex, hybrid, distributed, cognitive wholes. In such cases, it is the very fact that these additional elements trade in modes of representation and processing that are *different* from those of the cognitive core that makes the hybrid organization worthwhile. Tracing and understanding such deep complementarity are surely the most important tasks confronting the sciences of situated cognition. If we embrace the idea of such a cognitive core, we can happily accept, for example, that no genuinely cognitive system will turn out to consist *entirely* of the kinds of external resources that fans of extended cognition most typically invoke. This is fully compatible, however, with the claim that new integrated and genuinely cognizing wholes are sometimes brought into being on the back of those more basic, perhaps even cognitively indispensable, sets of skills and capacities.

Much opposition to EXTENDED, and the quite palpable unease it causes even in some of its most sensitive critics, may thus be rooted in the mistaken fear that by celebrating the power of new, hybrid, extended systems we lose sight of that crucial cognitive core.[14] The fear would be that to embrace hybrid cognitive forms is to lose sight of the unique importance of the core systems upon whose successful operation *the very possibility of such extended forms depend*. But such fears are groundless. It is not part of the EXTENDED agenda to attempt to wash out all the differences between various internal and external contributions or to downplay or undervalue the potentially unique contribution of the cognitive core. Indeed, the actual research program of distributed cognition is committed, above all, to plotting and charting the varied contributions made by a variety of biological and nonbiological resources and the potent and multilayered interactions between them. The agenda is thus not a negative but a purely positive one: to understand the larger systemic webs that, spun around the common core shared with so many other animals, help to give human cognition its *distinctive* power, character, and charm.

Consider, by way of partial analogy, the more mundane fact that human animals, apparently uniquely on the planet, display (in addition to the common core) a second, rather different set of skills. These are the skills of explicit, deliberative, "language-infected" reason and planning (see, e.g., Dennett 1996, and the more general discussion in chap. 3 of this book). Working together, these two very different sets of skills make us into especially potent cognitive engines. Nonetheless, if we contemplate these two kinds of cognitive resources, it seems compelling that in some very important sense, it is the skills of basic pattern recognition, learning, and affectively tuned response that are the most fundamental. By this I mean only that without these we would probably be unable to have thoughts at all and, ipso facto, unable to have the linguistically infected thoughts. The very same model (depicting an empirically essential core with some mind-bogglingly potent add-ons) may be invoked by the friends of the extended mind. It is surely entirely likely that many of the extended cognitive systems described in this literature are *in just the same sense* less fundamental. They are less fundamental in that no genuinely cognitive system could consist *entirely* of the most typical kinds of external resource (passive notebooks etc.) that currently augment the common core. The contributions are in that sense asymmetrical (Collins in press) or "lopsided" (Rupert in press-a). This, I think, is the important grain of truth underlying Adams and Aizawa's arguments concerning derived contents, conventional encodings, the "noncognitive" status of notebooks, and so forth. It is a grain of truth, however, that is no more damaging to the vision of the extended mind than it is to the vision of the language-infected mind. In each case, powerful new cognitive wholes are brought into being on the back of some set of more basic, and perhaps even cognitively indispensable, skills and capacities. And in each case, the new integrated systems that result are best seen as cognitive systems in their own right. They are, indeed, the cognitive systems whose fluid operation accounts for many of the unique and most characteristic achievements of the human mind.

Notice, finally, that attention to such new and larger systemic wholes in no way precludes a proper investigation of the special features of various parts, aspects, and components. A useful comparison is with the move toward systems-level neuroscience.[15] For much of its history, most serious neuroscientific research concerned the responses and behaviors of single cells. Then, with the advent of new techniques of recording, intervention, and investigation, attention began to be devoted to understanding the neural dynamics of whole populations of cells and the distinctive processing styles of different gross anatomical elements (e.g., the hippocampus and the neocortex). Contemporary neuroscience, courtesy of still newer techniques of imaging and analysis and by using increasingly biorealistic neural network simulations, is just beginning to make progress in understanding some of the key features and properties of even larger scale neural systems: whole processing cycles that involve the temporally evolving, often highly reentrant, activity of multiple populations of neurons spanning a variety of brain areas. The advent of true systems-level neuroscience does not (and should not) imply the inappropriateness of investigations that target the special properties and features of distinct cell types, populations, or neural areas. It simply adds to these investigations a new sensitivity to the value created by processing cycles that include multiple complementary operations, performed at various timescales and using various kinds of neural resources, and whose integrated action is responsible for much of the power and scope of an individual human intelligence. So, too, according to EXTENDED, whole brain-body-world systems can sometimes be the locus of extended processing cycles whose integrated action is responsible for much of what we deem mind and intelligence.

5.11 Hippo-world

Imagine a kind of Bizarro-world—call it Hippo-world—in which for half a century, all neuroscientific attention focused on the hippocampus, regarded (for some path-dependent historical reason let's assume) as the sole and obvious locus of human cognitive activity. Specific features of hippocampal processing and encoding are discovered and publicized. One day, a few researchers turn their attention to the rest of the brain. They discover many new and interesting features and begin to talk about the larger processing circuits that link, for example, hippocampal and neocortical processing and the way certain human memory phenomena seem to depend on the complex interactions between the components. But there is a problem. Some philosophers in Hippo-world believe that in discovering the characteristic causal processes that operate in the hippocampus, they were discovering *the scientific essence of cognition itself.* It is better, they now insist, to view *what the hippocampus does as cognitive* and the rest of the brain as merely sending inputs to, or receiving outputs from, that "truly cognitive part." Only the hippocampus, they suggest, exhibits the "mark of the cognitive." These other parts, after all, just don't do the same things as the hippocampus, so why regard what they do as cognitive? Others demur, for much of what they see as gross intelligent human behavior turns out to depend just as much upon the special features and properties of the other parts as upon the (important but limited) contribution of the hippocampus itself. The study of the extended mind presents no greater theoretical or practical difficulties than those, significant as they were, that might have attended the Hippo-worlders' first tentative moves toward a more inclusive cognitive neuroscience.[16] And it is justified, or so I believe, in very much the same way. In each case, we confront larger scale organizations, defined across a smorgasbord of heterogeneous elements, whose integrated operation makes us the peculiarly successful cognitive agents we are.

6

The Cure for Cognitive Hiccups
(HEMC, HEC, HEMC...)

6.1 Rupert's Challenge

Human cognitive processing, EXTENDED claims, may at times loop
into the environment surrounding the organism. Such a view should
be contrasted with a nearby, but rather more conservative, view according to which certain cognitive processes lean heavily on environmental
structures and scaffoldings but do not thereby include those structures
and scaffoldings themselves. This more conservative view, ably cham-
pioned in a series of papers by Robert Rupert (2004, 2006, in press-a, in
press-b) may be claimed to capture all that can be of philosophical or
scientific interest in such cases and to avoid some significant method-
ological dangers in the bargain. What positive value, it may be asked,
flows from the adoption of the extended perspective? And isn't there a
danger, in embracing such (often transient) larger wholes, of losing our
practical and theoretical grip on the very minds—the minds of more or
less stable individual agents persisting through time—that we hoped
better to understand?

I shall argue, by contrast, that (in the relevant cases) it is the conservative view that threatens to obscure much that is of value and that
a robust notion of cognitive extension thus earns its keep as part of the
emerging picture of the active embodied mind. To make this case, I first

sketch some quite general responses to the worries that motivate the more conservative view. I then present some new examples and arguments that aim to flesh out the skeleton responses and to further illuminate the nature and importance of cognitive extension itself.

6.2 The HEC Versus the HEMC

Rupert (2004) distinguishes two projects, which he sees as competing proposals for understanding situated cognition. The first, a version of what we have been calling EXTENDED, depicts human cognitive processing as sometimes quite literally including operations and capacities provided by the extraorganismic environment. Rupert dubs this the Hypothesis of Extended Cognition (HEC) and glosses it like this:

> According to this view...human cognitive processing literally extends into the environment surrounding the organism, and human cognitive states literally comprise—as wholes do their proper parts—elements in that environment. (2004, 393)

Rupert depicts the HEC as a radical hypothesis apt (if true) to transform cognitive scientific theory and practice and to impact our conceptions of agency and persons. But it needs to be assessed, Rupert argues, alongside a much more conservative (though still interesting and important) competitor perspective. This is the perspective he dubs the Hypothesis of Embedded Cognition (HEMC) according to which

> cognitive processes depend very heavily, in hitherto unexpected ways, on organismically external props and devices and on the structure of the external environment in which cognition takes place. (2004, 393)

Rupert (2004, 2006, in press-a, in press-b) presents a string of arguments meant to favor the HEMC over the HEC. The arguments start with a simple appeal to common sense. Common sense, Rupert suggests, rebels at the vision of extended cognition, so we need sound theoretical reasons to endorse it.[1] The HEMC, by contrast, is said to be much more compatible with common sense. Two main worries are then raised for the HEC.

The first worry, similar to one raised by Adams and Aizawa (see chap. 5), concerns the profound differences that appear to distinguish the inner and outer contributions. Thus, for example, we read that "the external portions of extended 'memory' states (processes) differ so greatly from internal memories (the process of remembering) that they should be treated as distinct kinds" (Rupert 2004, 407). Given these differences, there is no immediate pressure to conceive the internal and the external contribution in the same terms. But worse still, there is now (allegedly) a significant cost.

Hence, a second worry appears briefly in Rupert (2004, 2006) and at greater length in his later work (in press-a, in press-b). This concerns the apparent scientific cost of any wholesale endorsement of the HEC. For the wider applicability of the EXTENDED vision (its applicability, that is, beyond somewhat contrived cases such as Otto's ever-present notebook) requires us to be open to treating more transient external props and aids, assuming they are at least typically available in some problem-solving context, as aspects of human cognitive processing. But this robs us, Rupert fears, of the traditional target of psychological and cognitive scientific theorizing—namely, a suite of integrated, persisting, organismically grounded capacities[2] (those belonging to the persisting biological individual) whose responses can be, and historically have been, probed in a variety of differing environments and using a variety of inputs. Even in cases of developmental theorizing, where what is at issue (Rupert allows) is not so much stability as change, one still needs to find some persisting, though developing core. On the face of it, it seems, the HEC

> offers developmental psychologists no more reason to be interested in, for example, the series of temporal segments we normally associate with Sally from ages two-to-six than it offers to be interested in, say, Sally, aged two, together with a ball she was bouncing on some particular day, Johnny, aged five, together with the book he was reading on some particular afternoon, and Terry, aged seven, plus the stimulus item he has just been shown by an experimenter. (Rupert in press-a, 15)

The sciences of the mind, it thus seems, simply cannot afford to identify human cognitive processing with the activity of various short-lived coupled systems comprising neural, bodily, and worldly elements.[3] Adopting HEC, Rupert concludes, must either cost too high a price (nothing less than the loss of much of the progress that cognitive psychology has made thus far) or turn out to involve some ad hoc maneuver that allows us to preserve traditional means of systemic identification for experimental purposes while still perhaps embracing HEC in our rhetoric.

6.3 Parity and Cognitive Kinds, Again

These are important challenges. Nonetheless, Rupert's worries are misplaced and for two quite deep reasons. The first is that, as we saw at some length in chapter 5, none of the arguments for extended cognition turn on or otherwise require the *fine-grained* functional similarity of the inner and outer contributions. The second is that HEC need not, and in practice does not, accrue the prohibitive costs that Rupert fears.

Concerning the lack of similarity of the inner and outer contributions, part of the problem stems from a persistent misreading of the parity claim (see chap. 4 and 5) originally introduced in Clark and Chalmers (1998).[4] This was the claim that if, as we confront some task, a part of the world functions as a process which, were it to go on in the head, we would have no hesitation in accepting as part of the cognitive process, then that part of the world is (for that time) part of the cognitive process. But as we began to see in chapter 5, far from *requiring* any deep similarity between inner and outer processes, the parity claim was specifically meant to *undermine* any tendency to think that the shape of the present-day, human inner processes sets some bar (as, e.g., Adams and Aizawa 2001 suggest) on what should count as part of a genuinely cognitive process. The parity probe was thus meant to act as a kind of veil of metabolic ignorance, inviting us to ask what our attitude would be if currently external means of storage and transformation were, contrary to the presumed facts, found in biology. Thus understood, parity is not about the outer performing just like the human-specific inner. Rather, it is about equality of opportunity: avoiding a rush to judgment based on spatial location alone. The Parity Principle was meant to engage our rough sense of what we might intuitively judge to belong to the domain of cognition—rather than, say, that of digestion—but to do so without the pervasive distractions of skin and skull.

This point is nicely recognized by Wheeler (in press-b), who notes that the *wrong* way to assess parity of contribution is to "fix the benchmarks for what it is to count as a proper part of a cognitive system by identifying all the details of the causal contribution made by (say) the brain [then by looking] to see if any external elements meet those benchmarks" (3). To do things that way, Wheeler argues, is to open the door to the highly chauvinistic thought that only systems whose fine-grained causal profile fully matches that of the brain can be cognitive systems at all. Yet, as we saw in chapter 5, just because some alien neural system failed to match our own in various ways (perhaps they fail to exhibit the "generation effect" during recall; see Rupert 2004, for this example), we should not *thereby* be forced to count the action of such systems as noncognitive. The Parity Principle is thus best seen as a demand that we assess the bioexternal contributions with the same kind of unbiased vision that we should bring to bear on an alien neural organization. It is wholly misconstrued as a demand for fine-grained sameness of processing and storage. Rather, it is a call for sameness of opportunity, such that bioexternal elements *might* turn out to be parts of the machinery of cognition *even if* their contributions are unlike (perhaps deeply complementary to) those of the biological brain.

But even once we lay to rest the mistaken vision of the Parity Principle (as requiring fine-grained identity of causal contribution), there remains an important and closely related question. The question turns on the issue of natural or explanatory kinds. Thus, Rupert (2004) questions the idea, certainly present in Clark and Chalmers's original treatment, that treating the organism-notebook system as the supervenience base for some of Otto's dispositional beliefs was to be recommended on grounds of *explanatory unity and power*. Rupert's worry then takes as a premise the idea that a kind is natural if it is adverted to by the laws or explanations of a successful science. Biomemory thus meets the requirement because it falls under the laws and explanatory frameworks of a successful science—cognitive psychology or cognitive science more generally. But, the argument continues, "extended memory" doesn't fit the causal profile of memory as described by this body of successful science and hence should not be subsumed under the heading of "memory" at all.

We already saw (sec. 5.6) that acceptable forms of unification need not require all systemic elements to behave according to the same laws. Indeed, to assume they must do so is simply to beg the question against any science whose target is a genuinely hybrid system (e.g., a part-connectionist, part-classical computational organization). In such cases, one may, of course, hope to find *additional* principles governing the larger hybrid organization itself. At this point, it is surely worth remembering that the study of extended cognitive systems is just beginning, and it is no wonder that our best current unified understandings target the inner elements alone. That's where science has primarily been looking so far, after all.[5] Nonetheless, it is the substantive empirical bet of the extended systems theorist that the larger hybrid wholes, comprising biological and nonbiological elements, will *also* (and more on this later and in chap. 9) prove to be the proper objects of sustained scientific study in their own right.

A further reason to resist the easy assimilation of the HEC into the HEMC concerns the nature of the interactions between the internal and the external resources themselves. Such interactions, it is important to notice, may be highly complex, nested, and nonlinear. As a result, there may, in some cases, be no viable means of understanding the behavior and potential of the extended cognitive ensembles by piecemeal decomposition and additive reassembly. To understand the integrated operation of the extended thinking system created, for example, by combining pen, paper, graphics programs, and a trained mathematical brain, it may be quite insufficient to attempt to understand and then combine (!) the properties of pens, papers, graphics programs, and brains. This may be insufficient for just the same kinds of reasons advanced, within neuroscience itself, as reasons to study not *just* the various major neural substructures and their capacities but *also* their complex nonlinear interactions and the larger scale activities in which they participate. In the latter case, the larger explanatory targets are whole processing cycles, running on soft-assembled coalitions of neural resources, arising in response to some specific problem-solving purpose. Such soft-assembled neural packages involve the temporally evolving, often highly reentrant, activity of multiple populations of neurons spanning a variety of brain areas.[6] But why then suppose that the soft assemblies most relevant to human cognitive achievements are always and everywhere bounded by skin and skull? Why should we not recognize, in our peculiarly structured and artifact-rich world, a succession of similarly complex hybrid ensembles spanning brain, body, and world?

6.4 The Persisting Core

What, though, of the allegedly high costs of such an enlarged perspective? Here, it is important to see that there is no need, in taking extended cognition seriously, to lose our grip on the more or less stable, more or less persisting, core biological bundle that lies at the heart of each episode of cognitive soft assembly. Occasionally, under strict and rare conditions, we may confront genuine extensions of even that more or less persisting core: cases where even the persisting, mobile resource bundle is augmented (as in the case of Otto) in a potentially permanent manner. But in most other cases, we confront only soft-assembled, temporary medleys of information-processing resources comprising a dovetailed subset of neural activity and bodily and environmental augmentations. The mere fact that such circuits are temporary, however, does not provide sufficient reason to downgrade their cognitive importance. Many purely internal information-processing ensembles are likewise transient creations, generated on the spot in response to the particularities of task and context. As just one example, consider Van Essen, Anderson, and Olshausen's (1994) account according to which many neurons and neuronal populations serve not as direct encodings of knowledge or information but as (dumb) middle managers routing and trafficking the internal flow of information between and within cortical areas. These "control neurons" serve to open and close channels of activity and allow for the creation of a kind of instantaneous, context-sensitive modular cortical architecture. Control neurons thus weave functional modules "on the hoof" in a way sensitive to the effects of context, attention, and so on.[7] As Jerry Fodor once put it, in such cases, it is "*unstable instantaneous* connectivity that counts" (1983, 118; see also Fodor 2001). The resulting soft-wired ensembles, in which information then flows and is processed in ways apt to the task at hand, do not cease to be important just because they are transient creations ushered into being by a preceding wave of "neural recruitment."

Rupert worries that, by taking seriously the notion of cognitive extension in the special subclass of transient cases where the newly recruited organizations span brain, body, and world, we lose our grip on the persisting systems that we ordinarily take to be our objects of study. For indeed, as Rupert (in press-a, 15) points out, much work in cognitive and experimental psychology proceeds by assuming that subjects are "persisting, organismically bound cognitive systems."

The first and most important thing to notice is that there is no incompatibility whatsoever between EXTENDED and the notion of a persisting common biological core. Nor does anything in the present treatment threaten to deprive us of that common core as a proper object of scientific study. What we are invited to do, instead, is to let a thousand flowers bloom.[8] If our avowed goal is to discover the stand-alone properties of the neural apparatus, we might want to impede subjects from using their fingers as counting buffers during an experiment. Similarly, if our goal is to understand what the persisting biological organism alone can do, we might want to restrict the use of all nonbiological props and aids. But if our goal is to unravel the mechanically modulated flow of energy and information that allows an identifiable agent (a Sally, Johnny, or Terry) to solve a certain kind of problem, we should not simply *assume* that every biologically motivated surface or barrier forms a cognitively relevant barrier or that it constitutes an important interface from an information-processing perspective (see Haugeland 1998, and the discussion in chaps. 2 and 7). That this can be done while still respecting experimental requirements is shown, for example, by the careful investigations of skilled Tetris play described in chapter 4 and the various studies discussed in the next few sections.

Notice also that we don't find or individuate human agents by first finding their cognitive mechanisms! Instead, we find an agent by identifying (roughly speaking) a reliable, easily identifiable physical nexus of perception and action, apparently driven by a persisting and modestly integrated body of goals and knowledge. Then and only then do we ask, of some particular problem-solving performance displayed by *that very agent*, what and where are the underlying mechanisms that make possible that performance. It is at that point that we may sometimes be surprised to find that the target performance depends on a far wider variety of factors and forces than we initially imagined.[9] In so doing, we retain a perfectly good grip on the cognitive agents that are our primary objects of study.[10]

It is perhaps helpful to distinguish two possible explanatory goals at this point. One is to explain the persistence of specific cognitive agents. The other is to display the active machinery that underpins an agent's current mental state or that explains some specific cognitive performance. Thus, visual cortex, as David Chalmers (personal communication) notes, may be quite irrelevant to my persistence as a subject (I'd persist without it) while still being the supervenience base for some of my current mental states and performances. What is at issue, as far as the claims about cognitive extension are concerned, is simply which bits of the world make true (by serving as the local mechanistic supervenience base for) certain claims about a subject's here-and-now mental states or cognitive processing.

6.5   Cognitive Impartiality

Let us make the (surely uncontroversial) assumption that the biological brain is, currently at least, the essential core element in all episodes of individual human cognitive activity. A question we may then ask is: Does the brain care about the nature (biological or nonbiological) or location (organism bound or organism external) of the processing and storage resources soft-assembled to tackle some cognitive task?

In an important series of experiments, Wayne Gray and his colleagues have shown in compelling detail that it is a mistake to privilege any location or any type of operation in the online assembly of a cognitive routine. In the first set of such experiments (Gray and Fu 2004), subjects were required to program an on-screen simulation (see fig. 6.1) of a VCR control panel. The idea was to manipulate the time costs of accessing the information (concerning channel, start time, etc.) needed to program the VCR. This information was presented in a window

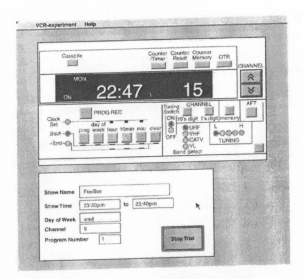

FIGURE 6.1   Screen shot of VCR and show-information window for the free-access condition. Notice that the fields of the show-information window are open at all times. For the gray-box and memory-test conditions, the fields would be covered by gray boxes during the trial. (From Gray and Fu 2004, by permission)

beneath the control panel and was either constantly visible by a flick of the eyes (free-access group) or available only by moving and clicking the mouse to remove an overlaid opaque cover (gray-box group). There was also a memory-test group (run under both the free-access and gray-box conditions), who, unlike the others, had previously memorized all the information required.

What the researchers found was that time costs of information retrieval, measured in milliseconds, appeared to determine the precise mix of resources (biomemory, motor actions, shifts of attention) recruited to solve the problem. That is, the subjects settled on whatever strategy yielded (at that phase of the programming) the least cost (measured by time) information retrieval. In fact, they did this even when the fastest mix of resources sacrificed perfect knowledge in the world for imperfect knowledge in the head.[11] Only when the in-the-world data could be accessed with less effort (measured by time) than the data stored in biological memory was it recruited and were calls to the external store "built into" the dominant strategy.

Gray and Fu present their results as a challenge to the idea that human cognitive strategies actively favor the use of information in the world over information in the head. The pendulum may have swung a little too far, they fear, in favor of reliance on external cognitive scaffolding. Instead, they argue that their results show that "the time spent retrieving something from memory is weighed the same as time spent in perceptual-motor activity" and that it is therefore a mistake to "presume the privileged status of any location or type of operation" (Gray and Fu 2004, 378, 380). They thus argue for a level playing field with time costs of access playing the key role in determining the mix of resources recruited as part of some cognitive routine.[12] That is,

The cognitive control of interactive behavior minimizes effort by using a least-effort [measured by time] combination of all the mechanisms available to it. All mechanisms or subsystems are on the table. There is no reason to think that one mechanism or subsystem has a privileged status in relation to another. (2004, 380)

Otherwise put:

The central controller[13] makes no functional distinction between knowledge in-the-head versus in-the-world or the means of acquiring that information (such as eye movement, mouse movement and click, or retrieval from memory). (Gray and Veksler 2005, 809)

This model is described as a "soft constraints" account of interactive behavior. Temporal cost–benefit trade-offs are said to provide a soft constraint (one that may always be overridden by various forms of explicit control) on the mix of motoric, perceptual, and biomemory-based resources that will, other things being equal, be automatically recruited to perform a given information-processing task on a given occasion. In subsequent work, Gray et al. (2006) directly compare this to a Minimal Memory Model (ascribed to Ballard, Hayhoe, and Pelz 1995 and to Hayhoe 2000) according to which the resource-recruitment process aims to *minimize* the use of biomemory and to *maximize* the use of environmental support. They thus agree with Ballard and others that the embodiment level (the level at which we observe delicate, short timescale interactions among motoric, perceptual, and bio-memory based resources; see Ballard, Hayhoe, and Pelz 1995; Ballard et al. 1997) is crucial for much of our problem-solving activity but differ in their account of exactly how the trade-offs are calculated. Where Ballard and others predict a bias toward the use of external encoding and storage, Gray et al. depict a level playing field[14] with fine temporal considerations calling the tune: "Milliseconds matter, and they matter the same regardless of the type of activity with which they are filled" (2006, 364).

This emerging empirical debate between the minimal memory account and the purely time-cost-based alternative is evidence, it seems to me, of an important turning point in the study of the embodied mind. For in place of a loose coalition of ideas concerning the cognitive importance of body and world, we begin to see the first stirrings of a science, complete with nuanced disagreements open to empirical investigation by broadly sympathetic practitioners. Further evidence of this development will be seen in the remaining chapters.

For my purposes, then, the resolution of this particular dispute is less important than the fact of its existence and the susceptibility of the issue to systematic empirical investigation. For we have here a sequence of controlled experiments targeting genuinely hybrid ensembles: soft-assembled coalitions comprising biostorage, motoric, and perceptual modes of access and bioexternal storage. The work by Gray et al. thus provides a clear demonstration of the susceptibility (despite the fears of Rupert, of Adams and Aizawa, and others) of such organizations to quite standard forms of cognitive scientific investigation. Even if Rupert and others are right that terms such as *memory* cannot, once extended to the nonbiological domain, themselves pick out explanatorily unified kinds, this does not mean that the extended organizations in which they participate are not proper objects of scientific enquiry, emerging and dissolving according to determinable principles, and operating in ways that maximize certain properties and features (in this case, speed of access). To the worry that there will be no unified science of heterogeneously constituted systems, we should reply that there not only can be, but already is, a nascent science both of the recruitment (of sets of neural and extraneural resources) and of the fine-tuned unfolding of activity in just such heterogeneous ensembles.

Gray et al. sum up their own preferred model with two claims. The first is that "the [neural] control system is indifferent to information source" (2006, 478). The second is that the only bias imposed by biology is that of finding the most cost-effective mix of elements (478) available. These very broad conclusions are, I should point out, compatible with a wide variety of cost functions (time taken may not always be the prime or sole determinant). But whatever the cost function or functions (which may turn out to vary with context and goals), what matters most, in my view, is the underlying vision of what I shall dub the Hypothesis of Cognitive Impartiality:

Our problem-solving performances take shape according to some cost function or functions that, in the typical course of events, accord no special status or privilege to specific types of operations (motoric, perceptual, introspective) or modes of encoding (in the head or in the world).

This is, in many ways, a quite natural accompaniment to the Parity Principle itself. It states that the biological control system doesn't care about differences of location or type of resource but simply uses whatever it can, relative to some cost–benefit trade-off, to get the job done.

6.6 A Brain Teaser

Simple as it may sound, the Hypothesis of Cognitive Impartiality hides something of a puzzle, at least for those who would depict cognition as not just embodied but also extended. For it threatens, unless delicately handled, to undermine the image of cognitive extension in quite a novel fashion.[15] Thus, suppose we now ask: Just *what is it* that is so potently impartial concerning its sources of order and information? The answer looks to be "the biological brain." So haven't we (rather deliciously) ended up firmly privileging the biological brain in the very act of affirming its own impartiality?

To see past this worry, we must notice that there are at least two explanatory targets in the immediate vicinity. The first is the recruitment of the extended organization itself.[16] We may ask just how, and according to what principles, the various elements (perhaps some subset of neural operations, "deictic" uses of eye movements, gestures, and scribblings) came to combine into a specific soft-assembled information-processing device. In this process of soft assembly, the brain surely plays a very special role. The second concerns the flow of information and processing in the newly soft-assembled extended device. Relative to that device we may ask just how information flows and is processed in ways that ideally solve some problem. HEC helps us to see that, as far as the second of these explanatory projects goes, the bounds of skin and skull are functionally transparent. HEMC, by contrast, both threatens to obscure the scientifically important distinction between the two projects and erects a firm skin-based boundary where the process of recruitment and use marks no boundary at all.

The puzzle concerning cognitive impartiality is thus resolved. Concerning the process of recruitment, it is indeed the biological brain (or perhaps some of its subsystems) that is in the driver's seat. That is to say, it is indeed some neurally based process of recruitment that (following Gray et al.) turns out to be so pointedly unbiased regarding the use of inner versus outer circuits, storage, and operations. But once such an organization is in place, it is the flow and transformation of information in (what is often) an extended, distributed system that provide the machinery of ongoing thought and reason.[17]

What this suggests (and this, too, is a theme that will recur in the remaining chapters) is that in rejecting the vision of human cognitive processing as *organism bound*, we should not feel forced to deny that it is (in most, perhaps all, real-world cases) *organism centered*. It is indeed primarily (though not solely) the biological organism that, courtesy especially of its potent neural apparatus, spins and maintains (or more minimally selects and exploits) the webs of additional structure that then form parts of the machinery that accomplishes its own cognizing.[18] Just as it is the spider body that spins and maintains the web that then (following Dawkins 1982) constitutes part of its own extended phenotype, so it is the biological human organism that spins, selects, or maintains the webs of cognitive scaffolding that participate in the extended machinery of its own thought and reason.[19] Individual cognizing, then, is *organism centered even if it is not organism bound*.

6.7   Thoughtful Gestures

At this stage of our discussion, it will help to introduce an additional worked example of extended cognizing in action. The example I shall take concerns the role of bodily gesture in thought and reason. The case is apt because gesture, though clearly itself an organismic activity, is not merely a *neural* activity. Moreover, bodily gesture turns out to exhibit some key features whose applicability looks to outrun the bounds of the organism itself.

Goldin-Meadow (2003), following an extensive inquiry into the nature and organization of human gesture, asks an intriguing question. Is gesture all about the expression of fully formed thoughts, and thus mainly a prop for interagent communication (listeners appreciating meanings through others' gestures), or might gesture function as part of the actual process of thinking? Some clues (136–149) that it might be more than merely expressive include:

> We do it when talking on the phone.
> We do it when talking to ourselves.
> We do it in the dark when nobody can see.
> Gesturing increases with task difficulty.
> Gesturing increases when speakers must choose between options.
> Gesturing increases when reasoning about a problem rather than merely describing the problem or a known solution.

Still, a deflationist might suggest that most of these effects are easily explained by mere association: that gesturing without a viewer is just a habit installed by our experience of gesturing in the normal communicative context. It turns out, however (141–144), that speakers blind from birth, who have never spoken to a visible listener and never seen others moving their hands as they speak, gesture when they speak. Moreover, they do so even when speaking to others they know are blind (see also Iverson and Goldin-Meadow 1998, 2001). Supposing for the sake of argument that gesture does play some kind of active causal role in thinking, just what role might that be? One way to find out is to see what happens when gesture is removed from the mix of available resources. To explore the impact of restricting gesture on thought, Goldin-Meadow and colleagues (2001; see also Goldin-Meadow 2003, chap. 11) asked two matched groups of children to memorize a list and then to carry out some mathematical problem solving before trying to recall the list. One group (call it the free-gesture group) could freely gesture during the intervening mathematical task; the other (call it the no-gesture group) was told not to gesture. The results were that restricting the use of gesture during the intervening mathematical task had a robust and significant detrimental effect on the separate memory task (remembering the list of words). The best explanation, according to Goldin-Meadow, is that the act of gesturing somehow shifts or reduces aspects of the overall neural cognitive load, thus freeing up resources for the memory task.

Before pursuing this idea, it is necessary to rule out a rather obvious alternative account. According to this alternative, the effort of remembering *not* to gesture (in the no-gesture group) is *adding* to the load rather than gesture (in the free-gesture group) reducing the load. If this were so, the no-gesture group would indeed not perform as well but not because gesturing lightens the load. Rather, remembering not to gesture increases it. As luck would have it, some children and adults spontaneously chose not to gesture during some of the episodes of mathematical problem solving. This allowed the experimenters to compare the effects of removing gesture by instruction and by spontaneous (hence, presumably effortless) inclination. Memory for the initial task turned out to be equally impaired even when the lack of gesture was a spontaneous choice (see Goldin-Meadow 2003, 155), supporting the claim that the gestures themselves play some active cognitive role.[20]

An important hint as to the nature of this active role emerges, Goldin-Meadow argues, when we look at cases of gesture–speech mismatches (2003, chap. 12). These are cases when what you say and what you gesture are in conflict (e.g., you gesture a one-one mapping while failing to appreciate the importance of such a mapping in your simultaneous vocal attempts at solving the problem).[21] Many such cases were found, and importantly, the gestures tended to prefigure the child's consciously finding the right solution in speech at a very slightly later point. Even if the right solution was not shortly found, the presence of the apt gesture turned out to be predictive of that child's being able to learn the right solution more easily than others, whose gestures showed no such tacit or nascent appreciation.

In the end, Goldin-Meadow is led to the following story (drawing also, as she clearly notes, on the groundbreaking work of David McNeill; see McNeill 1992, 2005). The physical act of gesturing, Goldin-Meadow suggests, plays an active (not merely expressive) role in learning, reasoning, and cognitive change by providing an alternative (analog, motoric, visuospatial) representational format. In this way,

> gesture...expands the set of representational tools available to speakers and listeners. It can redundantly reflect information represented through verbal formats or it can augment that information, adding nuances possible only through visual or motor formats. (2003, 186)

Encodings in that special visuomotor format enter, it is argued, into a kind of ongoing coupled dialectic with encodings in the other verbal format. Gesture thus continuously informs and alters verbal thinking, which is continuously informed and altered by gesture (i.e., the two form a genuinely coupled system). This coupled dialectic creates points of instability (conflict) whose attempted resolutions move forward our thinking, often (though of course not always) in productive ways. The upshot is "a dynamic mutuality such that activity in any one component of the system can potentially entrain activity in any other" (Iverson and Thelen 1999, 37).

Is it really the physical gestures that matter here, or do they merely reflect the transfer of load between two different neural stores? Does gesturing simply shift the burden from a neural verbal store to a neural visuospatial store? If so, then it should be harder to perform a separate spatial memory task when freely gesturing than when not. This was tested (Goldin-Meadow and Wagner 2004; Wagner, Nusbaum, and Goldin-Meadow 2004) by replacing the original word-recall task with a spatial one: that of recalling the location of dots on a grid. The results were unambiguous. The availability of gesture still helps (still yields improved performance on the memory task) even when the second task is itself a spatial one.

The act of gesturing, all this suggests, is not simply a motor act expressive of some fully neurally realized process of thought. Instead, the act of gesturing is part and parcel of a coupled neural–bodily unfolding that is itself usefully seen as an organismically extended process of thought. In gesture, we plausibly confront a cognitive process whose implementation involves machinery that loops out beyond the purely neural realm. This kind of cognitively pregnant unfolding need not stop at the boundary of the biological organism. Something very similar may, as frequently remarked, occur when we are busy writing and thinking at the same time. It is not always that fully formed thoughts get committed to paper. Rather, the paper provides a medium in which, this time via some kind of coupled neural-scribbling-reading unfolding, we are enabled to explore ways of thinking that might otherwise be unavailable to us. (Just such a coupled unfolding was eloquently evoked in the famous exchange between Richard Feynman and historian Charles Weiner reproduced in the Introduction.) If we allow that the actual gestures (not simply their neural pre- or postcursors) form part of an individual's cognitive processing, there seems no principled reason to stop the spread where skin meets air.[22]

At this point, however, Goldin-Meadow's talk of gesture "lightening the load" offers a possible hostage to fortune. For the skeptic might suggest that what this implies is that the physical gesturing itself is not part of the cognitive process but *merely impacts* it (recall our earlier discussion of the so-called causal-constitution error) by lightening the load on the *real* cognitive processes, whatever they are. I do not think we should set too much store on this choice of words. Such ways of speaking are more a reflection of our current scientific predisposition to locate all the machinery of cognition in the head than an argument for so doing. More important, the key distinction between "merely impacting" some inner cognitive process and forming a proper part of an *extended* cognitive process looks much less clear (as we shall soon see) in cases involving the systematic effects of *self-generated* external structure on thought and reason.

6.8 Material Carriers

McNeill (2005) offers a clear expression of the view that the physical gestures are elements in the cognitive process itself. McNeill's work is grounded in extensive empirical case studies on the use of gesture in free speech. The key idea that McNeill uses to understand and organize these studies is the notion of an ongoing imagery–language dialectic in which gesture acts as a material carrier.

The term *material carrier* is due to Vygotsky (1962/1986) and is meant to convey the idea of a physical materialization that has systematic cognitive effects. But once more, we should not be misled by the image of cognitive effects. For according to McNeill, "the concept [of a material carrier] implies that the gesture, *the actual motion of the gesture itself*, is a dimension of thinking" (2005, 98, emphasis in original). Our free (i.e., spontaneous, nonconventional) gestures are not, McNeill argues, merely expressions of or representations of our fully achieved inner thoughts but are themselves "thinking in one of its many forms" (99).

Notice that this is not to say that the gestures do not follow from, and lead to, specific forms of neural activity. They do, and McNeill has much to say about the neural systems preferentially involved in the generation and reception of spontaneous gesture (McNeill 2005; chap. 7 and 8). Rather, it is to see the physical act of gesturing as part of a unified thought-language-hand system whose coordinated activity has been selected or maintained for its specifically cognitive virtues.

There are important differences between McNeill's account and that of Goldin-Meadow, but they are united in seeing the physical gestures as genuine elements in the cognitive process. McNeill (2005) stresses the idea of "growth points," described as "the minimal unit of an imagery–language dialectic" (105). A growth point is a package of imagistic and linear propositional (linguistic) elements that together form a single idea (e.g., both conveying the concept of an antagonistic force as a speaker describes some series of events). The points of productive conflict stressed by Goldin-Meadow are not growth points in this technical sense (see, e.g., McNeill 2005, 137). But they are growth points in another, quite routine sense: They are collisions in meaning space, crucially mediated by gestural loops into the physical world, that are able to move our thinking along in productive ways.

These differences in emphasis do not amount, as far as I can tell, to any deep incompatibility between their underlying models of the cognitive virtues of gesture. In each case, the loop into gesture creates a material structure that is available to both speaker and listener. And just as that material structure may have a systematic cognitive effect upon the listener, so too it may have a systematic cognitive effect on the speaker. The role of gesture, if this is correct, is closely akin to that of certain forms of self-directed, overt or covert speech or (looping outside the organismic shell) to certain forms of writing for thinking (see McNeill 2005, 99).

To account for this special potency, McNeill invokes an evolutionary hypothesis that he dubs "Mead's Loop" (after G. H. Mead 1934). The background to McNeill's suggestion is the discovery of so-called mirror neurons. These are neurons, first discovered in the frontal lobes of macaques, that fire both when an animal performs some intentional action and when it sees another animal performing the same action (Rizzolatti, Fogassi, and Gallese 2001). McNeill's suggestion is that our own gestures activate mirror-neuron-dominated neural resources so that "one's own gestures [activate] the part of the brain that responds to intentional actions, including gestures, by someone else, and thus treats one's own gesture as a social stimulus" (McNeill 2005, 250).

Whether this is the correct evolutionary and mechanistic account is unimportant for present purposes. What matters is rather the guiding idea (versions of which we already met back in chap. 3) that by materializing thought in physical gesture we create a stable physical presence that may productively impact and constrain the neural elements of thought and reason.

Many other possibilities fall neatly under this broad rubric. Thus, Alač and Hutchins (2004) provide a useful and detailed analysis of a possible role for gesture among a group of interacting scientists, arguing that their microanalysis "reveals action as cognition, that is, actions that constitute thinking for the scientists" (629). One of the key roles of gesture, they suggest, is to highlight and explore possible relations between different *external* representations (in this case, between information on charts, brain scans, etc.). Physical gesture in the public space is here depicted as quite literally part of the cognitive process of conceptualization in which the scientists are engaged, acting as what Hutchins (in press) calls a "material anchor" for a conceptual blend.

Shaun Gallagher, in a rewarding recent discussion of gesture and thought, writes that "even if we are not explicitly aware of our gestures, and even in circumstances where they contribute nothing to the communicative process, they may contribute implicitly to the shaping of our cognition" (2005, 121). Gallagher approaches the topic of gesture in the larger framework of his account of the "prenoetic" role of embodiment. This is a term of art that Gallagher uses to signify the role of the body in structuring mind and consciousness. The idea is that facts about the body, and about bodily orientation and so forth, set the scene for conscious acts of perception, memory, and judgment (the "noetic" factors) in various important ways. A prenoetic performance, we are told, is "one that helps to structure consciousness but that does not explicitly show itself in the contents of consciousness" (Gallagher 2005, 32). Thus, to take a very simple example, embodied agents perceive the world from a certain spatial perspective. That perspective shapes what is given to us explicitly in phenomenal experience, but it is not itself part of what we experience. Instead, it "shapes" or "structures" experience (for this example, see Gallagher 2005, 2–3). In this manner, Gallagher speaks of the role of gesture in "shaping" cognition and (following Merleau-Ponty's usage in describing the cognitive role of speech) in the "accomplishment of thought." Such locutions neatly (though only superficially) sidestep the thorny issue of whether to see gesture as part of the actual machinery of thought and reason. In a footnote to the quoted passage, Gallagher is less evasive, suggesting that "it may be...that certain aspects of what we call the mind just are in fact nothing other than what we tend to call expression, that is, occurrent linguistic practices ('internal speech'), gesture, and expressive movement" (121). Gesture, Gallagher suspects, is both a means by which thought is accomplished *and* an aspect of mind—an aspect of the thinking itself.[23]

6.9   Loops as Mechanisms

Our own gestures, if the conjectures of the previous sections are correct, form part of an integrated language-thought-hand[24] system that has been selected for its specifically cognitive virtues.[25] Neural systems coordinate with, help produce, exploit, and can themselves be entrained by those special-purpose bodily motions that constitute free gestures. In this way, speech, gesture, and neural activity are able to form a single integrated system (Iverson and Thelen 1999) with clear problem-solving virtues not reducible to the virtues of any of its individual parts.

A single integrated system can, however, comprise a variety of distinct parts whose contributions are hugely different. Some of those parts, moreover, may be cognitive processes in their own right (i.e., they would remain cognitive processes even when considered in isolation from the others), whereas others are not. Thus, it seems obvious that a sequence of gross physical gestures alone could never implement a cognitive state or process. It is only in coordination with crucial forms of neural activity that the cognitive role of the gestures can emerge and be maintained. By contrast, some set of neural goings-on is often sufficient for the presence of some cognitive state or other. But this genuine asymmetry provides no reason to reject the notion that gestures form part of the machinery of cognition. To see this, we need only remind ourselves that the activity of a single neuron is likewise never sufficient for the existence of a cognitive state, yet that activity can, in the proper context, still form part of the machinery that implements a cognitive state or process.

It may or may not also be true that for any gesture-involving cognitive unfolding, there is a pure sequence of neural events such that *if* they were somehow held in place or ushered into being without the loop through physical gesture, the cognitive states of the embodied agent would be the same. It does not follow from this that the gestures play only a causal role and do not help constitute the machinery of cognition. For the same may also be true of a sequence of neural states held together by some internal operation. Achieve that very sequence some other way, and the chain of thoughts, let's assume, will come out the same. It doesn't follow (and see Hurley 1998, for more sophisticated versions of this argument) that the inner or the outer operations involved are thereby not, as things actually unfold, genuine aspects of the cognitive process. Thus, Hurley usefully cautions against what she calls "the 'causal-constitutive error' error," which is

> the error of objecting that externalist explanations give a constitutive role to external factors that are "merely causal" while assuming without independent argument or criteria that the causal/constitutive distinction coincides with some external/internal boundary. To avoid thus begging the question, we should not operate with prior assumptions about where to place the causal/constitutive boundary, but wait on the results of explanation. (in press)

In trying to get a grip on these matters, we are easily misled by various inessential features of many common cases where bioexternal factors and forces impact thought and reason. Thus, suppose the rhythmic pulse of rain on my Edinburgh window somehow helps the pace and sequencing of a flow of thoughts. Is the rain now part of my cognitive engine? No. It is merely the backdrop against which my cognizing takes shape. But this, I submit, is not because the rain is outside the bounds of skin and skull. Rather, it is because the rain is not part of (it is not even a side-effect or a "spandrel" within) any system selected or maintained for the support of better cognizing. It is indeed *mere* (but as it happens helpful) backdrop. Compare this with a robot *designed* to use raindrop sounds to time and pace certain internal operations essential to some kinds of problem solving. Such a robot would be vulnerable to (non-British) weather. But it is not clear, at least to me, that the whole drop-based timing mechanism is not usefully considered as one of the robot's cognitive routines. Consider finally the Self-Stimulating Spitting Robot. This is a robot that evolved to spit stored water at a plate on its own body for the same purpose, so as to use the auditory signal as a kind of virtual wire (Dennett 1991a) to time other key operations. Those self-maintained cognition-supporting signals are surely part of the cognitive mechanism itself. A neural clock or oscillator would count after all.

What these simple examples show is that (as Adams and Aizawa, see chap. 5, correctly stated) coupling alone is not enough. *Sometimes*, all coupling does is provide a channel allowing externally originating inputs to drive cognitive processing along. But in a wide range of the most interesting cases, there is a crucially important complication. These are the cases when we confront a recognizably cognitive process, running in some agent, that creates outputs (speech, gesture, expressive movements, written words) that, recycled as inputs, drive the cognitive process along. In such cases, any intuitive ban on counting *inputs* as parts of *mechanisms* seems wrong. Instead, we confront something rather like the cognitive equivalent of a forced induction system. A familiar example is the turbo-driven automobile engine. The turbocharger uses exhaust flow from the engine to spin a turbine that spins an air pump that compresses the air flowing into the engine. The compression squeezes more air into each cylinder, allowing more fuel to be combined, leading to more powerful explosions (that drive the engine that creates the exhaust flow that powers the turbo). This self-stimulating automotive arrangement provide up to 40 percent more power on demand. The exhaust flow is an engine output in good standing that also serves as a reliable, self-generated input. There can be little doubt that the whole turbocharging cycle should count as part of the automobile's own overall power-generating mechanism! The same is true, I submit, in the case of gesture: Gesture is *both* a systemic output and a self-generated input that plays an important role in an extended neural–bodily cognitive economy.[26]

6.10 Anarchic Self-stimulation

The most satisfying way to complete this picture involves one final (and still surprisingly vertiginous) step. This final step is not compulsory, and the case for cognitive extension stands even if one chooses not to take it.[27] But it provides a rather natural way to complete the account.

The step in question is to reject outright the idea of an inner executive—the "Central Meaner" (Dennett 1991a)—who "uses" practices of self-stimulation as a means to its own (preformed) cognitive ends. In place of such an all-knowing inner executive, we should consider the possibility of a vast parallel coalition of more or less influential forces, whose largely self-organizing unfolding makes each of us the thinking beings we are. Thus, Dennett (1991a, 1998) depicts the human mind in terms that more closely resemble a semianarchic parallel organization of competing elements, whose average level of intelligence remains well below that traditionally ascribed to the so-called central executive (a horde of competing miniexecutives or, better, maxiassistants with nobody to assist). Within this flatter competing–cooperating nexus, different elements gain control at different times. But crucially, no element in the dodging and bumping horde is the privileged source of thinking such that the job of the rest is just to articulate or store its fully formed (though perhaps as yet verbally unarticulated) thoughts. Within such an economy, our ongoing cycles of gestural and linguistic self-stimulation are neither simply the products of, nor the servants of, a single stable independent central reasoning element. In just this way, McNeill (2005, 98–99, fn. 11 and 12) presents his model of gesture as one that avoids the image of a central "thinking area" to which all cognitively potent representations need to be revealed, just as it avoids the image of gesture (and the spoken word) as a centrally manipulated cognitive tool.

Thus, consider the familiar observation that verbal encodings are the kinds of items we can temporarily maintain in special forms of short-term memory such as the "phonological loop" (Baddeley 1986), usually depicted as a subvocal resource comprising a kind of inner voice and a kind of inner ear.[28] According to the standard account, a central executive loads this circuit with some verbal content such as a telephone number. The central executive is "the part that runs the show and does the real work" (Reisberg 2001, 14). At the executive's beck and call are a number of "assistants" whose lowly tasks involve storing and cycling information as the executive bids. One such assistant is the aforementioned phonological loop. While the loop subvocally replays the verbal passage, the executive is free to attend to other matters, returning (as the trace decays) to read and refresh the verbal store by another subvocal launch. The overall effect is very much that of using a passive storage device, such as a notebook, perhaps with slowly vanishing ink.

It is instructive (and again, see Dennett 1991a, 1998) to try to imagine the role and functioning of something like the phonological loop in a system devoid of an inner executive, Central Meaner, or other form of stable top-level authority. The further we depart from that image (and there are, it is important to note, many intermediate options; see Shallice 2002; Carruthers 1998), the more space there seems to be to reconceptualize the cognitive contribution of our practices of self-stimulation. For example, instead of treating linguaform self-stimulation as fundamentally providing only as a kind of inner scratchpad useful for keeping prechosen verbal forms alive in working memory, we may begin to see it as one of the many simultaneously unfolding processes that contribute to the construction and origination of our thoughts and not merely to their short-term maintenance. In place of the Central Meaner, whose preformed ideas the self-produced input stream merely reflects, we may thus consider a more distributed, somewhat anarchic organization in which, for the most part, as Dennett (1998) nicely puts it, "the manipulanda have to manipulate themselves."

Our gestures, too, if Goldin-Meadow, McNeill, and others are right, act as elements in a loose-knit, distributed representational and information-processing economy, elements whose materialized imagistic contents may augment, refine, expand, and sometimes productively conflict with those of other elements in that same economy. The wrong image here is that of a central reasoning engine that merely uses gesture to clothe or materialize preformed ideas. Instead, gesture and (overt or covert) speech emerge as interacting parts of a distributed, semianarchic cognitive engine, participating in cognitively potent self-stimulating loops whose activity is as much an *aspect* of our thinking as its *result*.

6.11   Autonomous Coupling

There is one important sense, however, in which our practices of bodily or environmentally looping self-stimulation could not afford to be *fully* anarchic. For such practices are most potent when subject to what I shall term "soft control."

To creep up on this idea, consider first a small but suggestive set of simulations reported in Clowes and Morse (2005). The simulations investigate ways in which the internal reuse of a public symbol system might aid cognition. Internal reuse was enabled by the provision, in some agents, of a dedicated reentrant loop able to recycle "heard" linguistic inputs during subsequent processing. In the simulations, simple agents were evolved to find and move geometric figures in response to commands couched in a "public" code. The commands tell the agents (who are just simple recurrent neural nets with visual and word inputs) which of four different tasks to perform on objects in an on-screen arena. The tasks are to move the objects to the top ("up"), to move the objects to the bottom ("down"), to move the objects to the right ("right"), or to move the objects to the left ("left").

Groups of agents were evolved under three conditions:

1. A control condition, with no dedicated word reentrance loop. In this condition, the agent "hears" words as commands and must act on that basis alone (but the architecture is still that of a simple recurrent neural net, so there is memory available as the output

layer cycles back to the input layer alongside new inputs at the next time step).

2. Permanent word reentrance. In this condition, the "heard" command words are cycled back via a dedicated part of a recurrent loop while problem solving continues.

3. Self-controlled reentrance. This is as (2) except the net has an additional output unit that can gate the dedicated word reentrance loop on and off. "Heard" words can thus be recycled during processing at the agent's discretion.

Clowes and Morse found that under the control condition (no dedicated word reentrance), the agents take longer to learn to succeed at *any* of the tasks and seem unable to learn to succeed at all four. This is because improvements in one task seemed to always result in impairment to performance on one or more of the others. The nets with permanent word reentrance (condition 2) fared better. Good performance was quite rapidly evolved and typically displayed in at least three and often all four tasks. Most impressive of all, however, were the condition 3 nets with self-gateable word reentrance. These agents produced the best performance on all tasks and with the least evolutionary costs (in terms of numbers of generations required for competence). Such agents exhibit what Iizuka and Ikegami (2004) dub "autonomous coupling"—that is to say, coupling that can be turned on and off in ways dictated by current needs and projects.

Underlying this result may be something more fundamental. For the role of agent-controlled (i.e., gateable) recycling of public words may be understood as a simple example of the more general power of exploratory search via *loosely coupled processes*. This is an effect already observed in work on so-called GasNets (Husbands et al. 1998) in which the combination of (a simulation of) freely diffusing gaseous neurotransmitters and of more standard forms of neural network learning has been shown to improve performance and speeds evolvability. To explain this result, Phillippides et al. (2005) suggest that when an organism must accommodate conflicting pressures (just as in the four "contradictory" tasks confronting the Clowes–Morse net), the presence of various distinct but loosely coupled processes "allows the possibility of tuning one process against the other without destructive interference" (154).[29] The power of verbal rehearsal to aid cognition might thus be explained as another instance of the more general value of autonomous, loose couplings between dynamically distinct processes. Perhaps, that is to say (and here we pick up some of the themes first introduced in chap. 3) self-produced verbal outputs enter into loosely coupled forms of coordination dynamics with nonverbal neural processes, allowing the overall system to explore trajectories through "thinking space" that might otherwise be blocked by destructive interference among superficially conflicting current ideas, goals, or contexts.[30]

This general model seems to fit the case of gesture, too. Recall that the cognitive power of gesture, as understood by McNeill (2005) and Goldin-Meadow (2003), is partly due to the ability of the gestural system to enter into a kind of productive dialectic with the verbal reasoning system. For this to occur, the coupling needs to be in a certain sense loose so that the gestural and verbal systems can explore different spaces. And it is clearly gateable in that the gesturing can be (and often is) turned on and off as problem solving proceeds. Mere self-controlled gateability, however, should emphatically not be seen as reintroducing the inner executive. For the gateing routines themselves may be just more experience-driven microdemons added to the semianarchic mix: demons whose activity, though in some sense higher order, does not reflect the judgments of any highly informed inner homunculus monitoring or controlling the flow of thought and reason.[31]

In sum, it matters that gesturing, inner speech, and all the myriad forms of cognitively potent self-stimulation be subject to soft control, where that means simply that the self-stimulating routines can be turned on and off at appropriate moments during the flow of cognitive activity. But this is fully compatible with the kind of relatively flat, semianarchic organization that includes no central controller or all-knowing inner homunculus.

6.12   Why the HEC?

The chapter began with a double challenge. Show us that the Hypothesis of Extended Cognition (HEC) has not priced itself out of the market by depicting us as cognitively extended agents at the cost of identifying persisting subjects for scientific study, and show us that there is real added value in adopting the perspective of the HEC rather than its more innocuous-seeming cousin, the Hypothesis of Embedded Cognition (HEMC).

Both challenges have now been met. Concerning the first, we have arrived at a vision of human cognition as organism centered but not organism bound. Embracing the HEC does not require us to abandon the vision of a persisting biological (and within the biological, a neural) core that is a perfectly proper object of cognitive scientific study. The HEC simply asserts that we should also study larger, often temporary, ensembles as units of cognitive activity in their own right.

At that point, the second challenge becomes pressing. What is the added value accruing to the choice of the HEC over the HEMC? Both sides should concede the availability of alternative ways of carving the cognitive cake. Even in the hardest cases (for the HEMC), where the flow of information and control is deeply, densely, multiply, and reciprocally interwoven among inner and outer elements, we may still (if we so choose) designate only the inner neural activity as properly speaking cognitive. For the sheer complexity of flow across a borderline does not, as we saw in previous chapters, obliterate the borderline itself.

Some of the value of the HEC is prophylactic. It lies in its ability to nudge the theorist away from a complex of seductive but mistaken views about the nature and contribution of the neural machinery itself. In addition, there is a positive alternative vision whose key elements are just beginning to emerge. On the negative side, the HEC helps inoculate us against the following errors:

1. The "magic dust" error in all its many forms. The HEC reminds us that the neural goings-on are not blessed with some intrinsic property that makes them alone suitable to act as the circuitry of mind and intelligence. What matters is the functionality supported, and this in turn relies on nothing more mysterious than (or less mysterious than!) causal flow either within or beyond the bounds of skin and skull.

2. The "inner homunculus." The HEC reminds us that there is no single, all-powerful, hidden agent inside the brain whose job is to do *all the real thinking* and which is able to intelligently organize all those teams of internal and external supporting structure. Indeed, on the most radical model that we have scouted, it is (as it were) supporting structure "all the way down," with mind and reason the emergent products of a well-functioning swirl of (mostly) self-organizing complexity.

Suppose you also hold the following positive views concerning human cognitive organization:

3. The brain/CNS is "cognitively impartial": It does not care how and where key operations are performed.

4. Much human cognizing benefits from cycles of self-stimulating activity ("cognitive turbo-drives") in which we actively create the structures that drive and constrain our own evolving thought processes.

5. The flow of control is itself fragmented and distributed, allowing different inner resources to interact with, or call upon, differ-

ent external resources without such activity being routed via the bottleneck of conscious deliberation or the intervention of an all-seeing, all-orchestrating inner executive.

Point 5 bears elaboration. For it may be that some opposition to the idea of extended cognitive systems is rooted in the supposed availability of a simple alternative model in which a skull-bound intelligent agent decides to offload certain bits of work and storage onto bodily and environmental structures.[32] In many cases, however, there is no such act of conscious offloading and reloading to be found.[33] We do not consciously choose to gesture so as to lighten the load. The expert Tetris player (see sec. 4.6 and 4.7) does not consciously choose to use the rotate operation for epistemic ends. In such cases, the extended process involves complex subpersonally integrated routines that are selected and maintained for their peculiarly cognitive virtues. Nor need we imagine, in cases where conscious choice and orchestration are missing, that some highly intelligent, well-informed, though as it happens nonconscious, inner executive has made the choice for us. Instead (see also sec. 2.5, 2.6, and 4.7), the choice consists only in the emergence of an effective distributed problem-solving whole, where such emergence is guided by principles we are only just beginning (as in the work by Ballard, Gray, and others) to understand.

The HEMC thus threatens to repeat for outer circuits and elements the mistake that Dennett (1991a) warns us against with regard to inner circuits and elements. It depicts such outer resources as doing their work only by parading structure and information in front of some thoughtful inner overseer. In the absence of any such privileged inner component, the outer and the inner operations are free to emerge as well-tuned coactive participants in the construction of thought and reason.

To be sure, this overall vision (of cognition distributed among brain, body, and world) bequeaths a brand new set of puzzles. It invokes an ill-understood process of "recruitment" that soft-assembles a problem-solving whole from a candidate pool that may include neural storage and processing routines, perceptual and motoric routines, external storage and operations, and a variety of self-stimulating cycles involving self-produced material scaffolding. And at its most radical, it depicts that process as proceeding without the benefit of a central controller. But importantly, this all applies with equal force to the neural economy itself. Here, too, a cognitive task will often be addressed by a soft-assembled coalition of distributed (and often highly heterogeneous) neural components and brain areas, temporarily held together by a transient pattern of "functional connectivity."[34] The HEC thus gains in plausibility when the inner economy is itself seen aright: as multiple, fragmented, yet vastly empowered by an ill-understood capacity to form and re-form into a variety of surprisingly integrated (though temporary) wholes.

The HEMC depicts all our genuine cognizing as either neurally (Adams and Aizawa 2001) or organismically (Rupert 2004) circumscribed. But sweep away the magic dust, sack the inner executive, embrace the motley crew of cognitive processes and the fragmentation of the flow of control, take seriously the brain's own stunning indifference to what gets done where, and the familiar boundaries that the HEMC goes to such lengths to preserve begin to look ad hoc and unrevealing indeed. What the HEC allows us to see clearly is that where ongoing human cognitive activity is concerned, there are usually *many* boundaries in play, *many different kinds* of capacity and resource in action, and a complex and somewhat anarchic flux of recruitment, retrieval, and processing defined across these shifting, heterogeneous, multifaceted wholes. To identify the bounds of cognition with the bounds of the brain/CNS, or even with those of the biological organism, is to elevate just one or two of these many boundaries and interfaces to permanent cognitive glory at the expense of all the rest.

6.13   The Cure

An unexpected payoff of the HEC is its ability to help us see the human organism anew. From the perspective of the HEC, the ancient biological skinbag is the handy container of persisting recruitment processes and of a batch of core data, information, and body-involving skills. Thus equipped, the mobile human organism is revealed as a kind of walking BIOS, ever ready to bootstrap into existence the larger soft-assembled cognitive systems that are, quite literally, the information-processing engines of much advanced thought and reason.[35]

This turns Rupert's argument on its head. For having allowed that we could, if we so wished, choose to parse our cognitively potent coupled unfoldings according to either the HEC or the HEMC, we can now see that it is the choice of the HEMC that sometimes threatens to obscure much that is of value. We do indeed seek to carve nature at the most causally relevant joints, a task not accomplished by elevating anatomic and metabolic boundaries into make-or-break cognitive ones. The cure for cognitive hiccups (the unproductive argumentative oscillation from HEC to HEMC to HEC to...) is thus at hand. For the only real danger from the HEC is that it may blind us to the genuine extent to which human cognition, though not organism bound, remains importantly organism centered. To guard against that misreading, we may now scout:

Hypothesis of Organism-Centered Cognition (HOC)

Human cognitive processing (sometimes) literally extends into the environment surrounding the organism. But the organism (and within the organism, the brain/CNS) remains the core and currently the most active element. Cognition is organism centered even when it is not organism bound.

HEC, HEMC, HOC? We should not feel locked into some pale zero-sum game. As philosophers and as cognitive scientists, we can and should practice the art of flipping among these different perspectives, treating each as a lens apt to draw attention to certain features, regularities, and contributions while making it harder to spot others or to give them their problem-solving due.

The cure for cognitive hiccups is to stop worrying and enjoy the ride.

7

Rediscovering the Brain

7.1   Matter into Mind

Take 390 grams (about 14 oz.) of soft white-gray meat, tweak it, and pummel it, leaving the surface heavily convoluted. Place in a suitable (mobility-enabled) container, and steep for a few years in human society. Let the preparation grow, roam, and mature, and watch in amazement as human thought and reason slowly emerge from the motley pot of bones, muscles, sinews, sense organs, neurons, and synapses. Mental alchemy: meat made mind, and no cosmic cook (not even a Harry Potter) to sprinkle soul dust on the stew.

In this virtuoso display of cognitive unfolding, it would be madness to underplay the role of the biological brain. In the present chapter, I look at a number of worries about recent appeals to embodiment, embedding, and cognitive extension, all of which take, as their points of departure, the incontrovertible fact that we are very smart indeed and the (only slightly more controvertible) fact that the brain is where the major smarts start. Does work that stresses embodiment, embedding, distributed functional decompositions, and the well-groomed cognitive niche systematically distort the role of the biological brain? I shall argue that such worries are largely misguided. Attention to embodied, embedded, and extended cognition is simply what it takes to locate the right smarts in the right places at the right times. Indeed, such attention provides the essential lens through which to appreciate the startling power and elegance of the neural machinery, observed at home in its proper ecological setting.

7.2   Honey, I Shrunk the Representations

Confessions first. In one area at least, fans of radical embodiment *have* almost certainly overplayed their hand in a way that unjustifiably downgrades the contribution of the biological brain. This concerns the nature and implications of the interesting body of research sometimes called (perhaps misleadingly) "change blindness." This work (see, e.g., McConkie 1991; O'Regan 1992) showed that subjects are surprisingly poor at noticing changes made to visually presented scenes during saccadic eye movements. Subjects are poor, under such conditions, at noticing even quite major changes to the presently viewed scene. Nor is the change-blindness result limited to cases where the change is made during a saccade. Just about anything that takes out the motion transients that typically draw our attention to a locus of change seems to do the trick. Effective techniques include making the changes very slowly, or under the cover of flickers (brief blanks inserted between presentations of the pre- and postchange scene), during cuts in a film, in a real-world setting when the change takes place behind a passing occluding barrier, during blinks, and so on (see Simons and Levin 1997, and for a handy, more recent review, see Simons and Rensink 2005).

These results seemed to fit nicely with a rather minimalist vision of our persisting internal representation of the visual scene and were thus widely taken to be grist for a fairly radical mill. They were grist, that is to say, for the vision of human cognizing as accomplished using less by way of internal (specifically representational) resources and more by the way of ongoing world-engaging action. What the change-blindness work suggested, it seemed, was that instead of building up a rich, persisting internal model of the scene, we relied on our ability to saccade around the scene, retrieving what we need just in time for use. In place of the rich inner model, the world was to serve, in Rodney Brooks's famous phrase, as "its own best model." This was a satisfying fit, too, with Ballard et al.'s (1997; see sec. 1.3) account of repeated saccadic retrievals of momentarily relevant fragments of information and with O'Regan and Noë's (2001, and sec. 1.7, chapter 8 following) account of visual perception as *enactive*, as constructed by our ongoing active exploration of the scene.

The active nature of our visual exploration of the scene, on the enactive account, is also meant to explain "how it can be that we enjoy an experience of worldly detail that is not represented in our brains" (Noë 2004, 67). For our experience of rich worldly detail, Noë argues, is not explained by any matching detail in a suite of internal representations but by our capacity to access any part of the scene by a quick move of the head and body and/or by a rapid information-retrieving saccade. In this way, Noë suggests, the experiential content of perceptual experience is in a certain sense *virtual*: It is a matter of sensorimotor accessibility rather than inner encoding. Such facts about accessibility are claimed, in Noë (2004), to account for a wide variety of effects ranging from the one just mentioned (the experience of worldly detail that seems to exceed the detail of any momentary internal representational state) to the feeling of "presence": the feeling we have that we visually confront a whole object (e.g., a tomato) even though our retina is only stimulated by light reflected from one side of the object, or the way we seem to visually experience seeing a whole cat even when parts of the cat are occluded behind a picket fence. In all these cases, Noë argues, the depiction of the content of the experience as virtual (i.e., present in virtue of accessibility) allows us to do justice to a certain ambivalence in the experience itself—namely, that we seem to both see a whole cat or tomato *and* to see only those portions currently in full view (we do not, for example, fail to see certain portions of the picket fence because we have "filled in" the cat!).

Summarizing the view, Noë writes that

> according to the enactive approach, the far side of the tomato, the occluded portions of the cat, and the unseen environmental detail are present to perception virtually in the sense that we experience their presence because of our skill-based access to them... the features are present as available rather than as represented. (2004, 67)

This kind of view has roots in Dennett (1991a) and in Churchland, Ramachandran, and Sejnowski (1994). The main difference is that where both Dennett and Churchland et al. were prone to depict the experience of rich detail as in some sense illusory, because unsupported by an equally rich internal representation, Noë firmly depicts the experience as veridical. Virtual presence, Noë assures us, "is a kind of presence, not a kind of non-presence or illusory presence" (2004, 67).

In sum, appeals to striking change-blindness results have led many researchers to make strong claims predicated, at least in part, on the idea that this work reveals our internal visual representations to be minimal or perhaps even entirely absent. Things are not, however, quite as they meet the eye.

7.3   Change Spotting: The Sequel

From the outset, it was clear that there were a number of ways in which the change-blindness results might be accommodated. Simons and Rensink (2005, 18–19) nicely display the space of possibilities by suggesting four "requirements of scope" that need to be ruled out if the verdict of sparse or nonexistent internal representation is to be made to stick.

First, there is the possibility that detailed representations are created but decay fast and/or get overwritten. Second, there is the possibility that representations of the prechange stimulus persist but are not used for change detection due to some feature of their positioning (e.g., they are located outside the neural pathways whose encodings are available for spontaneous conscious judgment and report). Third, the representations might be in a format that makes them unusable for change detection. Finally, the representations might exist, in a usable (for change detection) format, be appropriately positioned to guide judgment, yet fail to do so because a comparison operation is never applied between the pre- and postchange representations.

These are not mere logical possibilities. Studies such as Hollingworth and Henderson (2002), Henderson and Hollingworth (2003), and Mitroff, Simons, and Levin (2004) effectively demonstrate the existence of some kinds of persisting, and not especially sparse, representation of the prechange stimulus. A central feature of many of these studies is their emphasis on the importance of visual fixation during the viewing of natural scenes. Hollingworth and Henderson (2002) showed that as long as a target object is fixated (i.e., directly targeted by foveated vision) and attended both before and after the change, subjects are able to detect even quite small and subtle alterations, such as the change of one telephone to another. Similar results obtain for experiments using the flicker paradigm (Hollingworth, Schrock, and Henderson 2001). There is also evidence, even when the change is not explicitly noticed, of covert awareness. Hollingworth et al. (2001) showed that fixation duration on the changed object (postchange) was longer than under normal (no change) conditions, while Silverman and Mack (2001) showed priming effects for "unnoticed" changes.

Pursuing a slightly different line, Simons et al. (2002) conducted an experiment in which an object (a red and white striped basketball) is surreptitiously removed during an exchange. The result was that

> although most subjects did not report noticing the change, when they were subsequently asked directed questions about what the experimenter had been carrying, most recalled the basketball and could even describe its unusual color pattern. (Mitroff, Simons, and Levin 2004, 1269)

Further experiments, described in Mitroff, Simons, and Levin (2004), suggest that some episodes of change blindness do indeed result not from failures of either encoding or simple accessibility but from a failure to compare pre- and postchange representations and that "multiple representations of the external world are stored internally and that these representations can be disrupted by later events" (1279). There is thus ample and mounting evidence for preserved representations of rather more information than the work on change blindness might initially have seemed to suggest.

It is important to notice, however, that we are not here seeing a return to anything like the classical model of scene recognition as the construction, from a sequence of fixated and attended regions, of a global, integrated ("composite") internal representation. All parties to the current debate agree that a tempting initial image, according to which a composite representation preserving information from previous fixations concerning shape, shading, texture, color, and so on, is not created (for compelling evidence, see Bridgeman and Mayer 1983; McConkie and Zola 1979; Irwin 1991; and the review by Hollingworth and Henderson 2002). It is simply not the case, as Hollingsworth and Henderson are careful to remind us, that "local high resolution information is painted onto an internal canvass, producing over multiple fixations a metrically organized composite image of previously attended regions" (2002, 113).

The idea of "detailed internal representation" is thus too vague as it stands. If it means the kind of composite sensory image just described, then there is good evidence that no such representations are formed. If it means simply the preservation of sufficient information, for example, to notice that the missing object was a strikingly patterned basketball, then there is mounting evidence that such representations may be formed and persist even when subjects initially indicate not noticing any change. For purposes of hygiene then, I propose to call the former "composite-detail representations" and the latter simply "informative encodings." Informative encodings, then, are what Mitroff, Simons, and Levin mean when they conclude that change blindness neither logically...nor empirically requires the absence of internal representations. Not only do we form multiple representations, but we form multiple representations that can be used to make multiple discriminations. The representations might be somewhat fragile and easily overwritten or disrupted, but they are sufficiently long-lived to allow for successful recognition performance. (2004, 1279)

Do these new findings put direct pressure on the enactive model of conscious, online, perceptual awareness? Certainly, it would be a mistake to think that the change-blindness results support the truly radical idea that we eschew persisting internal representations altogether, making do with the world (and our access to it on demand) instead. The best that can be said is that such results, taken alongside the other studies just mentioned, suggest (a) that we make do without any kind of composite-detail representations and (b) that our spontaneous conscious contact with the visual world often fails to alert us to quite large-scale changes in a presented scene. This is quite consistent with the creation and maintenance of plenty of informative encodings. As Noë himself more recently puts it:

Change blindness is evidence, then, that the representations needed to subserve vision *could* be virtual. Change blindness suggests that we don't make use of detailed internal models of the scene (even if it doesn't show that there are no detailed internal representations). In normal perception it seems that we don't have online access to detailed internal representations of the scene. (2004, 52)

More precisely, we can now say that it currently seems we don't create composite-detail visual representations at all, that we do create and maintain plenty of informative encodings, and that our reflective access to (and especially our spontaneous conscious comparative use of) those informative encodings is often rather more limited than we might have expected.[1]

The new findings are also consistent with (but importantly, lend no positive support to) the enactive account of the feeling of presence: the visual awareness of the whole tomato, the whole cat. Perhaps such feelings of presence are indeed due to our sensorimotor expectations—that is, due to our implicit knowledge of sensorimotor means of retrieving the missing information on demand. But it is equally possible that such feelings of presence have a somewhat (there are shades of gray here) more traditional explanation grounded in the presence of an informative encoding of "whole cat yonder." Compare, for example, Dennett's account of the visual experience of a kind of Andy Warhol wallpaper featuring repeated images of Marilyn Monroe. There is no need, Dennett rightly notes, for the brain to create a kind of composite representation by extrapolation. No need, that is, for the brain to "take...one of its high-resolution foveal views of Marilyn and reproduce it, as if by photo-copying, across an internal mapping of the expanse of wall" (Dennett 1991a, 354). Instead, the brain may just harbor a representation (an informative encoding) "*that* there are hundreds of identical Marilyns" (355). Ditto for the wholeness of the cat and the tomato. To assume that the way this is achieved is by implicit knowledge of the sensorimotor possibility of *retrieving* another fully foveated Marilyn on demand (or of the missing bits of cat and tomato) is to make an additional, and so far unwarranted, move.

Do the change-blindness results at least support the idea that our persisting internal visual representations are in some sense sparse, keyed mainly to the task of just-in-time access by visiting and revisiting the real-world scene? Certainly, the sheer amount of such online just-in-time retrieval (as we saw in the Ballard et al. experiments) suggests that the strategy is widely used. But it is a live possibility that we in fact combine a *large but fragmentary* suite of internal representations (multiple, partial, informative encodings) with a tendency to opt, wherever possible, for a kind of least-effort soft assembly of resources. The upshot of this is that we will sometimes use what Noë calls virtual representations (i.e., use eye- and head-movement-based access to the real world rather than call upon a stored representation) *even when appropriate stored representations exist*. But this is best seen as a form of what may be called *motor deference* rather than as an indication that no apt internal representations exist.

7.4 Thinking About Thinking: The Brain's Eye View

In chapter 3, it was suggested that words and language form a kind of "cognitive niche"—an animal-built structure that productively transforms our cognitive capacities. But here, too, it would be easy to overstate the case. For even if language cognitively empowers us in many deep and unobvious ways, it would be quite wrong to assume that such empowerment occurs in some kind of neural vacuum. All too obviously, only certain kinds of agents (people but not hamsters) are apt for the empowering effects of exposure to a public linguistic edifice. What we need to understand is thus a delicate balancing act between extraneural and neural innovation, such that the public material structures of language are enabled (in some beings but not in others) to play significant cognitive roles. This is clearly a large and ill-understood topic, so I shall restrict my comments to a single illustrative (though speculative) account of the possible inner neural scaffolding required to support one of the key cases examined in chapter 3.

The case I have in mind (sec. 3.2) is my much-loved example of token-trained chimps (*Pan troglodytes*) learning about relations between relations so as to succeed in a relational matching-to-sample task (Thompson, Oden, and Boysen 1997). In this case, so the story goes, the provision of concrete (well, plastic) tokens marking the relations of sameness and difference creates for the learner a new realm of perceptible objects (the associated tokens, tags, or linguistic labels) upon which to target more basic capacities of statistical and associative learning. The presence of the tags or labels, or (importantly) of inner images of such items, then alters the computational burdens involved in certain kinds of learning and problem solving, allowing the token-trained chimps (only) to solve more complex problems requiring judgments of higher order similarity and difference.[2] They do this, it was suggested, by allowing the chimp to internally generate images of the plastic sameness–difference tokens and then to judge *these* to be the same or different, thus reducing the higher order task to a more tractable lower order task.

Only language or token-trained animals (humans, or chimps with the token-training history) seem able to learn to perform the higher order task. The chimps' experience with concrete tags or tokens thus seems to be the difference that makes a difference. But not all animals are able to benefit from token training. Monkeys, unlike chimps, fail at the higher order task even after successful training with the tokens (Thompson and Oden 2000). Why might this be so?

One intriguing speculation is that to gain this kind of benefit from the token training requires the presence of neural resources keyed to the processing and evaluation of internally generated information. In particular, there is emerging evidence that the anterior or rostrolateral prefrontal cortex (RLPFC) is centrally involved in a variety of superficially quite different tasks, all of which involve the evaluation of self-generated information (Christoff et al. 2003). Such tasks include the evaluation of possible moves in a Tower of London task (Baker et al. 1996), the processing of self-generated subgoals during working memory tasks (Braver and Bongiolatti 2002), and remembering to carry out an intended action after a delay (Burgess, Quayle, and Frith 2001).[3] In general, the RLPFC is known to be recruited in a wide variety of tasks involving reasoning, long-term memory retrieval, and working memory. What unites all the cases, according to Christoff et al. (2003) is the need to explicitly (attentively, consciously) evaluate *internally generated information* of various kinds. The relational matching-to-sample task, Christoff et al. believe, requires just this kind of processing; that is, it requires the explicit directing of attention to internally generated information concerning, in this case, first-order relations of sameness and difference.[4] The involvement of the RLPFC in the inner processing needed to get the most out of the prior experience with concrete tokens for sameness and difference explains, the authors argue, the difference between the monkeys (who fail at the task), the chimps (who succeed), and the human five-year-olds (who seem to be even better at it). For the most relevant comparative brain area (Brodmann Area 10) is twice the relative size in humans as it is in the chimpanzee.[5]

Given the converging behavioral and neuroanatomical evidence, Christoff et al. speculate that

> [the] explicit processing of self-generated information may exemplify some of the highest orders of transformation in which the prefrontal cortex engages during the perception-action cycle...[and] may also be one of the mental processes that distinguish humans from other primate species. (2003, 1166)

Interestingly, while lateral BA10 seems to be engaged during the evaluation of self-generated information of the kinds discussed, *medial* BA10 has been shown to be activated during judgments of self-generated emotional states (Damasio 2000; Gusnard et al. 2001). The authors conclude that

> the ability to become aware of and explicitly process internal mental states—cognitive as well as emotional—may epitomize human mental abilities and may contribute to the enhanced complexity of thought, action, and social interaction observed in humans. (Christoff et al. 2003, 1166)

The speculations concerning the RLPFC may or may not turn out to be correct. What matters, for my purposes, is the general picture that rather concretely emerges. According to this picture, there are specific neural innovations that make it possible for some creatures, but not others, to benefit deeply from the ability to associate concrete tokens with abstract relations. To use that ability to leverage further abilities (e.g., thinking about higher order relations) requires capacities (e.g., those involved in the evaluation of internally generated information) that the external scaffolding alone does not provide. Nonetheless, the external scaffolding, in those equipped to make the most of it, can itself play a crucial role, as witnessed by the differences between the token-trained and token-free chimpanzees. The neural innovations and the structured cognitive niche are *both* differences that make a difference. The proper foci of our cognitive scientific attention are thus multiple and nonexclusive. This is all quite obvious yet apparently bears stating. We need to understand the key neural operations, *and* we need to understand how they conspire with various forms of extraneural scaffolding to yield the cognitive systems responsible for so much of our problem-solving success.[6]

7.5   Born-again Cartesians?

Grush (2003) takes issue with what he describes as

> a growing radical trend in current theoretical cognitive science that moves from the premises of embedded cognition, embodied cognition, dynamical systems theory and/or situated robotics to conclusions either to the effect that the mind is not in the head or that cognition does not require representation, or both. (53)

Grush's stalking horse is, in fact, a view that is in at least one crucial respect much more radical than EXTENDED itself. It is the view that

> the mind is not essentially a thinking or representing thing: it is a controller, a regulator, an element in a swarm of mutually causally interacting elements that includes the body and environment whose net effect is adaptive behavior. (55)

EXTENDED, however, need not deny that the mind is essentially a thinking or representing thing.[7] It is committed only to the much weaker claim that some of the thinking, and even the representing, may supervene on activities and encodings that criss-cross brain, body, and world. Nonetheless, it will be instructive to look at Grush's arguments in a little detail. I do not propose, in so doing, to enter yet again into an extended discussion of what should and should not count as an internal representation.[8] For present purposes, we can make do with the same basic account developed by John Haugeland and later quoted and endorsed by Grush.

> A sophisticated system (organism) designed (evolved) to maximize some end (such as survival) must in general adjust its

behavior to specific features, structures, or configurations of its environment in ways that could not have been fully pre-arranged in its design. If the relevant features are reliably present and manifest to the system (via some signal) when-ever the adjustments must be made, then they need not be represented.... But if the relevant features are not always pres-ent (manifest), then they can, at least in some cases, be repre-sented; that is, something else can stand in for them, with the power to guide behavior in their stead. That which stands in for something else in this way is a *representation*.... Here, however, we will reserve the term "representation" for those stand-ins that function in virtue of a general *representational scheme* such that: (i) a variety of possible contents can be represented by a corresponding variety of possible representations; (ii) what any given representation (item, pattern, state, event,...) rep-resents is determined in some consistent or systematic way by the scheme; and (iii) there are proper (and improper) ways of producing, maintaining, modifying, and/or using the various representations under various environmental and other condi-tions. (Haugeland 1991, 62)

Internal representations worth their salt, then, turn out to be iden-tifiable inner states or processes that stand in for features that may be distal or currently absent and where that mode of standing-in follows some kind of scheme determining a space of possible semantically related encodings. Grush (2003, 2004) argues that genuinely *cognitive* systems comprise all and only those systems able to combine effective real-world couplings with rich internal representational regimes and that such combinations are visible even in the biologically basic domain of motor control (see also Clark and Grush 1999).

At the heart of this vision of the cognitive lies the motor emula-tor circuit. In briefest outline (see Grush 2004, for a fuller account), the claim is that certain motor activities (fast intentional actions) involve the deployment of pseudo-closed-loop control. Closed-loop control (see, e.g., Barr 2002) is simply feedback-driven control. Feedback from the item to be controlled (the "plant," to use the jargon) is used to mod-ify the control signal that drives the plant, thus (ideally) keeping every-thing on track. A thermostat is an example of a closed-loop controller, as is the cruise control feature on an automobile. Closed-loop systems are entirely driven by feedback. Open-loop controllers, by contrast, don't exploit feedback. A standard example is a traditional microwave oven set for, say, two minutes defrosting. The button is pressed and the process unfolds for two minutes regardless of the state of (or feedback from) the item on the plate. Clearly, there are numerous advantages to the use of feedback. But in some cases, the process that needs to be controlled cannot be trusted to provide the required feedback in time. The fine control of intentional motor activity is a case in point. In the case of a fast, intentional reaching action, proprioceptive feedback from the bodily peripheries will arrive too late to be of use for effective error correcting. Yet we seem to make such corrections nonetheless. The explanation, according to Grush (drawing on original work by Ito 1984 and by Kawato, Furukawa, and Suzuki 1987) is that we rely, in such cases, on pseudo-closed-loop control.[9] A copy of the current motor command is sent to an onboard circuit (the motor emulator) that replicates the dynamics of the musculoskeletal system. The emulator's output is a prediction of what the sensory feedback should be. This "virtual feedback signal" is used to correct errors in the systemic unfolding and can itself be compared (at a later moment) with the actual feedback arriving from the bodily parts for purposes of calibration and learning.

A very simple implementation of this idea (Kawato 1990) would be a neural network whose units were trained to reproduce the evolution equations of key motor parameters (e.g., changes to shoulder and elbow angle, agonist and antagonist torques to the shoulder joint, etc.) and whose interconnectivity mirrored the interrelations between those very parameters. The inner model thus looks to be articulated in the sense that it is composed of identifiable components, each of which plays a specific representational role. Grush (2004) argues (and see also Clark and Grush 1999; Grush 1995) that such emulator circuits are the evolutionary entry-level versions of the strategy of using internal representations worthy of the name.

The next step, however, is the crucial one. Grush goes on to argue that this same kind of resource, running entirely offline, can explain mental imagery. An emulator circuit, running with the actual motor outputs inhibited, will yield a sequence of virtual sensory inputs corresponding (if the emulator is a good one) to those that would have resulted from the actual real-world activity. In the case of reaching, these will take the form of a sequence of mock proprioceptive signals. In other cases, they may be mock visual inputs corresponding, say, to those that we would obtain by revolving an object. Such resources could aid not just imagery but also motor planning because we may rapidly try out various motor signals to see which one yields the best outcome, as specified by the covert motor imagery (see Grush 2003, 77).

Grush claims that human cognition involves a great deal of this kind of emulation and that such strategies may mark the evolutionarily critical moment at which mere coupled unfoldings (adaptively potent, closed-loop, feedback-dependent processes) gave way to genuine cognizing. It is not hard to see how this might be so. A very simple phototropic robot strikes many of us (myself included) as embodying a noncognitive solution to the adaptive problem of finding light. By contrast, an agent that is able to operate upon internal models or representations so as to reason about what to do next, and to imagine what might happen were it to do such and such, looks much more like an agent engaged in thought and reflection. Motor emulation, according to Grush, marks the most basic point at which nature, still firmly fixated upon the support of real-time, real-world action, began to use the trick of representing that which was not readily at hand. This trick, Grush suggests, marks a real boundary between cognitive agency and other forms of adaptive success.[10] Cognizers use representations (surrogates that can be decoupled and run offline) in place of direct engagements with the world. Noncognizers, by contrast, remain trapped in a web of closed-loop interactions with the very aspects of the world upon which their survival depends.

It is a virtue of Grush's story that it suggests that the form of the internal representations will remain closely keyed to the sensorimotor capacities and experiences of the cognizing agent. It offers a vision of the internal economy that dispenses with much of the excess baggage of the classical, symbol-crunching vision while retaining the key insights concerning the use of inner models as the basis of much reasoning and planning. Moreover, it completely sidesteps the accusation that the use of internal representations must introduce an expensive bottleneck in online performance, since motor emulator circuitry seems to have evolved precisely as an aid to such performance (for more on these virtues, see Clark and Grush 1999). As an account of at least some aspects of the inner economy of the human cognizer, the story has a great deal to recommend it. But what does it mean for the account of cognition as embodied, embedded, and perhaps extended?

7.6   Surrogate Situations

Let us assume, for the sake of argument, that human cognition does indeed involve the use of many head-bound emulator-based strategies. Such a discovery would, it seems to me, in no way undermine the kinds of argument we have been pursuing in previous chapters. For these arguments neither depend on nor do they suggest the truth of any form of radical antirepresentationalism or anticomputationalism. They simply add a temporal sensibility and the many flavors of distributed functional decomposition to the mix. This was clear, for example, in the work on deictic pointers, the Tetris experiments, the Otto example, the work by Gray and Fu, and the case study of gesture. The positive vision thus displays the deep *complementarity* between the inner and the outer and between the neural and the bodily. It matters to this vision that skin and skull present no special barriers to the processes that support mind and cognition and that internal and external resources can sometimes combine as intimately as purely internal ones. It matters, too, that the nature of the internal encodings be, in many cases, *different from* that of the external ones, for it is from such differences that the special value of the inner–outer and neural–bodily combinations flows. But in all this, the nature and power of the neural engine, and its capacity to form and exploit internal representations of many kinds, are not (or should not be) at issue.

Grush is right, however, to note that most, though not all, of the really compelling accounts to emerge from the stables of dynamical and embodied cognitive science focus on cases of densely coupled unfolding. By this I simply mean that they typically display the use of a perceptuomotor routine whose operation exploits the continuing presence of some tangible target. The simplest example might be a wall-following or phototropic robot. More impressive demonstrations include the robot cricket that identifies and locomotes toward the call of its mate (Webb 1996) and many robotic models of the kind surveyed in Pfeifer and Scheier (1999).

In cases such as these (and there are many others), we confront a characteristic mix of constraints and opportunities that we may label the "basic signature." The basic signature involves a task that requires the agent to keep track of a situation unfolding in some constraining (absolute) time frame so that real timing (not just sequence) is essential to success. And it involves the use, to accomplish the task, of body, motion, and world as integral aspects of the problem solution. Examples include the use of head and eye motion and just-in-time sensing to retrieve information from the visual scene, thus (as Rodney Brooks put it) "using the world as its own best model." This signature mix of constraints and opportunities is indeed lacking in many cases of high-level human problem solving. We can plan next year's family vacation or design a new building. In such cases, we are forced to think and reason in the absence of the target situation. The vacation is not until next year. The building does not exist and may even be impossible. Instead, we seem forced into a mode of "offline reasoning." The tools, principles, and strategies that work so well for the online cases may falter, it is feared, in the face of such new demands and challenges.

It is in this general context that it makes sense for critics such as Grush to make much of the *apparent* fact that offline reason, now identified (at least for the sake of the present argument) as that which distinguishes the true cognizers from the rest, is entirely inner, involving emulator circuitry firmly located within the brain/CNS. Moreover, these brain-based unfoldings involve a rich suite of states and processes that seem to fully warrant description as internal representations, albeit ones that fail to fit the templates (or perhaps just the contemporary caricatures) of classical symbolic AI. The emulator-rich brain, Grush assures us, "can silently contemplate, dream, plan, all as a matter of the play of representations—pretty much everything Descartes thought the mind could do even in the absence of the world" (2003, 87). With this result in hand, Grush concludes that "the anti-Cartesian bandwagon looks to be on fire and headed directly for a cliff. I recommend getting off" (87).

But the cliff and fire are, it seems to me, illusory, spawned by a premature and restrictive vision of the range of possible anti-Cartesian projects. For there is absolutely no need for the anti-Cartesian to reject the claim that we often do lots of stuff (dreaming, planning, musing) entirely in our heads, perhaps even using inner representational surrogates for absent states of affairs. Instead, the real surprises lie in just how much of our cognitive activity is *not* that like and not just in the cases when we are in the presence of (indeed, closely coupled to) the very states of affairs with which we are attempting to deal.

In just this vein, the work discussed in part I aimed to show *not* that detached reflection using neural resources is impossible (that would be a brave goal indeed!) but *rather* that in a great many real-world cases, embodied action plays key information-processing roles creating cognitive circuitry that spans brain, body, and world.[11] Clearly, the fact that inner circuitry can *sometimes* be doing all the work goes no way at all toward casting doubt on this kind of claim. Moreover, if we now consider the class of cases at the very heart of Grush's own argument, we find suggestive evidence that brains like ours will go to extraordinary lengths to *avoid* having to resort to the kinds of fully environmentally detached reflection that Grush places at the center of the cognitive stage.[12]

Consider, for example, our remarkably extensive use of "surrogate situations" (Clark 2005a). By a surrogate situation, I mean any kind of real-world structure that is used to stand in for or take the place of an aspect of some target situation. By a target situation, I mean an actual, possible, or at least superficially possible real-world event or structure that is the ultimate object of my cognitive endeavor. For example, suppose I use a dotted line, or a small stick, to indicate on a rough drawing the proposed location of a supporting strut on a bridge that I am about to build. The target situation is the as yet nonexistent bridge, and the surrogate situation is the concrete context provided by the drawing (and the stick, if I am using one). Real-world processes of design, as Gedenryd (1998) has argued in great detail, are marked by multiple complementary uses of surrogate situations. Examining cases as diverse as designing a bridge or a building or laying out a magazine cover, Gedenryd details the different uses of sketches, prototypes, thumbnails, storyboards, and scenarios, to name but a few. What these all have in common is that they allow human reason to be disengaged (to reach out to that which is absent, distal, or otherwise unavailable) while at the same time providing a concrete arena to deploy perceptuo-motor routines of a fundamentally world-engaging kind. In such cases, human reason is disengaged from its ultimate target (the final copy, the unbuilt bridge) yet is still operating in a highly situated, world-exploiting fashion nonetheless. In such cases, courtesy of the special cognitive niche provided by the surrogate situation, reason is *disengaged but not disembodied.*

It is no doubt obvious enough that we often rely on such procedures, but their pervasiveness, variety, and importance are easily overlooked. Considered in the light of the typical worries about "scaling up" the embodied approach to higher human cognition, such tactics are revealing indeed. The mock-ups (etc.) serve no primary purpose other than that of allowing human reason to get a stable grip on what might otherwise prove elusive or impossible to hold in mind. Any given project will often rely on the use of multiple kinds of surrogate situations, each of which highlights or makes available some specific dimension of what Gedenryd calls "the future situation of use." In this way, surrogate situations are not simply miniature version of the real thing. Rather, they are selected to allow us to engage specific, and often quite abstract, aspects of the future situation of use. For example, a four-foot eye-level simulation of a walk-through of a new living and teaching space may be selected to address the need to develop a "safe and inspiring environment for 4–6 year olds" (Gedenryd 1998). In a similar fashion, page layout designers use very rough thumbnails to work out potential relations between graphic and textual objects and are explicitly counseled to omit distracting detail.

Nonetheless, the fact that the surrogate situation provides leverage for perceptuomotor engagement, real-world action, and concrete intervention is crucial. In cases such as these, the one thing the agent *cannot* do is "use the world as its own best model." A nonexistent building cannot act as its own best model, nor can a (merely) proposed route for a new road. Grush (2003, 86) rightly draws our attention to the fact that in many cognitively central cases, we simply *cannot* let the world serve as its own best model for the simple reason that the world (the target situation) is not yet present. But the alternative is not always to advert to a fully head-bound emulation-based strategy. Instead, in a great many cases, we prefer to *let a real physical model serve as its own best world*. We create a physical mock-up, a model, drawing, or prototype upon which to deploy more basic, coupling-style perceptuomotor strategies such as the use of just-in-time sensing and binding, leaving information in the world rather than putting it all in the head. These are the very strategies that Grush wants to depict as confining us to dealing with the here and now. In one sense, this is true: The model is indeed here and now, and that's why the strategies can work. On the other hand, the use of models and surrogate situations allow us to deploy such skills in the service of reasoning about the distal, absent, counterfactual, or impossible. In a certain sense, surrogate situations thus allow us to build *environmentally extended emulator circuits*. Neural subsystems, many of which will indeed involve internal representations in their own right, coupled to the real physical features of the model or mock-up then constitute hybrid ensembles that (just like purely internal emulators) enable us to explore a space of possibilities without the commitments and risks that would otherwise be involved. The image of coupled unfoldings as solely supporting simple, almost phototropic styles of behavior and response is thus wildly premature. Instead, such unfoldings play pivotal roles in cognition *all the way up*.

7.7   Plug Points

Another major theme in Grush's critique is that the brain is a *genuine component* in cognitive activity. Thus, in response to the bandwidth-based arguments deployed by Haugeland (see sec. 2.2), Grush correctly argues that even during high-bandwidth exchanges, the existence of "plug points" (points at which the biological organism can couple or decouple with external sources of order) bestows upon the brain (or perhaps the whole biological organism) the status of a genuine component. This, too, is not something that the fans of embodied, embedded, or even extended cognition should deny. The arguments and illustrations presented in part I work *not* by casting doubt on the presence of genuine interfaces (there are, as noted previously, plenty of these even within the brain itself) but by displaying special features (especially, rich temporal integration) of the flow of information across those interfaces and then by stressing the problem-solving properties of the new (typically, temporary) systemic wholes that result.

Consider, by way of analogy, the idea of a task-specific device (TSD) discussed by Bingham (1988). The notion of a TSD was introduced as a theoretical tool to help tackle the problem of understanding the organization of human action. In brief, a TSD is a temporary but highly integrated assembly created to accomplish some kind of goal. In the motor arena, a TSD is a soft-assembled (i.e., temporary and easily dissoluble) whole that meshes the dynamics inherent in the human action system and the so-called incidental dynamics contributed by various extraorganismic factors and forces. TSDs, that is to say, are "assembled over properties of both the organism and the environment" (Bingham 1988, 250). In each specific case, the biological action system will need to recruit some complex, nonlinear combination of contributions from the link-segment system, the musculoskeletal system, the circulatory system, and the nervous system and do so in a way expressly tailored to accommodate and exploit the incidental task dynamics introduced by, for example, a handle on a paint can, a bouncing ball, or a windsurf rig out on the open sea. (These examples span the three main kinds of incidental task dynamics identified by Bingham—viz., those tasks that simply introduce inertial and dissipative properties or mechanical constraints, as when we carry the paint can by the handle; those that involve absorbing, storing, and/or returning energy, as when bouncing a ball; and those that involve coupling with systems that have their own independent energy sources, such as the windsurf rig powered by the wind and waves of the open sea.)

Why study such task-specific devices? The most obvious reason is that these very ensembles are locally at work in many of the most distinctive cases of human action. We alone on the planet seem capable of creating and exploiting such a wide variety of action amplifiers, ranging from hammers and screwdrivers, to archery bows and bagpipes, to planes, trains, and automobiles. But a second reason, far less obvious, is that working backward from the analysis of these complex wholes may itself contribute important insights concerning the contributions and functioning of the biological human action system itself. Although a natural first thought would be to try to understand each of the four main biological subsystems in isolation, then perhaps to look at their coupled interactions, and finally to add in the incidental dynamics, it turns out that this simple stepwise approach may be doomed to failure. The reason is that the potential behaviors of the whole biological action system are determined by staggeringly complex nonlinear interactions between the four main subsystems and the incidental dynamics. The good news, though, is that in a TSD, the degrees of freedom of this large and unwieldy system are dramatically and productively reduced. The whole point, in fact, of soft assembling a task-specific device is to reduce the initially high-dimensional available dynamics to a much lower dimensional structure and thus to establish an effectively controllable resource (see, e.g., Fowler and Turvey 1978; Salzman and Kelso 1987). As a result,

> the challenge is to work backwards from a description of the reduced dynamics to an understanding of the manner in which subsystem dynamics couple and co-constrain one another to produce the observed dynamical system. Because information about both task-specific dynamics and the individuated resource dynamics is required, the strategy unites the efforts of behavioral scientists and physiologists in an integrated and coherent effort. (Bingham 1988, 237)

I have described this strategy in a little detail because many of the key ideas apply, I think, to the case of many extended *cognitive* systems. Most often, these larger problem-solving ensembles are likewise transient creations, geared toward a specific purpose (doing the accounts, writing a play, locating a star in the night sky), and combine core neural resources with temporary add-ons such as pen, paper, diagrams, instruments, and so on. We may refer to such temporary problem-solving ensembles as "transient extended cognitive systems" (TECSs). TECSs are soft-assembled (i.e., temporary and easily dissoluble) wholes that mesh the problem-solving contributions of the human brain and central nervous system with those of the rest of the body and various elements of local "cognitive scaffolding." Temporarily unified TECSs (just like TSDs) may thus be defined *across* the plug points that allow neural and bodily resources to couple and uncouple from external sources of order and energy.

Why study such transient ensembles? As before, the most obvious and highly motivating reason is that these very ensembles are locally at work in many of the most distinctive cases of human reasoning and problem solving. Here, too, we alone on the planet seem capable of creating and exploiting such a wide variety of cognition amplifiers, ranging from maps and compasses, to pen and paper, to software packages and digital music laboratories. (Once again, a second and perhaps less obvious motivation is that working *backward* from the analysis of these complex wholes may itself contribute important insights concerning the contributions and functioning of the biological brain itself.)

Perhaps, however, there is another way to turn the plug-points observation into a real objection. Jenann Ismael (personal communication) worries that to be able to design and use cognitive tools, the mind has to keep track of the line between the fixed parts of the functional architecture and prosthetic attachments. That is so, at least, if it is to be able to transition smoothly when the tool is absent or to exchange it easily for a different tool.

Ismael is right that without some such "keeping track" we would be impaired because we would never know what we could or could not reasonably hope to achieve at a given moment. It follows that the plug points must be somehow marked, or at least functionally distinguished, for the biological parts of the system. Such marking might be achieved by explicitly representing the tool or prop as temporary or detachable. More interestingly, however, it might be achieved indirectly by learning a fully dovetailed neural strategy that is then simply triggered by the presence of the appropriate tool.[13] Pen in hand, we simply find ourselves running neural routines that factor in the availability of writing and sketching as parts of the cognitive process. This would be analogous to the way the feel of prism goggles on the face has been shown to trigger a learned context-dependent adaption so that skilled users can don and doff inverting lenses without missing a beat (see Kravitz 1972; Wolpert, Miall, and Kawato 1998, 345).

In sum, then, the existence of well-defined (and perhaps even self-represented) plug points in no way undermines the vision of cognition as embodied and as sometimes extended. For it goes no way at all toward showing that unified information-processing ensembles are not soft assembled across the plug points themselves. In the natural order, interfaces abound. There are interfaces within the brain, between brain/CNS and body, and between organism and world. What counts are not interfaces but systems—systems that may come into being and dissolve on many different timescales but whose operation accounts for much of the distinctive power and scope of human thought and reason.

7.8 Brain Control

Keith Butler, in a wide-ranging critique of the notion of the extended mind, raises the following worry:

> There can be no question that the locus of computational and cognitive control resides inside the head of the subject [and involves] internal processes in a way quite distinct from the way external processes are involved. If this feature is indeed

the mark of a truly cognitive system, then it is a mark by means of which the external processes Clark and Chalmers point to can be excluded. (1998, 205)

Butler's suggestion is that even if external elements sometimes participate in processes of control and choice (the knot in the hanky, the entry in the notebook), still it is always the biological brain that has the final say and that here we finally locate the difference that, cognitively speaking, really makes a difference. The brain is the *controller and chooser* of actions in a way all that external stuff is not, and so the external stuff should not count as part of the *real* cognitive system.

Notice that there are at least two issues here. One concerns the functional poise of the neural computations and the claim that they alone are the "locus of computational and cognitive control." The other concerns the nature of the processes, which are said (echoing some of the worries due to Adams and Aizawa that we met in chapter 5) to act "in a way quite distinct from the way external processes are involved." This latter worry has hopefully been laid to rest. What of the former: that worry about the locus of ultimate choice and control?

The worry is interesting because it again highlights (recall sec. 5.6) the deceptive ease with which critics treat the inner realm itself as scientifically unified. Thus, suppose we reapply the "locus of control" criterion *inside the head*. Do we now count as *not part of my mind or myself* any neural subsystems that are not the ultimate arbiters of action and choice? Suppose only my frontal lobes have the final say. Does that shrink the real mind to just the frontal lobes? What if (as Dennett sometimes suggests; see Dennett 1987, 1991a; see also Dennett 2003, 122–126) no subsystem has the "final say." Has the mind and self just disappeared?

Perhaps opposition to the idea of nonbiological cognitive extension sometimes trades on a mistaken view of the thinking agent as some distinct, fixed inner locus of final choice and control.[14] But notice that even if there *were* some distinct inner locus of final choosing, that would provide no reason at all to identify the mind or the "cognitive agent" with that highly circumscribed faculty. My long-term stored knowledge is often called upon in my decision routines, but the long-term storage itself is no more an ultimate deciding routine than is, say, Otto's notebook. To treat all that falls beyond the mechanisms of ultimate choice and control as external to *my* cognitive mechanisms is to divorce my identity as an agent from the whole body of memories, skills, and dispositional beliefs that guide, shape, and characterize my behaviors. And this, I maintain, is to shrink the mind and self beyond recognition, reducing me to a mere bundle of final control processes and/or occurrent mental states.

Some may wish to embrace this conclusion. Thus, Brie Gertler, in a fascinating and provocative treatment (2007), argues that the best way to respond to the arguments of Clark and Chalmers (1998) is to reject the idea that standing beliefs (in fact, dispositional mental states and nonconscious mental operations of all kinds) are part of the mind. Instead, she stresses the role of occurrent (indeed, introspectible) mental states in the origination of all genuine actions. When nonoccurrent states have causal effects, such effects are not, she suggests, best thought of as actions belonging to the agent. In this way, Gertler (2007, 202), concedes the two main conditional claims that might be extracted from the original paper—namely,

> if standing beliefs are part of the mind, then the mind can be indefinitely extended: to notebooks, external computing devices, and even parts of others' minds.

And

> if nonconscious cognitive processes are part of the mind, then the mind can be indefinitely extended: to external computing devices and even parts of others' minds.

One issue that Gertler's argument raises is how to decide just when a belieflike state should count as occurrent. If occurrent just *means* conscious, then the kinds of worry about such a move raised in the original paper seem to bite. Shrinking the mind to the conscious is certainly one way to avoid the conclusions of the original paper. But do we really want to shrink the mind so far? For the most part, this is a route that even the staunchest fans of BRAINBOUND have tended to avoid. This seems sensible because it is hard to see what motivation one might really have (apart from the desire to avoid the conclusion of the Clark and Chalmers argument) for denying that standing beliefs are mental states of the agent. At least, it is hard to see why one might do this *unless* one is really an eliminativist about standing beliefs, thus rejecting common-sense psychology's appeal to such beliefs in the explanation of our actions, judgments, and choices. But this more radical route is not endorsed by Gertler, leaving unclear the force of the denial that such states are genuinely mental.[15]

What should be readily conceded, however, is that the arguments that seem to favor EXTENDED interact with vexing questions about personal identity and the nature of the self. A full defense of EXTENDED would need to resolve these matters. As things stand, the best we can say is that arguments for the extended mind provide further motivation, and perhaps some new kinds of scaffolding, for this important project.

7.9 Asymmetry Arguments

Rupert (in press-a) and Collins (in press) independently raise a related issue concerning the asymmetric relationship that obtains between the organism and its props and aids. Subtract the props and aids, they argue, and the organism may create replacements. But subtract the organism, and all cognitive activity ceases. As Rupert (in press-a) puts it,

> the volition of the organism, its intention to take up tools, and its capacities to do so are asymmetrically responsible for the creation of extended cognitive systems.

Such asymmetries (as seen in 5.1) may easily be exaggerated. For one thing, lone organisms may fare much worse than Rupert imagines. But in any case, the existence of asymmetries of this type is not something the fans of EXTENDED should deny. For example, it is true that the key microlocus of plasticity is the individual human brain. It is the brain's great plasticity and thirst for cheap, outsourced labor that drives the distributed engines of sociotechnological adaptation and change. It is true, too, that by subtracting those meaty islands of wet organismic plasticity, the whole process grinds to a standstill. There will be no new pens, paper, and software packages when the human organisms all dry up and die. But it by no means follows, from the fact that those wet organismic islands are in that way *lopsidedly essential* to all this, that the rest of the hybrid, distributed circuitry is not part of the mechanistic base for specific episodes of cognitive processing.

To take a mundane and noncognitive case, my index finger and I enjoy a similarly asymmetric relationship. I can persist without it, but it cannot persist without me. I can help repair it with a plaster, but it (working alone, as it were) can never repair me and so on. It does not follow that it is not part of me. Or recall Chalmers's example from chapter 6. Subtract the visual cortex and I can survive and attempt to compensate in various ways. But do whatever it takes to subtract *me*, and the leftover visual cortex won't try any such maneuvers. "I" thus stand in an asymmetric relationship to the operation of my own visual cortex. It hardly follows that the visual cortex is not, here and now, part of the mechanistic base of much of my perceptuocognitive functioning. The arguments from lopsidedness gain a thin veneer of persuasiveness only because we are unused to thinking of our brains as *themselves* not one single indivisible unity (question-beggingly "me") but simply as another collection of mechanisms.

7.10 EXTENDED in a Vat

I'd like to end this chapter by very briefly confronting a common, but I think informatively misguided, ploy that is often imagined[16] to establish the explanatory sufficiency of appeals to neural goings-on in the mechanistic[17] explanation of cognitive performances. The ploy invokes that familiar philosophers' toy, the brain in a vat. Surely, the argument goes, the brain in a vat enjoys all the very same mental and cognitive states as we do. The difference is just that it enjoys them courtesy, let's imagine, of some very fancy computer-supported buffering that simulates all the usual inputs and outputs to the brain, including those that might result from bodily activi-ties (e.g., gesture), from head- and eye-movement-based retrieval of information from the world, from the use of the notebook in the infamous Otto scenario, and so on. Doesn't this establish, in one fell swoop, the biological brain as the sufficient mechanistic locus of mind and cognition? Doesn't this demonstrate, once and for all, the sheer lunatic absurdity of attempts to depict bodily gestures, deictic codings, and even simple notebooks as part and parcel of an agent's cognitive apparatus?

But now consider a slightly different case: the case of the damaged brain in a (friendly) vat. Consider, to add one new figure to our shady pantheon, DB, a patient suffering from neural damage that has com-pletely destroyed motion area MT. As the superscientists program the hyperintelligent vat ready to receive DB's brain, it occurs to them that they might as well, while they are at it, indulge in a little bit of extra programming involving some new software and a bunch of additional vat-brain links. This extra programming re-creates, in perfect detail, the contributions that would have been made by an intact area MT. Sure enough, the envatted brain sends out signals that (converted to speech sounds courtesy of the vat buffer) express amazed delight at the sudden inexplicable recovery of visual motion, the newly restored capacity to cross busy roads in relative safety, the delights of baseball and tennis, and so on. In short, cognitive and phenomenal wholeness is restored.

What is the moral of this little exercise? Is it, perhaps, that neural area MT is not part of the "constitutive supervenience base" for human motion detection?[18] If we can restore motion detection in this way, should we conclude that MT is best treated merely (?) as a source of inputs to, and a receiver of outputs from, the rest of the brain? Surely not. All the vat scenario can directly establish is that, working together, the brain and the hyperintelligent vat conspire to support the usual panoply of cognitive and (I am willing to venture) phenomenal effects. But this fact alone can no more secure the conclusion that eye movement, gestures, and notebook entries do not form part of the constitutive supervenience base for those effects than it can establish that MT (and indeed, the whole biological brain!) does not form part of that base. The vat intuitions, supposing they are reliable, are simply silent on which bits of the overall system are doing the essential work.

Another way to see this is to consider Otto in the vat. Here, Otto's biological brain enjoys the support of a reliable notebook substitute—namely, the clever notebook-simulating work of the hyperintelligent vat. Otto in the vat, I want to say, shares all the standing beliefs of our worldly Otto. This should not come as much of a surprise because envatted Otto just *is* (functionally speaking) Otto the extended mind.

A metaphysically robust way to secure this conclusion is to argue (as per Chalmers 2005 and Clark 2005c) that envatted Otto is in fact fully and normally embodied and embedded, a constant physical notebook user albeit only courtesy of what would (to Otto) be some very surprising underlying physical and computational operations. (Note that we, too, might one day find ourselves surprised by the bottom-level story about what supports notebooks and the like. Perhaps many of us would already be thus surprised if only we had a better grip on what contemporary physics offers.) But for present purposes, it is enough to stress that the vat provides all the necessary opportunities to make the most (functionally speaking) of body and world. The envatted brain benefits, just as we do, from what seem to be passive dynamic contributions to the simplification of its neural strategies of locomotion, from the chance to use bodily gesture while reasoning, from the use of eye movements to retrieve information from the local scene, and from the use and functioning of language, notebooks, friends, family, lovers, labels, and yellow stickies. I conclude that appeals to brains in vats afford no leverage on the questions at issue in debates concerning embodiment, embedding, and cognitive extension.

7.11   The (Situated) Cognizer's Innards

There are good (I think compelling) reasons to depict the biological brain (a) as a genuine component in all cognitive activity, (b) as one capable of sustaining cognitive activity in relative isolation, and (c) as a biological hotbed of conscious awareness, executive control, and internal representational richness and multiplicity. Moreover, our striking abilities to make the most of the many forms of social and environmental scaffolding that surround us will surely itself turn out to depend on many key neural (and cultural) innovations and operations. The discussion of the RLTPF in section 7.4 affords one plausible illustration. None of this should give us pause. To see cognition as embodied, embedded, and even extended is not to deny any of these important truths, nor is it to take a fast track toward radical antirepresentationalism or the rejection of computational and functional approaches to understanding mind and intelligence.

To be sure, such strong negative theses do appear in the literature on the embodied mind. Thelen and Smith (1994, 388) are openly sceptical about the idea that the mind builds internal representations.[19] Van Gelder (1995) attempts to cast doubt on the value of computational approaches and of representational ones in about equal measure. Shapiro (2004) casts the appeal to embodiment as inimical to functionalist understandings of the mind.[20] By contrast, the positive story displayed in chapters 1 through 4 depicts embodied agents as benefiting from multiple forms of internal and external representation, as deploying a variety of computational transformations defined over those representations, and as apt to participate in extended functional organizations that allow cognitive processes to spread productively across brain, body, and world. The goal (pursued further in chap. 9) was thus to display a positive vision in which appeals to embodiment and cognitive extension go hand in hand with appeals to dynamics *and* to internal and external processes of representation and computation.

What does seem true, however, is that in the specific enabling context of embodied action within a persisting real-world arena, the *kinds* of internal representation we deploy, and the *forms* of computation and control required of the biological brain, are often importantly transformed. The inner economy is seen to be populated by motoric and perceptual forms of representation, closely geared to their primary roles in the control of action, and biological brains are driven toward "ecologically exploitative" (chap. 1 and 2) forms of control.[21] They are driven toward control strategies that push, nudge, and tweak some target system whose appropriate unfolding depends heavily on a variety of other sources of order and form, such as bodily biomechanics, environmental structures, and sometimes the actions and knowledge of other agents.[22] The primary lessons of embodiment are thus lessons in economy, efficiency, and spreading the load. Such lessons help display the strategies of representation, computation, and control that biological brains actually instantiate and deploy, revealing us as factory tweaked and primed for all manner of cognitive shortcuts, offloadings, and extensions. It is only thanks to this heady (?) combination of processing potency and openness to extension and transformation that the human brain succeeds as this world's most stunningly potent organ of cognitive success.

III

THE LIMITS
OF EMBODIMENT

8

Painting, Planning, and Perceiving

8.1   Enacting Perceptual Experience

Inner neural processes, we have seen, are often productively entangled with gross bodily and extrabodily processes of storage, representation, materialization, and manipulation. These extraneural elements play key information-processing roles as parts of extended organizations selected and maintained for their problem-solving virtues. Might this intimacy of brain, body, world, and action shed light on the nature and mechanisms of conscious perception? A positive answer is suggested by what I shall call "strongly sensorimotor" models of perception (O'Regan and Noë 2001; Noë 2004). According to such models, perceptual experience gains its content and character courtesy of an agent's implicit knowledge of the ways sensory stimulation will vary as a result of movement. Perceptual experience, on such accounts, is said to be *enacted* (Varela, Thompson, and Rosch 1991) via skilled sensorimotor activity.

Though correct to stress the importance of embodiment and action, strong sensorimotor models take us (or so I shall argue) one step too far. For despite the important role of embodied action both in information pickup and in initially tuning the circuitry that supports perceptual awareness, such models end up tying the contents and character of human experience too closely to the fine details of human embodiment.

In so doing, they fail to accommodate the substantial firewalls, disintegrations, and special-purpose streamings that form the massed strata of human cognition. In particular, they threaten to obscure the computationally potent and functionally well-motivated *insensitivity* of key information-processing events to the full subtleties of embodied cycles of sensing and moving.

8.2   The Painter and the Perceiver

Seeing, according to Noë (2004), is like painting. Painting is an ongoing process in which the eye probes the scene, then flicks back to the canvass, then back to the scene, and so on in a dense cycle of active exploration and partial, iterated cognitive uptake. It is this cycle of situated, world-engaging activity that constitutes the act of painting. Seeing (and more generally, perceiving) is likewise constituted, Noë claims, by a process of active exploration in which the sense organs repeatedly probe the world, delivering partial and restricted information on a need-to-know basis. This cycle of situated, world-engaging, whole animal activity is the locus, on Noë's account, of genuine cognitive interest, at least for perceptual experience. According to such a view, "Perception is not something that happens to us or in us, it is something we do" (Noë 2004, 1). Let's call this the Strong Sensorimotor Model (SSM) of perceptual experience.

The SSM does not merely claim that you need an active body as a platform for perceiving. Rather, the interesting claim is that skillful bodily action and perception are in some sense intimately entangled or intermingled. The starting point here is the correct and important observation that perception is *active*:

> Think of a blind person tap-tapping his or her way around a cluttered space, perceiving that space by touch, not all at once, but through time, by skilful probing and movement. This is, or at least ought to be, our paradigm of what perceiving is. (Noë 2004, 1)

Expanding on this, Noë adds that

> all perception is touch-like in this way: perceptual experience acquires content thanks to our possession of bodily skills. *What we perceive* is determined by *what we do* (or what we know how to do); it is determined by what we are *ready* to do ... we enact our perceptual experience: we act it out. (2004, 1, emphasis in original)

An important implication of this, according to Noë, is that appeals to internal representations (if such there be) cannot tell the whole story either for painting or for seeing:

> The causally sufficient substrate of the production of the picture is surely not the internal states of the painter, but rather the dynamic pattern of engagement among the painter, the scene and the canvass. Why not say the same thing about seeing? Seeing, on this approach, would depend on brain, body and world. (2004, 223)

In the case of seeing, and perceiving in general, a theoretical construct peculiarly well suited to this dynamic target is the notion of "sensorimotor dependencies" (first introduced as "sensorimotor contingencies" in O'Regan and Noë 2001 and also glossed as "sensorimotor expectations" in Noë 2006).

Sensorimotor dependencies are relations between movement or change and sensory stimulation. Such relations may be of many kinds, but what they all have in common is that they concern a kind of loop or cycle linking real-world objects and properties with systematically changing patterns of sensory stimulation. These changing patterns of sensory stimulation may be caused by the movements of the subject (this is the central case), as when we use head and eye movements to scan a visual scene. Or they may be caused by movements of the object itself or be due to other elements in the environmental frame (e.g., changes in illumination or light source). In addition, some features of these various kinds of changing patterns will be due to properties of the objects themselves (e.g., the self-similarity of a straight horizontal line along its length, giving rise to an unchanging pattern of retinal stimulation as the eye tracks along the line; see O'Regan and Noë 2001, 942). Other features (and this will loom large in our subsequent discussion) will be due to the idiosyncrasies of the human visual apparatus. For example, the same straight line projected onto the retina distorts dramatically as the eye moves up and down due to the curvature of the eyeball (941).

Different sense *modalities* also display generically different action-to-stimulation signatures. In vision, moving one's own body toward a visually fixated object causes an expanding flow pattern on the retina, whereas moving away causes a contracting flow pattern. No similar signature characterizes touch or audition. Or to take another case, human vision has dense central acuity and more restricted peripheral sampling. This means that motion of the eye along a perceived object yields a distinctive pattern of spatially alternating dense and shallower sampling.

The same action also yields a characteristic play of rich color information because this is made available mainly by central vision. Even the brute fact that blinks cause temporary blanks at the retinal input may be treated as part of the action-input signature for vision (see O'Regan and Noë 2001, 941) since blinking has no similar effect on touch or audition.

According to the SSM, then, to perceive the world is to draw upon our implicit knowledge of many kinds of sensorimotor dependence. It is our implicit knowledge of these sensorimotor dependencies that explains, according to the Strong Sensorimotor Model, both the contents and the character (visual, tactile, auditory, etc.) of our perceptual experiences. This stress on knowledge of (or expectations concerning) sensorimotor dependencies is meant as an alternative to standard appeals to qualia conceived as intrinsic, "sensational," properties of experience. Instead of appreciating such mysterious intrinsic qualities in experience, it is suggested, we *enact* (i.e., by acting, bring into being) perceptual experience. In the case of shape and spatial properties, for example,

> the enactive view denies that we represent spatial properties in perception by correlating them with kinds of sensation. There is no *sensation* of roundness or distance, whether tactile, visual or otherwise. When we experience something as a cube in perception, we do so because we recognize that its appearance varies (or would vary) as a result of movement, that it exhibits a specific sensorimotor profile. (Noë 2004, 101–102)

In sum, the SSM depicts conscious perceptual experience as quite literally consisting in a perceiver's active deployment of (her "exercise of") implicit knowledge of the rules or regularities relating sensory inputs to movement, changes, and action. "Our ability to perceive," Noë tells us, "not only depends upon, but is constituted by, our possession of this sort of sensorimotor knowledge" (2004, 2). Or to take a more recent formulation: "*Perception is an activity that requires the exercise of knowledge of the ways action affects sensory stimulation*" (Noë 2007, 532, emphasis in original).

8.3   Three Virtues of the Strong Sensorimotor Model

Noë's account, taken as a whole, has at least three apparent virtues, key aspects of which I shall be seeking, as far as possible, to preserve.

First and most important, there is the emphasis on skills rather than on qualia as traditionally conceived.[1] Skill-based accounts (see also Pettit 2003; Clark 2000a; Matthen 2005; and of course, Dennett 1991a) offer a powerful antidote to the venom of zombie thought experiments.[2] In particular, the strong sensorimotor account would, if all worked out according to plan, ensure that sameness of world-engaging sensorimotor skills and discriminatory capacities implied sameness of perceptual experience. More demonstrably, the emphasis on world-engaging loops and knowledge of sensorimotor dependencies affords an elegant and compelling account of a range of real-world phenomena involving sensory substitution and neural rewiring.

The classic example here (see chap. 2) is Tactile-Visual Substitution Systems (TVSS).[3] Equally impressive, though perhaps less well known, is the *auditory*-visual substitution system (discussed in some detail in O'Regan and Noë 2001) known as The Voice (see Meijer 1992). In this system, visual inputs to a head-mounted camera are systematically translated into audible patterns. Objects high in the visual field yield high-pitched sounds, while low ones yield low-pitched sounds. Lateral location is indicated by the balance of stereo sound, brightness by the loudness of sound, and so on. Crucially, as you move the camera around, the sound changes, and over time, subjects begin to learn the signature patterns (the sensorimotor dependencies) characteristic of different objects. In the original versions, subjects learned to distinguish plants from statues, crosses from circles, and so forth.

The overall effect, though powerful, fell short of creating a truly visual experience. But the claim of sensorimotor dependence theory is bold and clear: To whatever extent it is *possible* to re-create the same body of sensorimotor dependencies using an alternative route, you will re-create the full content and character of the original perceptual experience. This explains, according to O'Regan and Noë, why some of Bach y Rita's subjects report, for example, feeling as if they were *seeing* a looming ball when fitted with a TVSS system. By stressing similarities and differences in the profile of sensorimotor dependencies, Noë-style accounts neatly explain both the sense in which such systems create quasi-visual experiences and the ways in which the experiences thus generated (currently) fall short of those supported by the original routes. For example, there is a clear sensorimotor signature for a looming object whose invariant characteristics are as well captured by patterns of sound or tactile stimulation as they are by the more typical patterns of retinal stimulation. Very fine-grained color information, by contrast, is currently not well captured by these kinds of substitution systems. In each case, however, what is at issue is not the presence or absence of mysterious, ineffable qualia but simply the presence or absence of distinctive loops linking real-world objects and properties to changing patterns of sensory stimulation.

The same story explains, we are told, the remarkable results concerning the rewiring of visual inputs to auditory cortex in young ferrets (Sur, Angelucci, and Sharma 1999). Here, thanks to the early rewiring, "auditory" cortical areas become involved in the kinds of sensorimotor loops characteristic of vision and appear to support fully normal visual capacities in the modified ferret: "Appropriately embedded in a 'visual' sensorimotor dynamic, neural activity in 'auditory' cortex in young ferrets takes on 'visual' functions" (Noë 2004, 227). In short, appeals to the shape of a space of signature sensorimotor dependencies here replace appeals either to the intrinsic properties of sensations (qualia) or to their more hardnosed (but arguably equally unexplanatory) cousins, the putative special properties of specific neural regions.

The sensorimotor account is thus meant to be successful in cases "where neural accounts alone are explanatorily afloat" (Noë 2004, 226). What does the work is simply "the way neural systems subserve the activity of the embodied and embedded animal" (226). For Noë, then, experience is "not caused by and realized in the brain, although it depends causally on the brain. Experience is realized in the active life of the skillful animal" (2004, 226). In subsequent sections, we shall see that neural accounts need not be seen as thus "explanatorily afloat" even if we agree (as I think we should) that *certain* bodies of skill provide one of the keys to understanding perceptual experience.

Second in the list of possible virtues is the sensorimotor model's recognition of the importance, power, and scope of what (in the artificial neural network community) is known as prediction learning. Prediction learning is an ecologically plausible form of supervised learning. In supervised learning, an agent is provided with detailed feedback concerning the desired output for a given input. Since such training seems to require a well-informed, continually present teacher, its ecological plausibility, for most real-world learning situations, looks doubtful. In some cases, however, the world itself provides, at the very next time step, precisely the training information we need. Such is the case if, for example, the task (typically, as presented to a simple recurrent neural net; see, e.g., Elman 1995) is to predict the next sensory input itself, whether it is the next word in a sentence or the next frame in an evolving visual scene. Such prediction, for a mobile embodied agent, often requires a double input: information concerning the current sensory state and information (e.g., in the form of efferent copy) concerning any motion command currently in play. Given these items of information, a prediction can be made concerning the likely next sensory state. Such a prediction, in the visual case, will thus need to take into account both features of the scene and any motions of the agent and can immediately be tested against the actual sensory stimulations duly delivered by the world. Prediction learning has shown itself to be a valuable tool for the extraction of a number of important regularities, such as those characteristic of grammatical sentences, of shape, and of object permanence. In a sense, Noë and his collaborators are extending this proven paradigm to attempt to account for the full spectrum of perceptual experience, whose contents and character are said to sensitively depend on acquired expectations (implicit knowledge) concerning the ways sensory stimulation will morph and evolve with movement and other kinds of input-altering change. This is, it seems to me, precisely the kind of knowledge that would be embodied in the weights and connections of a neural network trained using a prediction-learning regime.

Prediction learning is computationally potent, demonstrably possible, and almost certainly biologically actual. The standard models are, however (as we just saw), resolutely subpersonal, with the predictions defined over sensory patterns that obtain without any conscious awareness. On Noë's account, however, a critically important subclass of cases is defined over *consciously experienced perspectival properties* ("P-properties"; see Noë 2004, 83) of objects. These are depicted as objective but relational properties: properties belonging to a perceiver-object pair situated in some larger environment: "That a plate has a given P-shape is a fact about the plate's shape, one determined by the plate's relation to the location of a perceiver, and to the ambient light" (Noë 2004, 83). Importantly, P-properties are *also* depicted as "looks of things, their visual appearances (84), and thus as able to participate in *phenomenologically salient* bouts of prediction learning. Thus,

> to see a circular plate from an angle, for example, is to see something with an elliptical P-shape, and it is to understand how that perspectival shape would vary as a function of one's (possible or actual) movements. (Noë 2004, 84)

But while agreeing that prediction learning is a powerful *knowledge-extraction tool*, especially in the perceptual arena, I am not convinced that mature perceptual experience is then constituted by the running of what might be thought of as the prediction software itself. That is to say, I am not convinced that appeal to predictions (or expectations) concerning the next sensory stimulation directly and exhaustively explain (subpersonally) or even characterize (personally) perceptual experience.

We shall return to these issues in subsequent sections. For the moment, it is useful simply to distinguish three different questions that may be asked.

1. What kinds of unconscious know-how drive or power our fluid sensorimotor engagements with the world?
2. What do we implicitly know about how our conscious perceptual experience will vary with movement or change?
3. What determines the content and character of our conscious perceptual experience itself?

These questions are all different, but the Strong Sensorimotor Model tends to offer the same kind of answer (one that invokes implicit knowledge of sensorimotor dependencies) to them all. I shall argue, however, that while the appeal to knowledge of sensorimotor dependencies might well be crucial to answering the first—as when an agent deploys "emulator circuitry" (see the discussion in chap. 7) to anticipate sensory input and hence drive smooth reaching and so on—it is by means obvious what role it should play in the other two. Probably, we do (regarding question 2) have *expectations* concerning the ways conscious experience will alter as we move and so forth, but it is not obvious that these expectations are crucial to the experience itself. Indeed (and moving on to question 3), there is considerable evidence that perceptual experience is linked to specific forms of neural processing that are systematically insensitive to much of the fine detail of the sensorimotor loops themselves, thus casting doubt on the strong sensorimotor response to both these questions.

The third and final virtue I want very briefly to mention is rather general but both important and surprisingly delicate. It is that the sensorimotor model is well poised to accommodate *narcissistic experience in an objective world*. Talk of cognitive agents that, by their own activity, "bring forth their worlds" can seem mysterious if not mystical (see Clark and Mandik 2002, for some discussion). But by linking the contents and character of perceptual experience rather directly to acquired expectations concerning patterns of sensorimotor dependence, the enactive framework is able to do justice both to the notion of an objective, mind-independent reality and to the sense in which the world as perceived is the world of a specific type of embodied agent. Such a perceived world is characterized by a suite of distinctive sensorimotor dependencies, whose nature sensitively determines the way the world is experienced through the senses.

According to this account, differently embodied beings will not be able to directly experience our perceptual world not because it is populated by its own mysterious qualia but because they lack the requisite "sensorimotor tuning" (Noë 2004, 156). It is a virtue of the sensorimotor model that it allows us to address this thorny topic in a straightforward manner. But it is a vice, or so I shall argue, that in doing so it implies that differently embodied beings *necessarily* inhabit different "perceptual worlds."

In general, then, the suspicion is that in several domains, the Strong Sensorimotor Model takes us one step too far. By stressing skills, abilities, and expectations, such accounts begin to offer a genuine alternative to traditional qualia-based approaches to perception and perceptual experience. But by focusing so much attention on the sensorimotor frontier, they deprive us of the resources needed to construct a more nuanced and multilayered model of perceptual experience and risk obscuring some of the true complexity of our own cognitive condition.

8.4   A Vice? Sensorimotor (Hyper)sensitivity

Strong sensorimotor models look to suffer from a form of sensorimotor hypersensitivity. Such models are hypersensitive to very fine details of bodily form and dynamics and, as a result, are prematurely committed on a variety of prima facie open (empirical) questions concerning the tightness or otherwise of the relations among perceptual experience, neural activity, and embodied action.

To begin to bring this rather general concern into focus, consider first the matter of what Clark and Toribio (2001) called "sensorimotor chauvinism." A sensorimotor chauvinist, as we used the term, is someone who holds, without compelling reason, that absolute sameness of perceptual experience requires absolute sameness of fine-grained sensorimotor profile. Noë (2004) is clear enough about this commitment. For example, in a discussion of the extent to which TVSS systems support "similarity of experience" (to normal vision), Noë asserts that

> tactile vision is vision-like to the extent that there exists a sensorimotor isomorphism between vision and tactile vision. But tactile vision is unlike vision precisely to the extent that this sensorimotor isomorphism fails to obtain. It will fail to obtain, in general, whenever the two candidate realizing systems differ...in their ability to subserve patterns of sensorimotor dependence. (2004, 27)

Expanding on this idea, Noë adds that

> only a vibrator array with something like the functional multiplicity of the retina could support genuine (full-fledged, normal) vision. To make tactile vision more fully visual, then, we need to make the physical system on which it depends more like the human's visual system. (2004, 27–28)

Despite the superficially liberal appeal in these quotes to "functional multiplicity," the required identity (for precise sameness of experience) thus reaches far down into the structure of the physical apparatus itself and demands very fine-grained similarities of body and gross sensory equipment. O'Regan and Noë are more explicit:

For two systems to have the same knowledge of sensorimotor contingencies *all the way down* they will have to have bodies that are identical *all the way down* (at least in relevant respects). For only bodies that are alike in low-level detail can be functionally alike in the relevant ways. (2001, 1015)

While later on, in Noë's single-author treatment, he asserts that

creatures with bodies like ours would have systems that are visual in the way ours are. Indeed, *only such systems can participate in the identical range of sensorimotor interactions that we participate in.* (2004, 159, emphasis added)

Or again:

It turns out that there is good reason to believe that the sensorimotor dependencies are themselves determined by low-level details of the physical systems on which our sensory systems depend. The eye and the visual parts of the brain form a most subtle instrument indeed, and thanks to this instrument, sensory stimulation varies in response to movement in precise ways. *To see as we do, you must have a sensory organ and a body like ours.* (2004, 112, emphasis added)

The position is thus that while some coarse-grained isomorphisms may be sufficient to begin to render the experience of a differently embodied being visual, the full glory of normal human visual experience depends on a gross sensorimotor profile that very sensitively tracks the fine details of human embodiment. Of course, even such a strong view need not be (as Noë 2004, 28, rightly points out) chauvinistic *if* the requirement of full sensorimotor isomorphism for identity of experience flows from a compelling theoretical model.

But does it? The claim in question (let's call it the claim of fine-grained sensorimotor dependence) is that every difference in fine-grained patterns of sensorimotor dependence will potentially impact any associated perceptual experience. Notice that this consequence does not in any way follow from the fact (if it is a fact) that prediction learning plays a key role in the *acquisition* of certain kinds of perceptual knowledge and understanding. For the upshot of such learning might well be forms of understanding that are systematically insensitive to some changes in sensory stimulation while exaggerating others.

Notice also that the patterns of sensorimotor dependence in question cannot *themselves* be patterns in experiential space (in the space of appearances) on pain of triviality. For, of course, every difference in experience implies some difference in experience. But if we step outside the phenomenological arena, then the claim of fine-grained sensorimotor dependence looks to involve the premature settling of what should be an open empirical question.

Thus, suppose, to imagine a concrete case, that certain patterns of sensorimotor dependence concern the relations between movement and retinal stimulation. And suppose that some very small difference in embodiment makes a very small difference to such patterns. It is surely an open empirical question whether every difference in respect to such stimulation *makes a difference* to the content and character of any conscious perceptual experience that ensues. And the same will be true wherever in the processing story we choose to focus, even if we opt for patterns of cortical rather than retinal stimulation.

Systematic insensitivities might, in fact, serve some functional purpose. It is easy to imagine design and engineering considerations that would favor various kinds of buffering, filtering, and recoding of perceptual inputs such that the contents and character of conscious perceptual experience might be determined at some considerable remove from the fine-grained details of sensorimotor loops. As we shall later see, there is some reason to believe that human perceptual experience is indeed determined at just such a remove and that it involves tweaked and optimized representations that do not march sensitively in step with the flow of gross sensory stimulation.

It might be objected that the kind of hypersensitivity I am contesting is simply the price one pays for appealing to embodied skills as an alternative to traditional appeals to qualia. But this is not so. For the skills to which such deflationary accounts (among which I count the strong sensorimotor theory) appeal may *themselves* be coarse- or fine-grained and may thus involve activities and capacities that are systematically insensitive to some of the goings-on at the sensorimotor frontier. For example, they may focus on what Matthen (2005, 229–232; see also Pettit 2003) calls "epistemic" skills: skills of sifting, sorting, classifying, selecting, choosing, reidentifying, and comparing. These skills (which must, in any deflationary context, be said to constitute rather than to call upon perceptual experience) may depend on modes of processing and forms of internal representation that ultimately float free of the full spectrum of fine sensorimotor detail. Nor, finally, need the appeal to skills (rather than qualia) force us to abandon the notion of a distinctive personal level at which a cognitive agent has access to some information. That is to say, it should not force us to abandon the notion of that which is in some important sense *manifest* (see Pettit 2003) to the agent concerned.

I suspect that in his admirable eagerness to avoid the qualia trap, Noë has been led to define appearances rather too directly in terms of objective relations between objects and perceivers, with the result that whatever impacts this objective relation (more precisely, whatever impacts the way this relation unfolds during sensorimotor activity) is said to impact, if only very subtly, how things look to the agent. Other ways of unpacking a skill-based account need not, as we'll see, buy into this kind of picture. But before exploring such a possibility, it helps to introduce a missing layer of complexity in (at least some versions of) the Strong Sensorimotor Model itself.

8.5   What Reaching Teaches

According to O'Regan and Noë (2001), we are conscious of a specific visually presented state of affairs only when our practical knowledge about the ways movement will yield sensory change is actively invoked *in the service of reason, planning, and judgment*. In such cases, we do not merely exercise our mastery of sensorimotor contingencies, for we do this even when we are unaware of our own actions, as when returning a fast tennis serve or absentmindedly driving along a familiar road. Rather, conscious awareness enters the scene when we make use of *that very same* knowledge of sensorimotor contingencies "for the purposes of thought and planning" (O'Regan and Noë 2001, 944). On this account, to consciously see is "to explore one's environment in a way that is mediated by one's mastery of sensorimotor contingencies, and to be making use of this mastery in one's planning, reasoning and speech behavior" (O'Regan and Noë 2001, 944).

The point of adding such a further requirement is clear. Very often, when we exercise our implicit knowledge of patterns of sensorimotor dependence, no corresponding perceptual awareness ensues. To explain the difference, O'Regan and Noë invoke use in reason, planning, and speech behavior as a kind of spotlight that allows some (but not all) of our active knowledge of sensorimotor contingencies to condition perceptual awareness.

Interestingly, this requirement, which is made much of by O'Regan and Noë, is nowhere in evidence in Noë's (2004) solo treatment. What we find there is just the bare idea of the active use of specific bodies of knowledge concerning sensorimotor dependencies in the guidance of behavior. Noë (personal communication) picks this issue out as one where his views are in a state of flux. The guiding thought, he writes, is that "being conscious of a feature is actively probing it—it's reaching out and making contact with it, as it were." But such active probing surely characterizes the intelligent saccades of the driver's eyes even when the driver is attending to other matters and not consciously experiencing the details of the road. Alternatively, if active probing means something like "probing in the context of attentive problem solving," then we are back to the full-strength role for reason and planning assigned by O'Regan and Noë.

There is, in any case, another possibility here that has significant empirical support and that is ultimately, or so I shall argue, suggestive of an alternative to the Strong Sensorimotor Model itself. This is the possibility (Milner and Goodale 1995, 2006; Goodale and Milner 2004; Clark 2001c, 2007; Jacob and Jeannerod 2003) that the contents of conscious perceptual experience are determined by the activation of a distinctive body of internal representations operating quasi-autonomously from the realm of direct sensorimotor engagement. Such representations are perceptual but are geared toward (and optimized for) the specific needs of reasoning and planning rather than those of fluent physical engagement. These representations are conditioned by a stream of inputs that do indeed originate at the sensors, but this stream proceeds in large part in parallel to the processing stream dedicated to the fluid control of online, fine-tuned, sensorimotor engagement and is systematically insensitive to much lower level detail.

These "dual-stream" models appear to differ from strong sensorimotor models (SSMs) in at least two crucial respects. First, they depict visual experience as depending on a suite of representations optimized for reasoning and planning, whereas strong sensorimotor models depict visual experience as occurring when (possibly very fine-grained) sensorimotor knowledge is either simply *active* or, more plausibly, when it is *put into contact with* or *used for the purposes of* reasoning and planning. Second, these models looks to be fully compatible with the idea (rejected outright by the SSM) that conscious visual experience might often (and perhaps always) depend on specific local aspects of internal representational activity rather than on whole animal sensorimotor loops.

A major part of the empirical impetus for the dual-stream story comes from Milner and Goodale (1995; see also Goodale and Milner 2004; and the important updates in Milner and Goodale 2006), who suggest that conscious visual awareness reflects information-processing

activity in a specific visual processing stream geared toward enduring object properties, explicit recognition, and semantic recall. This
stream—the ventral stream—is also in charge whenever real-world
objects are unavailable and governs our attempts to mime actions on
imagined or recalled objects. Actual object-based motor engagements,
by contrast, are depicted as the province of a semiautonomous processing stream—the dorsal stream—that guides fluent motor action in the
here and now. Milner and Goodale thus contrast capacities of visually
guided action and capacities of conscious visual perception, suggesting
that these come apart in a variety of unexpected and revealing ways.

In support of this hypothesis, Milner and Goodale invoke a rich body
of data concerning patients with damage to areas in either the dorsal or
ventral streams. The best known of these is the patient DF, a victim of
carbon monoxide poisoning suffering from widespread lesions of the so-
called ventral visual stream. DF cannot identify objects by sight (though
she can do so by touch) yet is able to pick up these very same objects
using fluent, well-oriented precision grips. Conversely, optic ataxics,
with dorsal stream lesions, are adept at visually identifying objects that
they cannot fluidly reach and grasp. Optic ataxics "have little trouble seeing [i.e., identifying objects in a visual scene] but a lot of trouble reaching
for objects they can see. It is as though they cannot use the spatial information inherent in any visual scene" (Gazzaniga 1998, 109).

DF, while claiming that she cannot see the orientation of a displayed slit, can nonetheless (on demand) successfully insert a letter
through the slit, with the letter preoriented so as to pass easily through
(see fig. 8.1). Optic ataxics, by contrast, are able to consciously perceive
and report the orientation of the slit but are unable (and not due to
any brute physical impairment) to preorient and insert the letter. Such
patients are aided somewhat if the slit is presented, then removed,
and the request is to orient the letter in the way that would have been
appropriate were the slot still available. This allows the use of a distinct, memory-based strategy. DF is unable to perform at all under
this delay condition. Thus, we see tight links between memory and
conscious visual report and a dissociation between both of these and
online object-engaged performance. DF reports that she cannot consciously perceive the orientation, and she does not succeed in the
delay condition, but the optic ataxics report that they can consciously
perceive the orientation and actually do better in the delay condition
(see Milner and Goodale 1995, 96–101, 136–138).

All of this, as Milner and Goodale stress, makes excellent computational sense. For fine-grained action control requires the extraction
and use of radically different kinds of information (from the incoming

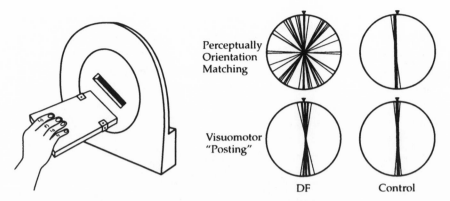

FIGURE 8.1 The diagram at the top of this figure illustrates the apparatus that was used to test sensitivity to orientation in the patient DF. The slot could be placed in any one of a number of orientations around the clock. Subjects were required either to rotate a hand-held card to match the orientation of the slot or to insert the card into the slot as shown in this figure. The polar plots at the right of the figure illustrate the orientation of the hand-held card on the perceptual matching task and the visuomotor posting task for DF and an age-matched control subject. The correct orientation on each trial has been rotated to vertical. Note that although DF was unable to match the orientation of the card to that of the slot in the perceptual matching card, she did rotate the card to the correct orientation as she attempted to insert it into the slot on the posting task. (From Milner and Goodale 1995, by permission)

visual signal) than does recognition, report, recall, and reasoning. The former requires a constantly updated, egocentrically specified, exquisitely distance- and orientation-sensitive encoding of the visual array. The latter requires a degree of object constancy and the recognition of items by category and significance irrespective of the fine detail of location, viewpoint, and retinal image size. A computationally efficient coding for either task precludes the use of the very same encoding for the other, a diagnosis also supported by work revealing the very different response characteristics of neurons in the dorsal and ventral streams (see Milner and Goodale 1995, 25–66).

The best interpretation of all these bodies of data, according to Milner and Goodale, is that memory and conscious visual experience depend on a type of mechanism and coding that is different from, and largely independent of, the mechanisms and coding used to guide visuomotor action in real time. The former depend on processing in the ventral stream leading from the primary visual cortex to temporal

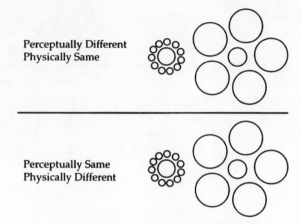

Perceptually Different
Physically Same

Perceptually Same
Physically Different

FIGURE 8.2 Diagram showing the Ebbinghaus or
Titchener circles illusion. In the top figure, the two
central discs are the same size but appear different;
in the bottom figure, the disc surrounded by an
annulus of large circles has been made somewhat
larger to appear approximately equal in size to the
other central disc. (From Milner and Goodale 1995,
by permission)

areas. The latter (the action-guiding resources) depend on the dorsal
stream leading to the parietal cortex.

Milner and Goodale also cite performance data from normal human
subjects using experimental paradigms such as Aglioti et al.'s ingenious use of the Ebbinghaus or Titchener circles illusion. In the standard
illusion (see fig. 8.2), subjects misjudge the relative size of two circles, each
surrounded by a ring of larger or smaller circles. In the topmost drawing,
the two central discs are equal in size, whereas in the lower drawing, they
are different in size. The effect of the surrounding rings of large and small
circles, in each case, leads us to in some way misrepresent the relative
sizes of the central discs, judging them to be different when they are the
same (top case) and the same when they are different (bottom case).

Conscious visual experience, in this case, appears to deliver a content that misrepresents the actual size of the center discs.[4] This mis-
representation surely occurs *within* the conscious visual experience
itself. For we are capable of altering our conceptual judgment without
thereby altering the way the visual scene appears to us in perceptual
experience. Once we know about the illusion, we may judge that the
center circles in the topmost picture are identical in size despite the
persistence, in our conscious visual experience, of the illusion.

Aglioti, Goodale, and DeSouza (1995) set up a physical version of the illusion using thin poker chips as the discs and then asked subjects to "pick up the target disc on the left if the two discs appeared equal in size and to pick up the one on the right if they appeared different in size" (Milner and Goodale 1995, 167). The surprising upshot was that even when subjects were unaware of—but clearly subject to—the illusion, their motor control systems produced a precisely fitted grip with a finger-thumb aperture perfectly suited to the *actual* (nonillusory) size of the disc. This aperture was not arrived at by touching and adjusting but was instead the direct result of the visual input. Yet, to repeat, it reflected not the illusory disc size apparently given in the subject's visual experience but the actual size. In short,

> grip size was determined entirely by the true size of the target disc [and] the very act by means of which subjects indicated their susceptibility to the visual illusion (that is, picking up one of two target circles) was itself uninfluenced by the illusion. (Milner and Goodale 1995, 168)

This was, indeed, a somewhat startling result, again suggesting that the processing underlying visual awareness may be operating quite independently of that underlying the visual control of action. In a little more detail, the explanation, according to Goodale and Milner (2004, 88–89), is that the conscious scene is computed by the ventral stream in ways that are at liberty to make a variety of assumptions on the basis of visual cues (e.g., attempting to preserve size constancy by treating the smaller circles as probably farther away than the larger ones). The dorsal stream, by contrast, uses only the kinds of information that are metrically reliable and exploit specific opportunities for elegant, fast, metrically accurate diagnosis. For example, the dorsal stream may make great use of binocular depth information (information that, they claim, "makes only a small contribution to our [conscious] *perception* of depth"; Goodale and Milner 2004, 91). These differences in processing, combined with the quasi-independent modes of operation of the two streams, account for the illusion's ability to impact conscious visual experience while leaving our visuomotor engagements splendidly intact.

More recently, a similar effect has been shown using the so-called hollow face illusion. In this illusion (see fig. 8.3), a concave model of a human face appears convex due to the influence of top-down knowledge concerning normal human faces. This suggests it is a purely ventral-stream-based illusion. Kroliczak et al. (2006) showed that in a task where subjects were asked to flick small targets off the actually

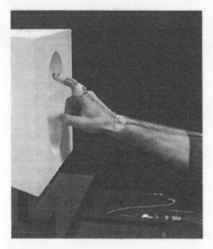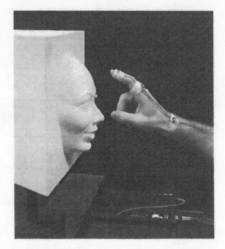

FIGURE 8.3 Fast flicking and the hollow-face illusion.

hollow (though visually convex) face, the flicking movements found the real (nonillusory) locations of the targets. According to Milner and Goodale,

> this demonstrates that the visuomotor system can use bottom-up sensory inputs...to guide movements to the veridical locations of targets in the real world, even when the perceived positions of the targets are influenced, or even reversed, by top-down processing. (2006, 245)

The claims concerning the immunity of visuomotor action to visual illusions have spawned a large industry devoted to the search for counterexamples, alternative explanations, exceptions, refinements, and additional support (for some useful reviews, see Carey 2001; Clark 2001c, 2007; Goodale and Westwood 2004). For example, it has been shown that some visual illusions do affect visuomotor engagement. Importantly, however, this seems to be the case only when the illusion is rooted in very early stages of visual processing (in primary visual cortex) and is thus "passed on" to both streams when they subsequently diverge (Dyde and Milner 2002; Milner and Dyde 2003). This is, of course, fully compatible with the strong dual-systems view. Moreover, several other perceptual illusions have subsequently been shown to affect conscious experience without impacting visuomotor acts of grasp scaling and reaching, including the Ponzo ("railway lines") and Müller-Lyer illusions (see Goodale and Milner 2004, 89).[5] In such cases, motor effects *are* observed when delays are introduced between viewing the illusion and producing the motor response. But this is as predicted by the model, which treats time-delayed actions as "pantomimed" in that they cannot rely on the here-and-now computations of the dorsal stream and are instead driven by the illusion-prone deliverances of the ventral stream (see Milner and Goodale 1995, 170–173).

8.6 "Tweaked" Tele-assistance

Despite their stress on the relative independence of the dorsal and ventral visual-stream contributions, Milner and Goodale accept that there has to be some kind of important interaction between the two. As they themselves comment (1995, 201–204), the two streams must act harmoniously, noncompetitively, and—in some sense—cooperatively. Even the neuroanatomy exhibits multiple instances of cross-connectivity between the streams and displays certain neuroanatomical areas as common ground between the two (e.g., areas V3A and MT; see Felleman and Van Essen 1991). This makes obvious functional sense. We are clearly able to factor stored high-level information into basic action routines, for example, when our reach and grip are adjusted to the known weight and slipperiness of a visually encountered object. In this vein, Milner and Goodale (1995, 202) explicitly allow that part of the process of visuomotor grasping probably involves "the transfer of high-level visual information between the two streams" and add that "understanding these interactions would take us some way towards answering what is one of the central questions in modern neuroscience: how is sensory information transformed into purposeful acts?" (202).

One question, then, is how to capture the shape of the crucial interactions. Milner and Goodale's suggestion is that such interaction occurs largely at the level of target- and action-type selection. Roughly speaking, the conscious visual contents (supported, they claim, by activity within the ventral stream) are said to figure prominently in our *selection* of goal objects and in our choice of *types* of action, while a largely independent (and, they suggest, dorsal-stream-based) coding provides the spatial and physical form information needed for the fine-grained control and maintenance of the ensuing activity. The process of selection of objects to be acted upon may, it is speculated, involve mechanisms of attention that "flag" the goal object and initiate the retrieval of whatever high-level information needs to be factored into the visuomotor routine. The act of grasping a fork, for example (see Milner and Goodale 1995, 203), requires not *simply* the provision of an accurate precision grip but a grip appropriate to the intended *use* of the fork.[6]

And this requires the dorsal stream to be influenced by the high-level products of ventral-stream processing. Interaction thus occurs and is vital to normal functioning. But the influence is high level and does not posit a common representational format used both to guide fine-grained action and to support report and recognition.

A good (though potentially somewhat blunt and overdramatic, as we shall see) way to focus the intended difference is by means of an analogy (Goodale 1998; Goodale and Milner 2004) with tele-assistance approaches to the control of distant robots in distant or hostile environments. In a typical tele-assistance setup, a human operator and a semi-intelligent distal robot combine forces to perform actions in some environment. A familiar example might be a Mars rover, where the human operator reviews images on a screen and flags items of interest (e.g., a strangely shaped rock in the top left of the screen). The operator commands the robot to retrieve the flagged item, perhaps adding commands that specify the use of one of several retrieval modes (according to estimated weight, fragility, etc.). The robot rover then does the rest, locomoting to the spot and calculating the local commands needed to deploy the robot body and gripper to achieve the goal. Such approaches should be contrasted with *tele-operation* solutions, in which the human operator controls all the spatial and temporal aspects of the robot's movements (perhaps via a joystick or a set of sensors that relay the operator's own arm and hand movements to the robot). In a tele-assistance solution,

> the human operator doesn't have to worry about the real metrics of the workspace or the timing of the movements made by the robot; instead, the human operator has the job of identifying a goal and specifying an action towards that goal in general terms. [The robot then uses] its on-board range-finders and other sensing devices to work out the required movements for achieving the specific goal. (Goodale and Milner 2004, 99)

The tele-assistance analogy identifies the human operator with the ventral stream (working with stored memory and various "executive control" systems). The task of this coalition, the analogy suggests, is to identify objects and to select types of action that are appropriate, given the agent's current goals, background knowledge, and currently attended perceptual input. The task of the dorsal stream (and associated structures) is then to turn these high-level specifications into metrically accurate, egocentrically specified forms of world-engaging action. The dorsal stream (+) thus plays the robotic Mars rover to the ventral stream (+)'s human operator. In this way, "both systems have to work together in the production of purposive behavior—one system to select the goal object from the visual array, the other to carry out the required metrical computations for the goal-directed action" (Goodale and Milner 2004, 100).

The tele-assistance model can, however, as Goodale and Milner go on to note, make it seem as if the ventral stream (and associated resources) "plays only a very distant role in the implementation of action, rather like a chief executive officer in a corporation, setting goals and writing mission statements, and then delegating the real work to others" (Goodale and Milner 2004, 103). For *some* aspects of the motor programming, however, the ventral system does rather more than this. As we already noted, it provides information about the action type (if the object is a screwdriver, it provides information about which end to grip and, in what way, actually use the tool; see, e.g., Goodale and Milner 2004, 105–107). The patient DF, with ventral damage, though able to scale her grip to the shape of the (to her, unidentifiable) tool, will often grip the tool from the wrong end. Moreover, the programming of grip force required to take account of an object's likely weight turns out to require ventral involvement, too, and not just in respect of familiar objects whose weight is known and stored in memory. In effect, the dorsal resource has nothing beyond visual attributes, processed "bottom-up" on the spot, to go on. So even to use knowledge of material (lead vs. plastic) to determine grip force requires information beyond its means. Grip force turns out to be left to the ventral stream, so much so that illusions of size (in this case, using a special version of the Ponzo, or railway lines, illusion) have been shown (Jackson and Shaw 2000) to affect the scaling of grip force even in cases when grip size is computed correctly, presumably by the dorsal stream. This suggests that the computation of size that determines the applied grip force is the one carried out by the ventral (illusion-prone) resource, even though the computation of size that determines the precision grip itself is not. Nonetheless, the broad notion of a relatively high-level executive interaction between conscious seeing and fine-grained motor control is highly attractive. It helps make sense of the interesting linkages between conscious visual report and memory and of the equally interesting dissociations between both of these (on the one hand) and fine-tuned, object-engaging action (on the other). Thus, consider Prinz's (2000, 252) suggestion that "the key to connecting consciousness with action might involve memory systems rather than motor systems." Prinz's idea is that conscious awareness is intimately bound up with the use of attentional systems to put sensory systems into contact with working and episodic memory. Such contact developed, he conjectures, to allow stored memories of specific incidents to guide planning and action selection. It was the relatively recent coevolution of consciousness and new memory systems (especially episodic memory) that, on this account, then freed certain creatures from the here and now and opened the doors to planning and reason as we know them. The upshot was to drive a new wedge between sensing and acting, rendering the relation at times indirect. The role of conscious visual perception, on this model, is to support reason, recall, and reflection. It is only indirectly to guide (better, to select; see Clark 2001c, 2007) actions in the here and now.

8.7   Sensorimotor Summarizing

At this point, it is useful to locate the dual visual systems hypothesis in a wider framework. This framework depicts conscious visual perception as depending on forms of encoding and representation optimized for (or simply specialized for) their role in reasoning, choice, and action selection rather than for their role in actual sensorimotor engagement. Thus, in the Titchener circles experiment, the representations that support conscious visual experience would be specialized, just as Milner and Goodale suggest, to guide the choice of *which* disc to pick up and the choice of what *kind* of grip to deploy (one apt for picking up and not, e.g., for throwing). The conscious illusion of one circle being larger than another may then be best explained by the visual system's delivering a representation enhanced in the light of information about relative size—a trick that is effective for reasoning and choice in most ecologically realistic situations but that would be damaging (resulting in a mass of failed or botched encounters) were it replicated by fine sensorimotor control systems.

Similarly, a study by Carrasco et al. (2004) found that the allocation of attention affected the appearance of a visual stimulus, causing an enhanced contrast effect in a cued grating. Reporting on this effect, Treue (2004) comments that

> attention turns out to be another tool at the visual system's disposal to provide an organism with an optimized representation of the sensory input that emphasizes relevant details, even at the expense of a faithful representation of the sensory input. (436–437)

This general model of the role of conscious awareness is found in, among others, the work of Koch (2004), who speaks of "summaries" apt to aid frontal regions in the selection of one among a set of possible types of action or response. It is also suggested by Campbell's (2002) "targets" view of consciousness and in Jacob and Jeannerod's (2003) delicately nuanced version of the dual visual streams view.[7] Common to all these views is the image of conscious perceptual experience as dependent on representations whose special cognitive role is to enable the deliberate selection of targets for action and of types of action and to support a range of "epistemic skills" such as sorting, sifting, comparing, and the like (see Matthen 2005; Pettit 2003). Representations optimized for such purposes need not, and typically do not, reflect the full intricacies of our actual ongoing sensorimotor engagements with the world.[8] Instead, they are geared, tweaked, and nuanced to inform reason, selection, comparison, and choice. They thus reflect only the very broad outlines of a space of possible targets and possible *kinds* of sensorimotor engagements. They are "sensorimotor summarizing" resources whose computational form is geared to use in reason, planning, and action selection. And though they must be sensitive to sensory input, they need not (indeed, must not) be sensitive to every nuance in the ongoing mass of sensory stimulation.

The representations that ultimately determine visual experience are quite distinct, this alternative account insists, from those that support the sensorimotor loops by means of which we successfully engage the very world we perceive. They are, nonetheless, still distinctively visual insofar as they represent the special kinds of information gathered (in normal agents) by part of the visual pathway: features such as rough spatial location, color, shape, and so on. TVSS systems, on this account, aim to make the same kinds of information available by means of superficially different sets of signals and will succeed to whatever extent this turns out to be possible (which will in turn depend both on the nature and extent of neural plasticity and on the ability of these alternative input devices to make the same bodies of information available and at roughly the same timescale; for this take on TVSS, see Bach y Rita and Kercel 2003).

Hence, the proper way to think about TVSS, The Voice, and other such systems is that they aim to make available the same gross information that is normally carried by the optic nerve and thus feed both ventral and dorsal processing streams. As such, the successes of TVSS and other systems provide no reason to prefer the Strong Sensorimotor Model to the sensorimotor summarizing alternative that highlights implicit knowledge of poise over a rather coarse-grained action space. It is true that the adaptation of visuomotor action and of visual experience march closely in step (e.g., as in the well-known cases of adaptation to inverting lenses etc.; see the discussion in Clark 1997a). But all this shows is that visuomotor activity helps tune and organize the neural resources that support and maintain conscious visual experience, whereas cases of selective impairment (e.g., DF's visual form of agnosia and optic ataxia) then provide evidence of the activity of distinct systems underlying achieved competence.

Noë (2004, 19) claims that such dual visual systems ideas are "at best orthogonal to the basic claims of the enactive approach." The reason given (see also Noë 2004, 11) is that the enactive approach makes no claims about what conscious visual perception is *for* and hence remains neutral on the topic of vision for action versus vision for conscious perception. More positively, O'Regan and Noë (2001, 969) claim that, with a few provisos, there is actually a good fit between the Strong Sensorimotor Model and the dual visual systems ideas because the requirement (for conscious experience) that sensorimotor knowledge be active in the service of reason and planning predicts the kinds of dissociation found in the literature.

I think it should be clear (and see Block 2005, for some nice discussion) that such direct attempts at reconciliation cannot succeed. For what is at issue is not simply the evidence of substantial dissociation but the best *functional and architectural explanation* of that evidence. And the best functional and architectural explanation, according to Milner, Goodale, and others, is that conscious perceptual experience reflects the activation of representations that have less to do with the fine details of world-engaging sensorimotor loops and more to do with the need to assign inputs to categories, types, and relative locations so as better to sift, sort, select, identify, compare, recall, imagine, and reason.

The contrast between the two views emerges in, for example, O'Regan and Noë's surprising description of DF as a case of "partial awareness" in which "she is unable to describe what she sees but is otherwise able to use it for the purpose of guiding action" (2001, 969). DF, recall, is able to use visually presented information for some purposes (e.g., to insert a letter into a slot) even though she claims not to visually experience the shape, color, or orientation of the slot. O'Regan and Noë depict this as a case of partial awareness since visual information is still playing an action-guiding role in the overall organism–environment loop. But this surely conflates visual awareness with the use of visual information, precisely the knot that Milner and Goodale were trying to untie. For this reason, Goodale (2001, 984) rejects O'Regan and Noë's account of DF, pointing out that she "shows almost perfect visuomotor control in the absence of any evidence that she actually 'sees' the form of the object she is grasping."

Here, I suspect, the enactive framework is trying to wag the empirical dog. For the enactive framework is, as we saw, precommitted to linking the perceptual facts to facts about whole animal embedded, embodied activity. Perception, including conscious perception, is thus said to be "a kind of skillful activity on the part of the animal as a whole" (Noë 2004, 2; see also Varela, Thompson, and Rosch 1991). But this pre-commitment works against taking truly seriously the evidence for deep dissociations between vision for action and vision for perception.[9]

In contrast with this whole animal view, dual-stream models are open to the possibility that specific perceptual capacities and experiences depend on (and can be brought about by) the activity of specific aspects of neural circuitry. In the case of conscious visual experience, such models embrace the idea that processing in the ventral stream plays a special role in the construction of conscious experience and that there is serious functional decomposition (coupled with dense online integration; Jacob and Jeannerod 2003) between systems for conscious experience and systems for fluent, fine-tuned visuomotor action.[10]

Such models retain the important emphasis on skills rather than qualia as traditionally conceived. But they do so while recognizing the very large extent to which the human agent is a *fragmented bag of embodied skills*, only some of which are potentially relevant to the contents and character of perceptual experience. In particular, these will be skills geared rather directly toward reasoning and planning, such as abilities of sifting, sorting, classifying, selecting, choosing, reidentifying, recalling, and comparing (again, see Pettit 2003). This special focus opens up a significant buffer zone between the fine details of movement and of motion-dependent sensory input and the rather more specialized skill base that determines the contents and character of perceptual experience. What counts for perceptual experience is then this suite of epistemic skills, *however they happen to be supported by cycles of low-level sensorimotor pickup*. And there is, as far as I can see, no compelling reason to believe that *these* kinds of epistemic skills need to march in lockstep with a being's full sensorimotor profile. Indeed, they may depend on representational forms that are deliberately (i.e., productively and for good computational reasons) insensitive to many fine details of bodily orientation and sensory stimulation. If this is correct, then the perceptual experience of differently embodied animals could in principle be identical, not merely similar, to our own.

8.8   Virtual Content, Again

This general story applies equally, it seems to me, to the account of virtual content and the experience of detail. Thus, recall the claim (Noë 2004, 67, and the discussion in sec. 7.3) that "experiential content is itself virtual." The idea is that experience presents all the detail in a visual scene as present but virtually so, rather like "the way that a web site's content is present on your desktop" (50). In the latter case, it can seem just as if, to use Noë's own example, you have the entire contents of the online version of the *New York Times* encoded on your hard drive. But of course, this is not so. Rather, information is accessed from the distant site on a kind of just-in-time, need-to-know basis. Similarly, according to Noë, we perceptually experience the visual scene as rich in detail. But this experience, while not illusory (pace the Grand Illusion idea popularized by Dennett and others; see Noë 2004, 50–67), is rooted not in the presence of a rich neurally encoded representation of all that detail but in our skill-based access to the requisite detail as and when needed: "The detail is present—the perceptual world is present—in the sense that we have a special kind of access to the detail, an access controlled by patterns of sensorimotor dependence with which we are familiar" (Noë 2004, 67).

This stress on access is correct and, I think, profoundly important. But what *exactly* is the role of the actual sensorimotor loops by means of which such access is provided? How, that is to say, should we conceive the role of the *specific routines* by means of which we thus engage the world, retrieving more visual information as and when needed?

One radical possibility is that certain specific kinds of sensorimotor activity (actually retrieving externally stored information via certain means) are now part of the minimal supervenience base for the present experience of richness.[11] Another, only slightly less radical, possibility is that our implicit knowledge of the availability of these specific sensorimotor loops is part of the minimal supervenience base for the present experience of richness. But still another possibility is that the present experience of richness is simply a present experience of the easy accessibility (of certain kinds of information) as and when needed and that the specific world-engaging loops provide merely the *contingent means to this end*. The minimal supervenience base for the perceptual experience of richness, on this model, would not include the routines that actually retrieve such information. Indeed, the very same experience of perceptual richness then looks compatible with the running (behind the scenes, as it were) of a wide variety of quite different retrieval routines.

The deepest question raised by the Strong Sensorimotor Model is thus surely this: To what extent does the detailed "how" of information pickup (the specific details of some sensorimotor retrieval routine) matter *for perceptual experience itself*? My own suspicion, which I have tried to at least begin to make plausible in the previous sections, is that such details may be merely the contingent means by which a certain higher level information-processing poise, itself essential for conscious experience, is achieved. The kind of poise required will vary from case to case but will typically be pitched at some remove from the full details of our active sensorimotor repertoire.

8.9 Beyond the Sensorimotor Frontier

The moral of all this is that appeals to embodiment, environmental structure, and action need to be handled with care. For while it seems increasingly clear that embodiment, action, and situation make a large contribution to the contents and character of human thought and experience, we should not be too quick to assume that such contributions are direct or that they must be kept fixed if the contents and character of thought and experience are to remain the same. Strong sensorimotor models of perceptual experience do us a service by foregrounding embodied skills and eschewing appeals to qualia as traditionally conceived. But they fail to do justice to the many firewalls, fragmentations, and divisions of cognitive labor that characterize our engagements with the world our senses reveal. Strong sensorimotor models paper over this complex motley crew by casting everything prematurely in the single currency of implicitly known patterns of fine sensorimotor dependence. By trying to distill all that matters about human perceptual experience from the homogeneous mash of implicit knowledge concerning sensorimotor dependencies, such models are congenitally blind to the computationally potent *insensitivity* of key information-processing routines to the full subtleties of embodied cycles of sensing and moving. In place of this common sensorimotor currency, we need to consider a more complex picture that displays a cognitive economy replete with special-purpose streamings and with multiple, quasi-independent forms of internal, and external, representation and processing.

9

Disentangling Embodiment

9.1 Three Threads

Drawing on the various work and case studies presented in previous chapters, we can now display three distinct but sometimes overlapping ways in which embodiment seems to matter for mind and cognition. The three ways are:

1. **Spreading the Load.** The body and brain, thanks to evolution and learning, are adept at spreading the load. Bodily morphology, development, action, and biomechanics, as well as environmental structure and interventions, can reconfigure a wide variety of control and learning problems in ways that promote fluid and efficient problem solving and adaptive response.
2. **Self-Structuring of Information.**[1] The presence of an active, self-controlled, sensing body allows an agent to create or elicit appropriate inputs, generating good data (for herself and for others) by actively conjuring flows of multimodal, correlated, time-locked stimulation.
3. **Supporting Extended Cognition.** The presence of an active, self-controlled, sensing body (a) provides a resource that can *itself* act as part of the problem-solving economy and (b) allows for the

co-opting of bioexternal resources into extended but deeply integrated cognitive and computational routines.

The three threads are joined by a supporting hypothesis that we encountered back in chapter 6:

Hypothesis of Cognitive Impartiality

Our problem-solving performances take shape according to some cost function or functions that, in the typical course of events, accord no special status or privilege to specific types of operation (motoric, perceptual, introspective) or modes of encoding (in the head or in the world).

In fact, we have also seen (sec. 7.3) some evidence for a slightly stronger hypothesis:

Hypothesis of Motor Deference

Online problem solving will tend to defer to perceptuomotor modes of information access. That is, we will often rely on information retrieved from the world even when relevant information is also neurally represented.

However, the results surveyed in section 6.5 cast doubt on any fully general version of motor deference and seem to indicate temporal factors as the "level playing field" determinants of which information sources an agent will implicitly prefer. For present purposes, then, I shall adopt cognitive impartiality as a working hypothesis. Cognitive impartiality explains why it is that organizations (both long and short term) emerge in which the storage, processing, and transformation of information is spread so indiscriminately among brain, body, and world. Taken as a whole, the three threads and the supporting hypothesis cash out the claim that human cognition respects something like a Principle of Ecological Assembly (sec. 1.3), according to which information-processing organizations are repeatedly soft assembled from a motley crew of neural, bodily, and external resources.

Examples of (1) included the work on passive dynamic walking, on sensor placement, and on the productive use of environmental structure (sec. 1.1 and chap. 4). Examples of (2) included Ballard's work on just-in-time sensing and deictic pointers and Yu et al.'s work on learning visually grounded meanings (sec. 1.3 and 1.6). In addition, the studies of sensory substitution systems further underlined the importance of self-controlled temporally nuanced cycles of sensor movement and (resultant) input in tuning bodily and sensory equipment in ways apt to support perception and action. Examples of (3) included the Otto thought experiment (chap. 4) and empirical work on gesture for thought (chap. 6) and on cognitive niche construction in general (chap. 3 and 4). Chandana Paul's robot (sec. 9.7) adds one final illustration to this (the most contentious) category.

In this final substantive chapter, I hope to show that (despite some recent publicity) these appeals to embodiment, action, and cognitive extension are best understood as fully continuous with computational, representational, and (broadly speaking) information-theoretic approaches to understanding mind and cognition. In so doing, I hope to display at least something of the likely shape of a mature science of the embodied mind.

9.2   The Separability Thesis

Larry Shapiro, in a recent review article on embodied cognition, glosses it in part as "an approach to cognition that departs from traditional cognitive science in its reluctance to conceive of cognition as computational."[2] While Rohrer (2006) claims that "unlike the computationalist-functionalist hypothesis, embodiment theorists...argue that the specific details of how the brain and body embody the mind do matter to cognition" (2).[3]

Of course, even the most traditional of machine functionalists allowed (indeed, insisted) that cognitive processes be implemented in physical stuff. The point was just that the physical stuff mattered only in virtue of what were broadly speaking its functional or organizational properties. Cognition, for the machine functionalist, was independent of its physical medium in the sense that *if* you could get the right set of abstract organizational features in place (typically, some set of input to internal-state transitions to output functions), you would get the cognitive properties "for free." Importantly, as long as the right abstract organization could be instantiated, you would (it was claimed) get the very same mental and cognitive properties regardless of the materials you were using (see, e.g., Cummins 1983) and regardless of any details of gross physical shape or form. The traditional functionalist thus held that cognition was in *some* sense "platform independent." The question then arises, does work in embodied cognition really cast doubt on such claims of platform independence?

Shapiro (2004) seems to suggest that it does.[4] He presents an argument against one version of the claim of platform independence that he dubs the Separability Thesis (ST). According to ST, a humanlike mind could perfectly well exist in a very nonhumanlike body. Against the ST, Shapiro urges us to embrace what he calls the Embodied Mind Thesis (EMT), which holds that "minds profoundly reflect the bodies in which they are contained" (167).

Why reject ST? One reason, Shapiro tells us, turns on quite basic facts about sensing and processing. Human vision, for example, involves a great deal of sensor movement. We move our heads to gain information about the relative distances of objects because nearer objects will (courtesy of parallax effects) appear to move the most. Such movements, Shapiro argues, are not simply an aid to vision. They are part and parcel of the visual processing itself. They are "as much a part of vision as the detection of disparity or the calculation of shape from shading" (Shapiro 2004, 188). Similar points can be made about audition and the placement of the ears on the head. The idea is that

> psychological processes are incomplete without the body's contributions. Vision for human beings is a process that includes features of the human body … this means that a description of various perceptual capacities cannot maintain body-neutrality, and it also means that an organism with a non-human body will have non-human visual and auditory psychologies. (Shapiro 2004, 190)

Body neutrality, for Shapiro, is the idea that "characteristics of bodies make no difference to the kind of mind one possesses" and is associated with the idea that "mind is a program that can be characterized in abstraction from the kind of body/brain that realizes it" (175). Work on the role of bodily movements in visual processing suggests, according to Shapiro, that body neutrality fails and that human-style vision requires a human-style body.

We have already met another corpus of research that appears to contest claims of body neutrality, at least regarding the contents of perceptual awareness. This is the enactive approach to perception discussed in chapter 8. Laying out this approach, Noë commented that

> If perception is in part constituted by our possession and exercise of bodily skills … then it may also depend on our possession of the sorts of bodies that can encompass those skills, for only a creature with such a body could have those skills. To perceive like us, it follows, you must have a body like ours. (2004, 25)

Another very different way of rejecting ST appeals to considerations of the role of the body in structuring human concepts. The *locus classicus* here is Lakoff and Johnson's (1980, 1999) work on the role of body-based metaphors in human thought and reason. Many of our basic concepts, they argue, are quite evidently body based—concepts like front and back, up and down, inside and outside: "If all beings on the planet were uniform stationary spheres floating in some medium and perceiving equally in all directions, they would have no concepts of *front* and *back*" (Lakoff and Johnson 1999, 34).

But these basic concepts, they go on to argue, end up structuring our understandings (and our inferences) in more rarefied domains. Happiness and sadness, to take the standard example, are humanly conceived in terms of upness and downness. The specifics of embodiment thus shape the basic concepts that in turn inform, so it is argued, the rest. Summing up the Lakoff and Johnson line, Shapiro suggests that

> organisms that didn't have bodies like our own would develop other metaphors to characterize happiness and sadness. *Happy* and *sad* would be structured in other ways and would thus assume different meanings. (2004, 201)[5]

The common upshot of all these arguments, then, is a kind of principled body centrism, according to which the presence of humanlike minds depends quite directly on the possession of a humanlike body.

9.3 Beyond Flesh-eating Functionalism

It is revealing, I think, that Shapiro's spirited defense of profound bodily[6] involvement in the mental comes in the larger context of a series of arguments aimed at a different, logically independent, but thematically related target. That target was the thesis of multiple realizability, a staple of nonreductionist philosophy of mind ever since the heady days of early machine functionalism. At about that time, the notion that minds like ours might be directly identified with their specific *neural* underpinnings was widely cast as a kind of unacceptable meat or species chauvinism, to be replaced by the identification of mind as a functional kind—a kind capable in principle of being realized by many different physical substrates (Putnam 1975b; see also Putnam 1960, 1967). In this new regime, mindware stood to neural hardware rather as software stood to the physical device. Just as the same software could run on different bedrock machines, so the same kinds of mind might, it was supposed, turn up in various kinds of material form. What mattered was not the bedrock physical forms as much as the abstract patterns (of input to internal-state transitions to output) that the material structures were able to support. Sameness at this rather abstract level was meant to guarantee sameness at the mental level. Or at any rate, any remaining slack was to be taken up by rather arcane details of history and/or distal environmental embedding. As far as the *local machinery* of mind itself was concerned, functional identity fully fixed any contribution to mentality.

Shapiro's appeal to work in embodied, embedded cognitive science depicts it as in spirit rather inimical to the platform-neutral machine functionalist model of mind.[7] But the notion of platform neutrality is a slippery beast. For as we saw, even the standard machine functionalist need not (and should not) deny that properties of the bodily "platform" *matter* to mind and cognition. The only necessary claim is that insofar as the bodily platform matters, it matters by virtue of the suite of abstract opportunities (encodings, operations) that it makes available, and contrariwise, the suite of encodings and operations that it makes unnecessary (recall the discussion of Wilson's notion of "exploitative representation" in sec. 4.5).[8] Thus, the machine functionalist, to take a simple example, need not (and should not) ignore the potent effects of passive dynamics (sec. 1.1) on the requirements for a control system supporting powered goal-driven locomotion. For the presence of rich passive dynamics reconfigures the problem space to enable biological organisms to produce and control locomotion in amazingly efficient ways. Moreover, and in line with our earlier (sec. 1.9) discussion of dynamics and soft computationalism, we should not be misled into thinking that the kinds of operation and encoding at stake must be restricted to the familiar (digital, discrete, typically local, often temporally impoverished) suite of possibilities explored by classical artificial intelligence. Instead, as we have seen repeatedly in previous chapters, human intelligent performance may be best understood by approaches that recognize the role of analog elements that change continuously in time or that exploit continuous state; of coupled unfoldings that crisscross brain, body, and world; of motor-loop-involving self-stimulating routines; and of the active self-structuring of the flow of information.[9]

Thus, consider once again Ballard's claim (sec. 1.3 and 1.4) that the brain creates its programs so as to minimize the amount of working memory that is required and that eye motions are recruited for just-in-time retrieval of information from the environment. Ballard et al. (1997) were able to systematically alter the particular mixes of biological memory and active, embodied retrieval recruited to solve different versions of the problem, concluding that, in this kind of task at least, "eye movements, head movements, and memory load trade off against each other in a flexible way" (732). The Ballard et al. work is, as noted earlier in the text, an example of the kind of approach that we dubbed (sec. 1.4 and 4.5) distributed functional decomposition. Such an approach analyzes a cognitive task as a sequence of less intelligent sub-tasks (in this case, using recognizable computational and information–processing concepts), but it does so relative to a larger (not merely neural) organizational whole. Such approaches recognize the profound contributions that embodiment and environmental embedding make to the solution of the problem and display those contributions clearly and distinctly. They do this by identifying the information-processing role of specific (both gross bodily and neural) operations in our perfor-mance of the task. Bodily actions and worldly encodings and transfor-mations might thus emerge as among the means by which certain key operations are implemented. In this way, bodily and worldly elements emerge as genuine parts of extended problem-solving regimes apt for formal description in either (or both) dynamical and information-processing terms.

Or to take one final example, recall the discussion of bodily ges-ture in chapter 6. Our suggestion, following work by McNeill, Goldin-Meadow, and others, was that actual spatially extended physical gestures sometimes act as cognitive elements in their own right so that speech, gesture, and neural activity unite to form a single integrated cognitive system. If that were indeed the case, then, for a being like us, the body might thus provide for a kind of cognitive functionality that neural unfoldings alone do not typically support. But viewed from a greater distance, this merely represents one way of implementing a much more abstract routine whose essence was seen to lie in the pro-ductive tension between two forms of loosely coupled encoding: one visuospatial (and here involving self-stimulating loops via embodied action) and the other verbal. The increasingly popular image of func-tional, computational, and information-processing approaches to mind as flesh-eating demons is thus subtly misplaced. For rather than *neces-sarily* ignoring the body, such approaches may instead help target larger organizational wholes in ways that help reveal where, why, how, and even how much (see sec. 9.8) embodiment and environmental embed-ding really matter for the construction of mind and experience.[10]

9.4   Ada, Adder, and Odder

We are now in a position to reconsider Shapiro's (2004) opposition (mounted, recall, in the name of embodied cognition) to the idea that "the same kind of mind can exist in bodies with very distinct properties"

(175). On the basis of the kinds of evidence described in section 9.3, Shapiro rejects the idea that "snakelike organisms and creatures of science fiction" (174) might share our kind of mind. If the theorists of embodied cognition are correct, Shapiro suggests, body neutrality—the idea that "characteristics of bodies make no difference to the kind of mind one possesses" (175)—is false.

It should now be clear that something has gone by rather too swiftly. For imagine now a case in which we have two intelligent beings. One of them is a snakelike creature lying on top of an advanced touch-screenlike environment. In this flat-screen setting, every little wriggle of the snake can cause specific external symbolic tokens to appear elsewhere on the screen—tokens that are themselves apt for perceptual uptake (perhaps via a kind of Braille). The snake being (call it Adder) uses this setup, let us suppose, to carry out the same complex accounting as the standard, pen-and-paper accountant Ada, whom we met in section 4.5. As far as the distributed functional decomposition (DFD) story goes, there is no reason to suppose (from anything we have said so far) that the accounting-relevant states of Ada and Adder need differ in any respect. Each implements the same extended computational process. They even, we may suppose, divide the biological and nonbiological contributions in the same way, making use of external storage and notations at exactly the same points in their distributed problem-solving routines.

More radically, however, we may next imagine a case where there are differences at the level of what gets done where. Enter Odder. Odder performs certain computations internally that Ada and Adder both perform using action and perception routines in the nonbiological arena. Here, too, the DFD theorist is at liberty to assert that the very same cognitive routines are being implemented, with nothing distinguishing the cases apart from some nonessential matters of location. Just as, on a standard internalist model, we need not care exactly where *within* the brain a given operation is performed, so, too (it might now be urged), we should not care whether, in some extended computational process, a certain operation or encoding occurs inside or outside some particular membrane or metabolic boundary. (Such was, of course, the intended moral of the original Otto thought experiment.)

DFD-style work in embodied, embedded cognition thus lends no support to the idea that minds like ours require bodies like ours, even though it insists that bodily and worldly operations can be active and crucial participants in extended information-processing routines. What matters, the DFD theorist insists, is just the full suite of encodings and operations made available by the some combination of neural, gross bodily, and worldly opportunities. Creatures with radically different bodies, brains, and worlds from us might thus contrive to use their varying resources to implement many of the very same cognitive and information-processing routines.

9.5   A Tension Revealed

All this reveals a tension at the heart of the program that is sometimes so easily (so unitarily) glossed as the study of "embodied, embedded cognition." It is the tension between seeing body (and world) as expanding the palate of opportunities for the realization of cognitive processes and mental states and something more fundamentally—but I fear mysteriously—fleshy: the idea that embodiment vastly restricts the space of "minds like ours," tying human thought and reason inextricably and nontrivially to the details of human bodily form.[11] It is nontrivial in that, of course, the encountered (seen, touched) shape and propioceptively sensed unfolding activity of the body will be part of what is given in conscious experience and is thus apt to impact and inform our self-image and attitudes in many well-understood ways. To that extent, the details of specific forms of embodiment clearly *make* a difference. The question is, must all differences in bodily form make differences that go beyond these direct and, as it were, instrumental effects?

Thus, consider Shapiro's observation that

> the instructions by which the human brain computes relative depth do not work in creatures with eye configurations other than those in a human being. This is the sense in which depth perception is embodied. The procedures by which human beings perceive depth—a fact about human psychology—are contingent on a fact about human bodies. (2004, 188)

Recall that from facts such as these, Shapiro (2004) concludes that "human vision needs a human body" (189). Such a claim is, however, importantly ambiguous. It might mean only that the brain's algorithms factor in the bodily structures and opportunities. This is surely correct and, as we saw, fully compatible with platform-flexible forms of distributed functional decomposition. Or it might mean that being able to make the kinds of gross visual discrimination that we can make *requires* having exactly the same kind of body (in respect of eye configuration at least) as we do.[12] But this claim is surely false because an alternative distribution of the very same information-processing steps, in some differently brained and differently bodied being, would be capable of implementing that same algorithm.[13] Or finally, it might mean that any such alternative implementation need not preserve the qualitative feel of human depth perception—a qualitative feel that is somehow tied, and nontrivially tied, not to the abstract algorithm but to the use of two gross physical eyes of such-and-such shape and character located a certain distance apart.

The wild card in this debate is thus our old friend phenomenal experience itself. Might the body be making some special kind of contribution, one that cannot help but impact (in nontrivial ways) certain qualitative aspects of our mental life? This is probably the best way to understand Noë's previously quoted assertion that "the character of our experience depends on...idiosyncratic aspects of our sensory implementation" (2004, 26). If you think that the sensory implementation plays a unique (suprafunctional) role that contributes directly and nontrivially to experiential content, you are at liberty to think that every difference in implementation makes a real (though perhaps vanishingly small) difference to the felt nature of the experience itself.[14]

It is by no means obvious, however, that we should endorse, even where conscious experience is concerned, any such full and principled sensitivity to the fine details of a being's embodiment and/or sensory apparatus. From a mechanistic standpoint, it seems compelling that two beings could be very different in respect of gross sensory apparatus and embodiment and yet, courtesy perhaps of compensatory differences in key aspects of downstream processing, end up realizing the same set of experience-determining operations and state transitions. Noë (2004; see also O'Regan and Noë 2001) seem to leave no room for this even as a bare possibility. Recall from chapter 8 that Noë is explicit that "to see *as we do*, you must...have a sensory organ and a body like ours" (Noë 2004, 112, emphasis in original).[15]

Perhaps this is right, and experience *is* nontrivially permeated by the full details of biological embodiment. My own view, as defended in chapter 8, is that this is most unlikely to be true. By simply *identifying* the contents of experience with implicit knowledge of the full suite of contingencies defined at the sensorimotor surfaces, this kind of strong sensorimotor account leaves no room for compensatory downstream adjustments to yield identical experiences despite surface dissimilarities.[16] Nor does it leave room for small differences at the sensorimotor surfaces to be such as to make no experiential difference, courtesy of failing to deliver any *salient* differences in signals to downstream processors. Perhaps, that is to say, downstream processing provides a kind of grid relative to which certain differences at the level of the sensory inputs (and associated contingencies) simply fail to *make* a difference.

A related worry threatens at least the strongest versions of Lakoff and Johnson's claims concerning the tight links between forms of embodiment and basic conceptual repertoires. For what embodied experience actually delivers as the baseline for learning and metaphorical thought surely depends on some complex mixture of bodily form, environmental structure, and (possibly innate) downstream internal processing. Here, too, compensatory adjustments in either of the two nonbodily arenas look likely to make available forms of thought and reason that are not tethered in any simple way to the gross bodily bedrock.

For these general reasons, I think it would be unwise to rest content with any account according to which conscious perceptual experience is nontrivially tied to the fine details of specific bodily form. But perhaps we can nonetheless understand the body as playing a distinctive functional and/or computational role: one that impacts both conscious and nonconscious cognitive strategies and that explains why the body *matters* without making the body matter mysteriously. It is to this option that I now turn.

9.6 What Bodies Are

Over the previous eight chapters, we have seen that for many problems there is an elegant, often computationally and representationally low-cost, solution that makes the most of gross physical properties of the bodily platform and local situation. For example, consider the concrete details of sensor placement. A system with a certain spatial distribution of sensors for heat or light will not need to deploy multiple steps of inference to determine whether certain ecologically salient signature patterns of heat or light are present or absent. Moreover, the fixed relations between bodily mounted sensors obviate the need to constantly determine how input at point X relates to input at point Y. Such relations may be either constant (as between two fixed eyes) or else vary systematically (where X and Y are independently controllable or movable, as in the case of the left and right index fingers). In either case, the gross properties of the body keep the sensory inputs in a certain kind of alignment, and this can be simply assumed (rather than explicitly represented) by algorithms that use the sensory inputs as sources of problem-solving information.

The body is also the point at which willed action, if successful, first impacts the wider world. This sounds trivial, but it is actually profoundly important. When conjoined to the observation that, in the typical human case, these points of willed action include all our voluntary sensor movements, it yields the intuitive understanding of the body as the common and persisting locus of sensing and action.[17] Extensive work on the technologies of telepresence (for a review, see Clark 2003, chap. 4) suggests that the human sense of presence, of being at a certain place in space, is fully determined by our ability to enter into closed-loop interactions, in which willed sensor motions yield new sensory inputs, and by our ability to act upon at least some of the items thus falling within sensory range.

Finally, the body, by being the immediate locus of willed action, is also the gateway to intelligent offloading. The body, as we saw in earlier chapters, is the primary tool enabling the intelligent use of environmental structure. It acts as the mobile bridge that allows us to exploit the external world in ways that simplify and transform internal problem solving. The body is thus the go-between that links these two different (internal and external) sets of key information-processing resources. Hence, the body's role in such cases is that of a bridging instrument enabling the repeated emergence of new kinds of distributed information-processing organization. This role may, without too much exaggeration, be likened to that of the corpus callosum. Both are key physical structures whose cognitive role is in part to allow distinct sets of resources to engage in highly integrated forms of problem-solving activity.

At this point, it may seem as if the body is, just as it happens, the locus of willed action, the point of sensorimotor confluence, the gateway to intelligent offloading, and the stable (though not permanently fixed) platform whose features and relations can be relied upon (without being represented) in the computations underlying some intelligent performances. But I am inclined to go further and to assert not just that this is what the body *does* but that this (or something quite like it) is what, at least for all cognitive scientific purposes, the body *is*. I am inclined, that is, to simply identify the body[18] with whatever plays these (and doubtless some additional[19]) roles in the genesis and organization of intelligent behavior.

9.7   Participant Machinery and Morphological Computation

A recurrent theme in previous chapters has been the ability of body and world to act as what might now be dubbed "participant machinery"—that is, to form part of the very machinery by means of which mind and cognition are physically realized and hence to form part of the local material supervenience base for various mental states and processes.

FIGURE 9.1   The XOR robot. This robot has one wheel with two actuated degrees of freedom. The motor M_1 is responsible for turning the wheel so that the robot moves forward. The motor M_2 is responsible for lifting the wheel off the ground. Each motor is controlled by a separate perceptron network, which takes as inputs A and B. M_1 is controlled by a network that computes A OR B, and M_2 by a network that computes A *and* B. Using only these controllers, the robot is able to display the XOR function in its behavior. (From Paul 2004, by permission)

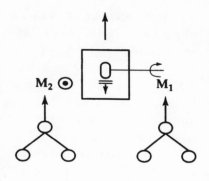

Since this has seemed to many quite an exotic claim (witness the lively debates presented in chap. 5–7), it may be worth adding one final, and just about maximally simple, illustration—one that simultaneously supports the picture (sec. 9.5) of suites of cognitively critical operations that may be realized by varying admixtures of gross bodily and neural processing.

Chandana Paul (2004, 2006) describes a toy example designed to demonstrate "that a robot body can be used for computation in addition to merely acting as an effector for the controller." The backdrop to the demonstration involves a very simple class of neural networks known as perceptrons (Rosenblatt 1962). It is well known that a perceptron, if given two inputs, A and B, can compute OR and AND functions (in fact, all linearly separable functions) but not linearly inseparable ones such as exclusive OR. Exclusive OR, normally written XOR, is true if either *but not both* disjuncts are true.

Paul's demonstration involves a simple "vehicle" of the kind made famous by Braitenberg (1984) whose behavior is determined by the activity of two perceptrons (see fig. 9.1). Perceptron 1 computes OR and controls M_1, a forward drive delivered to the single central front wheel of a front-wheel-drive vehicle. This means that power is delivered to the single central front wheel if either or both inputs are active (it is thus computing the standard inclusive OR function). Perceptron 2 computes the standard AND function and controls M_2, a lifting device that will raise the single front wheel of the forward drive vehicle off the ground if and only if both inputs are active.

TABLE 9.1   Behavioral profile of the XOR robot.

A	B	Behavior
F	F	stationary
F	T	moving
T	F	moving
T	T	stationary

Source: From Paul 2004, by permission.

You can probably see where this is going. When A and B are both reading OFF (zero, false), both nets output zero, the wheel is on the ground, but no power is delivered so the robot stays stationary. When only A is ON, the AND net delivers zero, the wheel stays grounded, and the OR net outputs a one. The wheel turns and the robot goes forward. The same type of scenario occurs when only B is ON. But (and this is the crucial case) when A and B are both ON, the OR net causes M1 to move but the AND net lifts the wheel from the ground so the robot stays stationary. The embodied system's response profile to the different possible values of the A and B inputs thus has the form of the standard XOR truth table *despite* the fact that the computational controllers are perceptrons, congenitally unable to compute nonlinearly separable functions such as XOR. Lifting the front wheel in response to the conjunction of the two inputs now stands in for the "missing line" of the XOR truth table. In this way, the physical vehicle, despite having only perceptrons for controllers, is able to behave exactly as if it were controlled by an XOR net. For it now behaves in the way displayed in table 9.1.

The active body of the robot is providing the functional equivalent of the missing second layer of neural processing: the extra processing that would be required to solve the linearly inseparable problem of computing XOR (see fig. 9.2). The overall embodied system thus provides the missing functionality, equivalent to performing a NOT on the first input, followed by an AND. In this way, "the example shows that through its configuration a robot body can perform a quantifiable operation on its inputs" (Paul 2004, 33).

At this point, a skeptic might argue that this XOR computation is in some way unreal—more in the eye of the observer than a true resource for a reasoning robot. And there is, as things stand, some truth in this. For what the robot currently displays is what Paul nicely dubs "latent morphological computation": computation that is visibly (to us)

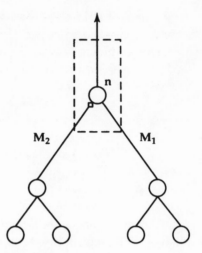

FIGURE 9.2 Computational structure
equivalent to the XOR robot. The
body of the XOR robot acts as if it is
performing a NOT on its first input
followed by an AND. (From Paul 2004,
by permission)

implicit in the response profile of the overall physical device but not
yet available *to the device itself* as a general-purpose problem-solving
resource. A simple (and as we shall see, biologically unexceptional)
tweak, however, makes the new functionality available to the device
itself. Thus, Paul next describes a "vacuum cleaning robot" (the precise
details of which need not concern us here). The vacuum cleaning robot
is like the XOR robot except that this time it is augmented with a sensor informing it of the behavioral consequences of its own action. Thus
augmented, the robot can learn (or be programmed) so as to incorporate
the body-involving XOR circuit into an open-ended set of other routines, routing various A, B signals through the body circuit and reading
the XOR result off from a rapid, self-perceived bodily twitch of the front
wheel, a twitch that need not even persist long enough to cause actual
forward motion. The body-involving XOR computation, which may
previously have appeared merely in the eye of the beholder, is now a
general-purpose resource that can be invoked much like a regular logic
gate. Quite generally, then,

> when a robot with latent morphological computation is aug-
> mented with a sensor which can sense the behavioral con-
> sequences, it makes the computational function defined by
> the morphology explicit, such that it can be used as a stan-
> dard computational sub-unit at any stage of the processing.
> (Paul 2004, 36)

It might seem that this is all just a clumsy trick: Why use the robot
body to perform a computation that would be so cheaply and easily

handled using a simple three-layer neural network? To think this, however, is to miss the point and force of the demonstration. For the idea is that evolved biological intelligences, unlike the more neatly engineered solutions with which we are still most familiar as designers, are perfectly able to find and exploit unexpected forms of *multiple functionality*.[20] That is to say, they may find and exploit solutions in which a single element (e.g., a bodily routine or motion) plays many roles, some of them merely practical and others more "epistemic" in nature (see Kirsh and Maglio 1994, and the discussion in sec. 4.6). The clean division between mechanical (body) design and controller design that characterizes many humanly engineered solutions looks quite unimportant (indeed, often counterproductive) if what we seek is efficiency and maximal exploitation of resources. Paul's demonstration may be compared to Thompson, Harvey, and Husbands' (1996) and Thompson's (1998) work using genetic algorithms to evolve real electronic circuits. The evolved circuits turned out to exploit all manner of physical properties usually ignored or deliberately suppressed by human engineers (for a discussion, see Clark 2001a, chap. 5). The lesson, according to the authors, was that

> it can be expected that all of the detailed physics of the hardware will be brought to bear on the problem at hand: time delays, parasitic capacitances, cross-talk, meta-stability constraints and other low-level characteristics might all be used in generating the evolved behavior. (Thompson et al. 1996, 21)

What thus goes for the brain (the hardware chip) goes for the rest of the physical body, too. It may also be exploited, in all manner of unexpected ways, as an essential part of an information-processing organization. In real-world cases, Paul goes on to suggest, we should expect to find that the computational roles played by bodily acts are much more complex than the computation of a common binary function, perhaps involving analog functions of quite unexpected degrees of complexity. The case of gesture for thought (sec. 6.7) may be an example of just this kind, in which actual hand and arm motions look to implement encoding and processing operations that are, as McNeill suggests, holistic and analog rather than local, symbolic, and discrete.

This possibility is also underscored by recent work on the computational role of the tendon network of the fingers. Using a combination of real-world cadaveric experiments (here, experiments using fresh cadaveric hands resected at the midforearm) and computer simulations, Valero-Cuevas et al. (2007) demonstrate the existence of anatomically distributed information processing for the control of finger motions.

In particular, they show that such control is not enabled solely by the nervous system but involves complex and essential contributions from the network of linked tendons such that

> the distribution of input tensions in the tendon network itself regulates how tensions propagate to the finger joints, acting like the switching function of a logic gate that nonlinearly enables different torque production capabilities. (Valero-Cuevas et al. 2007, 1161)

The network of linked tendons is itself a kind of complex "tensegrity" (Fuller 1961; Paul, Valero-Cuevas, and Lipson 2006) structure in which rigid elements (here, bones) are joined together by an interlinked web of continuous tensile elements (here, the tendon network).[21] The nervous system and the tendon network are thus said to "work synergistically to preferentially reach different regions of torque activation" (Valero-Cuevas et al. 2007, 1164). Working together, they allow the production of a much wider range of directions and magnitudes of fingertip forces than would otherwise be possible, thus solving a problem of "versatile finger joint actuation."

We have already encountered this kind of load sharing in the work on passive-dynamic walking (sec. 1.1). But in the present case, the authors suggest, it is not just that the load is spread but that the *control function* itself is distributed across the nervous system and tendon network, such that "part of the controller is embedded in the anatomy, contrary to current thinking that attributes the control of human anatomy exclusively to the nervous system" (Valero-Cuevas et al. 2007, 1165).

As I read the authors, this is because the structure of the tendon network itself modifies, in a complex and systematic manner, what they describe (1165) as the *interpretation* of signals delivered by the nervous system. It does this by acting like a kind of logic gate performing a nonlinear switching function affecting the way that tensions propagate to the finger joints. The way the tensions propagate is thus transformed in a manner that significantly expands the space of possible joint actuation patterns (compared to the simple case where each tendon path connects a muscle to a single bone). Such a function, *were it performed by the nervous system itself*, would surely be counted as part of the evolved control apparatus. By a kind of internal extension (!) of the Parity Principle (sec. 4.8) then, it seems that we should indeed count this contribution of the tendon network as a contribution to the control function itself (for discussion, see Valero-Cuevas et al. 2007, 1165–1166).[22]

Returning to Paul's robotic demonstration, we may now appreciate that, simple though it is, it also helps reveal deep links between the bedrock notion of a trade-off between morphology and control (sec. 1.1), the superficially more exotic notion of epistemic actions (sec. 4.6), and the superficially even more exotic notion of the extended mind (sec. 4.8). For once we start to question our received visions of the normal division of labor among brain, body, and world, it becomes clear that there is no barrier to the realization of cognition and control supporting organizations by very complex admixtures of neural, bodily, and environmental elements.

Paul's robot also provides one last example of the power of cognitive self-stimulation (sec. 6.9). For the step from latent to explicit morphological computation depends essentially on the agent's ability to sense its own bodily states. As embodied agents replete both with systems for efferent copy and for sensing what our own bodies are doing, we are ideally placed to profit from our own bodily actions and to exploit our own bodily acts for cognitive and computational ends. Daily embodied activity may thus be playing many subtle, yet-to-be-understood cognitive roles. To take just one concrete example, there is a growing body of work on the possible role of eye movements in thought, reason, discourse comprehension, and recall (for a useful review, see Spivey, Richardson, and Fitneva et al. in press). Studies include Ballard et al.'s work on deictic (fixation-based) pointers in block copying (sec. 1.3), Richardson and Spivey's (2000) account of the cognitive role of eye movements in recall, Richardson and Kirkham's (2004) exploration of the role of eye movements in six month olds as spatially indexing auditory information, and Richardson and Dale's (2004) model of the role of coupling between speaker and listener's eye movements in discourse comprehension.

9.8   Quantifying Embodiment

I'd like to end by bravely (if briefly) broaching a topic whose very label causes raised eyebrows among some of the more radical friends of embodied cognition The topic is quantifying embodiment—that is, measuring exactly *how much* difference embodiment makes with regard to some behavior, capacity, or ability.

At first blush, the question sounds peculiar. What can it mean to quantify the effects of embodiment? Relative to *what* might we measure them? The question sounds less peculiar, though, once we begin to view embodiment through a broadly speaking information-theoretic lens—that is to say, once we attempt to understand the cognitive roles of body, action,[23] and environment by understanding their roles in the elicitation, storage, transformation, and processing of information and in securing its poise for use in the control of intelligent action. It is, in fact, quite a small step from viewing body, world, and action as elements in extended dynamical-computational routines to attempts at quantification. As early as 1995, we read that

> it is necessary to understand the way various external actions fit into an overall strategy of computation. This requires identifying mental functions served by external actions and changes, and enumerating the resources saved in specific cognitive components such as visual memory, articulatory loop, attention, and perceptual control. (Kirsh 1995a, 31)

In the same paper, Kirsh measured the performance benefits gained by the "cognitive use" (as he put it) of hands, fingers, and surrounding material objects in a variety of tasks. More recently, Maglio, Wenger, and Copeland (2003, and sec. 4.6) plotted the increase in the value of the so-called hazard function that results from information self-structuring during expert Tetris play. (The hazard function, recall, is the instantaneous probability of completing a process in the next move and serves as a rough measure of information-processing payoff.) We have also already encountered Gray and Fu's (2004, and sec. 6.5) attempts to measure the information-theoretic costs and savings achieved by various mixes of neural processing and embodied action using time taken as a rough measure of effort.

Such attempts at quantifying the benefits of embodiment and action remain in their infancy. But there is cause for optimism. Lungarella et al. (2005) describe a variety of methods for quantifying increases in the information present in raw sensory experience as a result of coordinated sensorimotor activity (information self-structuring, as described in sec. 1.6). The experimental setup involved a robot able to deploy active vision (in the form of a robot-controlled camera) so as to detect informational structure in a video data stream. The study investigated the extent to which the ability to produce self-generated motor activity (activity that actively structures the sensory input that guides the ongoing motor activity itself) increases the information structures present in the sensory signals used to guide learning and response. The results were unambiguous. The presence of coordinated self-generated motor activity (when compared to a control condition) resulted in a suite of measurable differences in the information structure implicit in the sensory array. For example, there were measurable increases in

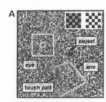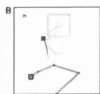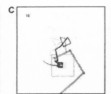

FIGURE 9.3   Creature and environment. (A) Sample frame showing color distribution in environment, object, eye including fovea, and arm with touchpad. Insert at top right shows visual (left) and tactile features (right) of the object. (B) Sample frame (color environment omitted) showing behavior before evolutionary selection (random genomes). (C) Sample frames showing behavior after evolutionary selection for complexity of sensory information (cost function Cplx). (From Sporns and Lungarella 2006, by permission)

mutual information (the statistical dependence of one variable in the simple experiment and the state of an individual pixel in the visual array on another), in integration (the total amount of statistical dependence among the variables, hence the degree to which they share information), and in complexity (the degree to which elements manage to be specialized, reporting statistically independent events, while also sharing information).[24] Such increases in the information structure present in the sensory signal provide, the authors argue, a clear functional rationale for the evolution and use of coordinated sensorimotor behavior as a means of actively structuring our own sensory experience.

In a neat inversion, these informational measures can also be used to drive the evolution of artificial agents. By using the measures as part of a fitness function, Sporns and Lungarella (2006) were able to investigate the morphologies and behaviors that result from direct pressure to maximize the information structure in the sensory signal. The idea was tested in simulation using a simple creature and environment (see fig. 9.3). The creature was provided with vision and touch in the form of an eye (a 25-by-25 pixel moving window with a 5-by-5 pixel central fovea) that could sweep the environment and an arm-hand/touchpad appendage that could also move across the environment. The environment itself was just a 100-by-100 pixel area where each pixel and each time step displayed a randomly generated color (either red, green, or blue). Across this little world, a single-colored object (5 by 5 pixels) moved at a constant speed in a random path. The object, unlike the rest of the environment, had tactile features, too (either ridges or knobs). When the touchpad encounters the object, the object stops, thus allowing the pad to sweep the surface to detect tactile properties. Once touch is broken,

TABLE 9.2   Behavioral (B), information-theoretical (I), and control (C) cost functions.

Cost Function		Description
B	*foveation*	Maximizing time for which distance between eye and object is less than 2.5 pixels
	touch	Maximizing time for which object is touched
	fovtouch	Conjunction of *foveation* and *touch*
	maxred	Maximizing color red in the fovea
I	*negH*	Minimizing entropy
	MI	Maximizing mutual information
	Intg	Maximizing integration
	Cplx	Maximizing complexity
C	*H*	Maximizing entropy
	negCplx	Minimizing complexity

Source: From Sporns and Lungarella 2006, by permission.

the object resumes its random walk. Controlling the simple body was a neural system appraised of the visual and tactile inputs and provided with an attention system involving the use of a salience map to drive eye and arm activity. Using a mixture of behavioral and information-theoretic cost functions (see table 9.2), Sporns and Lungarella were able to evolve agents capable of coordinated visuomotor action. Before evolution, the accidental touch of the target object did not yield foveation, tracking, or prolonged object "capture." After evolution, arm and eye worked together to acquire and scan the objects. Maximizing specific forms of information structure was thus seen to lead to the emergence of key adaptive strategies, including visual foveation, tracking, reaching, and tactile exploration of objects. In this way, actively maximizing key parameters relating to the self-structuring of information flows helps explain the emergence of coordinated sensorimotor activity in embodied agents and provides a new design tool for evolving artificial agents able to profit from various forms of embodied intervention and, hence, information self-structuring.

9.9   The Heideggerian Theater

The contemporary tendency to speak of mind as embodied is, according to one recent writer, just "a lexical band-aid covering a 350 year old wound generated and kept suppurating by a schizoid metaphysics"

(Sheets-Johnstone 1999, 275). Where some see a band-aid, others see a panacea, finding in the appeal to embodiment and environmental embedding a sweeping radical alternative to standard forms of cognitive scientific exploration and understanding. Neither view should compel our assent. To take embodiment seriously is simply to embrace a more balanced view of our cognitive (indeed, our human) nature. We are thinking beings whose nature qua thinking beings is not accidentally but profoundly and continuously informed by our existence as physically embodied, and as socially and technologically embedded, organisms.

To understand how this is so, where it is so, how much it is so, and just what kinds of difference it makes, we will need all the tools currently at our disposal and probably several more. We will need to combine a dynamic sensibility to the importance of action, timing, and closely coupled unfolding with, I predict, the use of a variety of more familiar tools and constructs. These will include the various computational, representational, and information-theoretic lenses that currently seem to provide our best understanding of the rich and complex space of adaptive trade-offs among neural, bodily, and environmental contributions and operations. But despite the use of some familiar and some unfamiliar tools, the object of study here is not the same as before. Our target is not just a neural control system but a complex cognitive economy spanning brain, body, and world. Within this complex economy, the body plays a crucial role. It is the organ of active sensing, the means to information self-structuring, and the enabling structure supporting a variety of extended problem-solving organizations. The body is—dare I say it?—the Heideggerian Theater: the place where it all comes together, or as together as it comes at all.

10

Conclusions: Mind as Mashup

Richard Dawkins, at the start of his classic treatment of the extended phenotype, encourages readers to try a "mental flip" (1982, 4–5). Whereas before we saw only whole organisms (albeit replete with smaller parts and themselves forming and re-forming into larger groups and wholes), we are now to imagine those bodies falling transparent so as to reveal the near-seamless play of replicating DNA. Through this special lens, the spider's web appears as a proper part of the spider's extended phenotype, and the organism emerges as no more (and no less) than an adaptively potent nonrandom concentration of DNA. This perspective, Dawkins suggests, is not compulsory nor can it be simply proved or disproved by experiment (1982, 1). Its virtues lie rather in the different ways of seeing familiar phenomena that it may breed in the flip of perspective that invites us to view the larger organism–environment system in a new and illuminating light.

Work on embodiment, action, and cognitive extension likewise invites us to view mind and cognition in a new and, I believe, illuminating manner. Such work invites us to cease to *unreflectively* privilege the inner, the biological, and the neural. This in turn should help us better understand the nature and importance of the inner, biological, and neural contributions themselves. The human mind, viewed though this special lens, emerges at the productive interface of brain, body, and social and material world.

To unravel the workings of these embodied, embedded, and sometimes extended minds requires an unusual mix of neuroscience, computational, dynamical, and information-theoretic understandings, "brute" physiology, ecological sensitivity, and attention to the stacked designer cocoons in which we grow, work, think, and act. This may seem a daunting prospect, but there is cause for optimism. In learning, development, and evolution, trade-offs among neural control, bodily morphology, action, and the canny use of environmental resources and opportunities are regularly and reliably achieved. Since such "messy" but powerful solutions are reliably found, there is a good chance that they can be systematically understood. Better still, the sciences of the mind are already well on the way to developing frameworks and forms of analysis that make headway with this difficult task. A mature science of the embodied mind will, I have tried to show, need to combine dynamical insights such as the stress on various forms of coupled organism–environment unfolding with a much better understanding of the broad space of adaptive trade-offs: an understanding currently best achieved, or so I have argued, by use of the more familiar tools provided by computational, representational, and information-theoretic approaches.

The appeal to embodiment, if this is correct, signals not a radical shift as much as a natural progression in the maturing of the sciences of the mind. It does not call into question all "machine metaphors," and it need involve no rejection of (though it is no longer exclusively committed to) accounts couched in terms of representations and computations. Confronted by the kaleidoscope of cases encountered in the previous chapters, the proper response is to see mind and intelligence themselves as mechanically realized by complex, shifting mixtures of energetic and dynamic coupling, internal and external forms of representation and computation, epistemically potent forms of bodily action, and the canny exploitation of a variety of extrabodily props, aids, and scaffolding. Minds like ours emerge from this colorful flux as surprisingly seamless wholes: adaptively potent mashups extruded from a dizzying motley of heterogeneous elements and processes. These kinds of minds are supersized only relative to some impoverished expectations. Seen aright, our mashup minds are just mindsized after all.

Appendix: The Extended Mind

Andy Clark and David Chalmers

[The authors are listed in order of degree of belief in the central thesis.]

Where does the mind stop and the rest of the world begin? The question invites two standard replies. Some accept the demarcations of skin and skull, and say that what is outside the body is outside the mind. Others are impressed by arguments suggesting that the meaning of our words "just ain't in the head," and hold that this externalism about meaning carries over into an externalism about mind. We propose to pursue a third position. We advocate a very different sort of externalism: an *active externalism*, based on the active role of the environment in driving cognitive processes.

Extended Cognition

Consider three cases of human problem solving:

(1) A person sits in front of a computer screen which displays images of various two-dimensional geometric shapes and is asked to answer questions concerning the potential fit of such shapes into depicted "sockets." To assess fit, the person must mentally rotate the shapes to align them with the sockets.

(2) A person sits in front of a similar computer screen, but this time can choose either to physically rotate the image on the screen, by pressing a rotate button, or to mentally rotate the image as before. We can also suppose, not unrealistically, that some speed advantage accrues to the physical rotation operation.

(3) Sometime in the cyberpunk future, a person sits in front of a similar computer screen. This agent, however, has the benefit of a neural implant which can perform the rotation operation as fast as the computer in the previous example. The agent must still choose which internal resource to use (the implant or the good old fashioned mental rotation), as each resource makes different demands on attention and other concurrent brain activity.

How much *cognition* is present in these cases? We suggest that all three cases are similar. Case (3) with the neural implant seems clearly to be on a par with case (1). And case (2) with the rotation button displays the same sort of computational structure as case (3), although it is distributed across agent and computer instead of internalized within the agent. If the rotation in case (3) is cognitive, by what right do we count case (2) as fundamentally different? We cannot simply point to the skin/skull boundary as justification, since the legitimacy of that boundary is precisely what is at issue. But nothing else seems different.

The kind of case just described is by no means as exotic as it may at first appear. It is not just the presence of advanced external computing resources which raises the issue, but rather the general tendency of human reasoners to lean heavily on environmental supports. Thus consider the use of pen and paper to perform long multiplication (McClelland et al. 1986, Clark 1989), the use of physical re-arrangements of letter tiles to prompt word recall in Scrabble (Kirsh 1995b), the use of instruments such as the nautical slide rule (Hutchins 1995), and the general paraphernalia of language, books, diagrams, and culture. In all these cases the individual brain performs some operations, while others are delegated to manipulations of external media. Had our brains been different, this distribution of tasks would doubtless have varied.

In fact, even the mental rotation cases described in scenarios (1) and (2) are real. The cases reflect options available to players of the computer game Tetris. In Tetris, falling geometric shapes must be rapidly directed into an appropriate slot in an emerging structure. A rotation button can be used. David Kirsh and Paul Maglio (1994) calculate that the physical rotation of a shape through 90 degrees takes about 100 milliseconds, plus about 200 milliseconds to select the button. To achieve the same result by mental rotation takes about 1000 milliseconds. Kirsh and Maglio go on to present compelling evidence that physical rotation is used not just to position a shape ready to fit a slot, but often to help *determine* whether the shape and the slot are compatible. The latter use constitutes a case of what Kirsh and Maglio call an "epistemic action." *Epistemic* actions alter the world so as to aid and augment cognitive processes such as recognition and search. Merely *pragmatic* actions, by contrast, alter the world because some physical change is desirable for its own sake (e.g., putting cement into a hole in a dam).

Epistemic action, we suggest, demands spread of *epistemic credit*. If, as we confront some task, a part of the world functions as a process which, *were it done in the head*, we would have no hesitation in recognizing as part of the cognitive process, then that part of the world *is* (so we claim) part of the cognitive process. Cognitive processes ain't (all) in the head!

Active Externalism

In these cases, the human organism is linked with an external entity in a two-way interaction, creating a *coupled system* that can be seen as a cognitive system in its own right. All the components in the system play an active causal role, and they jointly govern behavior in the same sort of way that cognition usually does. If we remove the external component the system's behavioral competence will drop, just as it would if we removed part of its brain. Our thesis is that this sort of coupled process counts equally well as a cognitive process, whether or not it is wholly in the head.

This externalism differs greatly from standard variety advocated by Putnam (1975a, 1975b) and Burge (1979). When I believe that water is wet and my twin believes that twin water is wet, the external features responsible for the difference in our beliefs are distal and historical, at the other end of a lengthy causal chain. Features of the *present* are not relevant: if I happen to be surrounded by XYZ right now (maybe I have teleported to Twin Earth), my beliefs still concern standard water, because of my history. In these cases, the relevant external features are *passive*. Because of their distal nature, they play no role in driving the cognitive process in the here-and-now. This is reflected by the fact that the actions performed by me and my twin are physically indistinguishable, despite our external differences.

In the cases we describe, by contrast, the relevant external features are *active*, playing a crucial role in the here-and-now. Because they are coupled with the human organism, they have a direct impact on the organism and on its behavior. In these cases, the relevant parts of the world are *in the loop*, not dangling at the other end of a long causal chain. Concentrating on this sort of coupling leads us to an *active externalism*, as opposed to the passive externalism of Putnam and Burge.

Many have complained that even if Putnam and Burge are right about the externality of content, it is not clear that these external aspects play a causal or explanatory role in the generation of action. In counterfactual cases where internal structure is held constant but these external features are changed, behavior looks just the same; so internal structure seems to be doing the crucial work. We will not adjudicate that issue here, but we note that active externalism is not threatened by any such problem. The external features in a coupled system play an ineliminable role—if we retain internal structure but change the external features, behavior may change completely. The external features here are just as causally relevant as typical internal features of the brain.[1]

By embracing an active externalism, we allow a more natural explanation of all sorts of actions. One can explain my choice of words in Scrabble, for example, as the outcome of an extended cognitive process involving the rearrangement of tiles on my tray. Of course, one could always try to explain my action in terms of internal processes and a long series of "inputs" and "actions," but this explanation would be needlessly complex. If an isomorphic process were going on in the head, we would feel no urge to characterize it in this cumbersome way.[2] In a very real sense, the re-arrangement of tiles on the tray is not part of action; it is part of *thought*.

The view we advocate here is reflected by a growing body of research in cognitive science. In areas as diverse as the theory of situated cognition (Suchman 1987), studies of real-world-robotics (Beer 1989), dynamical approaches to child development (Thelen and Smith 1994), and research on the cognitive properties of collectives of agents (Hutchins 1995), cognition is often taken to be continuous with processes in the environment.[3] Thus, in seeing cognition as extended one is not merely making a terminological decision; it makes a significant difference to the methodology of scientific investigation. In effect, explanatory methods that might once have been thought appropriate only for the analysis of "inner" processes are now being adapted for the study of the outer, and there is promise that our understanding of cognition will become richer for it.

Some find this sort of externalism unpalatable. One reason may be that many identify the cognitive with the conscious, and it seems far from plausible that consciousness extends outside the head in these cases. But not every cognitive process, at least on standard usage, is a conscious process. It is widely accepted that all sorts of processes beyond the borders of consciousness play a crucial role in cognitive processing: in the retrieval of memories, linguistic processes, and skill acquisition, for example. So the mere fact that external processes are external where consciousness is internal is no reason to deny that those processes are cognitive.

More interestingly, one might argue that what keeps real cognition processes in the head is the requirement that cognitive processes be *portable*. Here, we are moved by a vision of what might be called the Naked Mind: a package of resources and operations we can always bring to bear on a cognitive task, regardless of the local environment. On this view, the trouble with coupled systems is that they are too easily *decoupled*. The true cognitive processes are those that lie at the constant core of the system; anything else is an add-on extra.

There is something to this objection. The brain (or brain and body) comprises a package of basic, portable, cognitive resources that is of interest in its own right. These resources may incorporate bodily actions into cognitive processes, as when we use our fingers as working memory in a tricky calculation, but they will not encompass the more contingent aspects of our external environment, such as a pocket calculator. Still, mere contingency of coupling does not rule out cognitive status. In the distant future we may be able to plug various modules into our brain to help us out: a module for extra short-term memory when we need it, for example. When a module is plugged in, the processes involving it are just as cognitive as if they had been there all along.[4]

Even if one were to make the portability criterion pivotal, active externalism would not be undermined. Counting on our fingers has already been let in the door, for example, and it is easy to push things further. Think of the old image of the engineer with a slide rule hanging from his belt wherever he goes. What if people always carried a pocket calculator, or had them implanted? The real moral of the portability intuition is that for coupled systems to be relevant to the core of cognition, *reliable* coupling is required. It happens that mostreliable coupling takes place within the brain, but there can easily be reliable coupling with the environment as well. If the resources of my calculator or my Filofax are always there when I need them, then they are coupled with me as reliably as we need. In effect, they are part of the basic package of cognitive resources that I bring to bear on the everyday world. These systems cannot be impugned simply on the basis of the danger of discrete damage, loss, or malfunction, or because of any occasional decoupling: the biological brain is in similar danger, and occasionally loses capacities temporarily in episodes of sleep, intoxication, and emotion. If the relevant capacities are generally there when they are required, this is coupling enough.

Moreover, it may be that the biological brain has in fact evolved and matured in ways which factor in the reliable presence of a manipulable external environment. It certainly seems that evolution has favored on-board capacities which are especially geared to parasitizing the local environment so as to reduce memory load, and even to transform the nature of the computational problems themselves. Our visual systems have evolved to rely on their environment in various ways: they exploit contingent facts about the structure of natural scenes (e.g., Ullman and Richards 1984), for example, and they take advantage of the computational shortcuts afforded by bodily motion and locomotion (e.g., Blake and Yuille, 1992). Perhaps there are other cases where evolution has found it advantageous to exploit the possibility of the environment being in the cognitive loop. If so, then external coupling is part of the truly basic package of cognitive resources that we bring to bear on the world.

Language may be an example. Language appears to be a central means by which cognitive processes are extended into the world. Think of a group of people brainstorming around a table, or a philosopher who thinks best by writing, developing her ideas as she goes. It may be that language evolved, in part, to enable such extensions of our cognitive resources within actively coupled systems.

Within the lifetime of an organism, too, individual learning may have molded the brain in ways that rely on cognitive extensions that surrounded us as we learned. Language is again a central example here, as are the various physical and computational artifacts that are routinely used as cognitive extensions by children in schools and by trainees in numerous professions. In such cases the brain develops in a way that complements the external structures, and learns to play its role within a unified, densely coupled system. Once we recognize the crucial role of the environment in constraining the evolution and development of cognition, we see that extended cognition is a core cognitive process, not an add-on extra.

An analogy may be helpful. The extraordinary efficiency of the fish as a swimming device is partly due, it now seems, to an evolved capacity to couple its swimming behaviors to the pools of external kinetic energy found as swirls, eddies, and vortices in its watery environment (see Triantafyllou and Triantafyllou 1995). These vortices include both naturally occurring ones (e.g., where water hits a rock) and self-induced ones (created by well-timed tail flaps). The fish swims by building these externally occurring processes into the very heart of its locomotion routines. The fish and surrounding vortices together constitute a unified and remarkably efficient swimming machine.

Now consider a reliable feature of the human environment, such as the sea of words. This linguistic surround envelops us from birth. Under such conditions, the plastic human brain will surely come to treat such structures as a reliable resource to be factored into the shaping of on-board cognitive routines. Where the fish flaps its tail to set up the eddies and vortices it subsequently exploits, we intervene in multiple linguistic media, creating local structures and disturbances whose reliable presence drives our ongoing internal processes. Words and external symbols are thus paramount among the cognitive vortices which help constitute human thought.

From Cognition to Mind

So far we have spoken largely about "cognitive processing," and argued for its extension into the environment. Some might think that the conclusion has been bought too cheaply. Perhaps some *processing* takes place in the environment, but what of *mind*? Everything we have said so far is compatible with the view that truly mental states—experiences, beliefs, desires, emotions, and so on—are all determined by states of the brain. Perhaps what is truly mental is internal, after all?

We propose to take things a step further. While some mental states, such as experiences, may be determined internally, there are other cases in which external factors make a significant contribution. In particular, we will argue that *beliefs* can be constituted partly by features of the environment, when those features play the right sort of role in driving cognitive processes. If so, the mind extends into the world.

First, consider a normal case of belief embedded in memory. Inga hears from a friend that there is an exhibition at the Museum of Modern Art, and decides to go see it. She thinks for a moment and recalls that the museum is on 53rd Street, so she walks to 53rd Street and goes into the museum. It seems clear that Inga believes that the museum is on 53rd Street, and that she believed this even before she consulted her memory. It was not previously an *occurrent* belief, but then neither are most of our beliefs. The belief was sitting somewhere in memory, waiting to be accessed.

Now consider Otto. Otto suffers from Alzheimer's disease, and like many Alzheimer's patients, he relies on information in the environment to help structure his life. Otto carries a notebook around with him everywhere he goes. When he learns new information, he writes it down. When he needs some old information, he looks it up. For Otto, his notebook plays the role usually played by a biological memory. Today, Otto hears about the exhibition at the Museum of Modern Art, and decides to go see it. He consults the notebook, which says that the museum is on 53rd Street, so he walks to 53rd Street and goes into the museum.

Clearly, Otto walked to 53rd Street because he wanted to go to the museum and he believed the museum was on 53rd Street. And just as Inga had her belief even before she consulted her memory, it seems reasonable to say that Otto believed the museum was on 53rd Street even before consulting his notebook. For in relevant respects the cases are entirely analogous: the notebook plays for Otto the same role that memory plays for Inga. The information in the notebook functions just like the information constituting an ordinary non-occurrent belief; it just happens that this information lies beyond the skin.

The alternative is to say that Otto has no belief about the matter until he consults his notebook; at best, he believes that the museum is located at the address in the notebook. But if we follow Otto around for a while, we will see how unnatural this way of speaking is. Otto is constantly using his notebook as a matter of course. It is central to his actions in all sorts of contexts, in the way that an ordinary memory is central in an ordinary life. The same information might come up again and again, perhaps being slightly modified on occasion, before retreating into the recesses of his artificial memory. To say that the beliefs disappear when the notebook is filed away seems to miss the big picture in just the same way as saying that Inga's beliefs disappear as soon as she is no longer conscious of them. In both cases the information is reliably there when needed, available to consciousness and available to guide action, in just the way that we expect a belief to be.

Certainly, insofar as beliefs and desires are characterized by their explanatory roles, Otto's and Inga's cases seem to be on a par: the essential causal dynamics of the two cases mirror each other precisely. We are happy to explain Inga's action in terms of her occurrent desire to go to the museum and her standing belief that the museum is on 53rd Street, and we should be happy to explain Otto's action in the same way. The alternative is to explain Otto's action in terms of his occurrent desire to go to the museum, his standing belief that the museum is on the location written in the notebook, and the accessible fact that the notebook says the museum is on 53rd Street; but this complicates the explanation unnecessarily. If we must resort to explaining Otto's action this way, then we must also do so for the countless other actions in which his notebook is involved; in each of the explanations, there will be an extra term involving the notebook. We submit that to explain things this way is to take *one step too many*. It is pointlessly complex, in the same way that it would be pointlessly complex to explain Inga's actions in terms of beliefs about her memory. The notebook is a constant for Otto, in the same way that memory is a constant for Inga; to point to it in every belief/desire explanation would be redundant. In an explanation, simplicity is power.

If this is right, we can even construct the case of Twin Otto, who is just like Otto except that a while ago he mistakenly wrote in his notebook that the Museum of Modern Art was on 51st Street. Today, Twin Otto is a physical duplicate of Otto from the skin in, but his notebook differs. Consequently, Twin Otto is best characterized as believing that the museum is on 51st Street, where Otto believes it is on 53rd. In these cases, a belief is simply not in the head.

This mirrors the conclusion of Putnam and Burge, but again there are important differences. In the Putnam/Burge cases, the external features constituting differences in belief are distal and historical, so that twins in these cases produce physically indistinguishable behavior. In the cases we are describing, the relevant external features play an active role in the here-and-now, and have a direct impact on behavior. Where Otto walks to 53rd Street, Twin Otto walks to 51st. There is no question of explanatory irrelevance for this sort of external belief content; it is introduced precisely because of the central explanatory role that it plays. Like the Putnam and Burge cases, these cases involve differences in reference and truth-conditions, but they also involve differences in the dynamics of *cognition*.[5]

The moral is that when it comes to belief, there is nothing sacred about skull and skin. What makes some information count as a belief is the role it plays, and there is no reason why the relevant role can be played only from inside the body.

Some will resist this conclusion. An opponent might put her foot down and insist that as she uses the term "belief," or perhaps even according to standard usage, Otto simply does not qualify as believing that the museum is on 53rd Street. We do not intend to debate what is standard usage; our broader point is that the notion of belief *ought* to be used so that Otto qualifies as having the belief in question. In all *important* respects, Otto's case is similar to a standard case of (non-occurrent) belief. The differences between Otto's case and Inga's are striking, but they are superficial. By using the "belief" notion in a wider way, it picks out something more akin to a natural kind. The notion becomes deeper and more unified, and is more useful in explanation.

To provide substantial resistance, an opponent has to show that Otto's and Inga's cases differ in some important and relevant respect. But in what deep respect are the cases different? To make the case *solely* on the grounds that information is in the head in one case but not in the other would be to beg the question. If this difference is relevant to a difference in belief, it is surely not *primitively* relevant. To justify the different treatment, we must find some more basic underlying difference between the two.

It might be suggested that the cases are relevantly different in that Inga has more *reliable* access to the information. After all, someone might take away Otto's notebook at any time, but Inga's memory is safer. It is not implausible that constancy is relevant: indeed, the fact that Otto always uses his notebook played some role in our justifying its cognitive status. If Otto were consulting a guidebook as a one-off, we would be much less likely to ascribe him a standing belief. But in the original case, Otto's access to the notebook is very reliable—not perfectly reliable, to be sure, but then neither is Inga's access to her memory. A surgeon might tamper with her brain, or more mundanely, she might have too much to drink. The mere possibility of such tampering is not enough to deny her the belief.

One might worry that Otto's access to his notebook *in fact* comes and goes. He showers without the notebook, for example, and he cannot read it when it is dark. Surely his belief cannot come and go so easily? We could get around this problem by redescribing the situation, but in any case an occasional temporary disconnection does not threaten our claim. After all, when Inga is asleep, or when she is intoxicated, we do not say that her belief disappears. What really counts is that the information is easily available when the subject needs it, and this constraint is satisfied equally in the two cases. If Otto's notebook were often unavailable to him at times when the information in it would be useful, there might be a problem, as the information would not be able to play the action-guiding role that is central to belief; but if it is easily available in most relevant situations, the belief is not endangered.

Perhaps a difference is that Inga has *better* access to the information than Otto does? Inga's "central" processes and her memory probably have a relatively high-bandwidth link between them, compared to the low-grade connection between Otto and his notebook. But this alone does not make a difference between believing and not believing. Consider Inga's museum-going friend Lucy, whose biological memory has only a low-grade link to her central systems, due to nonstandard biology or past misadventures. Processing in Lucy's case might be less efficient, but as long as the relevant information is accessible, Lucy clearly believes that the museum is on 53rd Street. If the connection was too indirect—if Lucy had to struggle hard to retrieve the information with mixed results, or a psychotherapist's aid were needed—we might become more reluctant to ascribe the belief, but such cases are well beyond Otto's situation, in which the information is easily accessible.

Another suggestion could be that Otto has access to the relevant information only by *perception*, whereas Inga has more direct access—by introspection, perhaps. In some ways, however, to put things this way is to beg the question. After all, we are in effect advocating a point of view on which Otto's internal processes and his notebook constitute a single cognitive system. From the standpoint of this system, the flow of information between notebook and brain is not perceptual at all; it does not involve the impact of something outside the system. It is more akin to information flow within the brain. The only deep way in which the access is perceptual is that in Otto's case, there is a distinctly perceptual phenomenology associated with the retrieval of the information, whereas in Inga's case there is not. But why should the nature of an associated phenomenology make a difference to the status of a belief? Inga's memory may have some associated phenomenology, but it is still a belief. The phenomenology is not visual, to be sure. But for visual phenomenology consider the Terminator, from the Arnold Schwarzenegger movie of the same name. When he recalls some information from memory, it is "displayed" before him in his visual field (presumably he is conscious of it, as there are frequent shots depicting his point of view). The fact that standing memories are recalled in this unusual way surely makes little difference to their status as standing beliefs.

These various small differences between Otto's and Inga's cases are all *shallow* differences. To focus on them would be to miss the way in which for Otto, notebook entries play just the sort of role that beliefs play in guiding most people's lives.

Perhaps the intuition that Otto's is not a true belief comes from a residual feeling that the only true beliefs are occurrent beliefs. If we take this feeling seriously, Inga's belief will be ruled out too, as will many beliefs that we attribute in everyday life. This would be an extreme view, but it may be the most consistent way to deny Otto's belief. Upon even a slightly less extreme view—the view that a belief must be *available* for consciousness, for example—Otto's notebook entry seems to qualify just as well as Inga's memory. Once dispositional beliefs are let in the door, it is difficult to resist the conclusion that Otto's notebook has all the relevant dispositions.

Beyond the Outer Limits

If the thesis is accepted, how far should we go? All sorts of puzzle cases spring to mind. What of the amnesic villagers in *One Hundred Years of Solitude*, who forget the names for everything and so hang labels everywhere? Does the information in my Filofax count as part of my memory? If Otto's notebook has been tampered with, does he believe the newly-installed information? Do I believe the contents of the page in front of me before I read it? Is my cognitive state somehow spread across the Internet?

We do not think that there are categorical answers to all of these questions, and we will not give them. But to help understand what is involved in ascriptions of extended belief, we can at least examine the features of our central case that make the notion so clearly applicable there. First, the notebook is a constant in Otto's life—in cases where the information in the notebook would be relevant, he will rarely take action without consulting it. Second, the information in the notebook is directly available without difficulty. Third, upon retrieving information from the notebook he automatically endorses it. Fourth, the information in the notebook has been consciously endorsed at some point in the past, and indeed is there as a consequence of this endorsement.[6] The status of the fourth feature as a criterion for belief is arguable (perhaps one can acquire beliefs through subliminal perception, or through memory tampering?), but the first three features certainly play a crucial role.

Insofar as increasingly exotic puzzle cases lack these features, the applicability of the notion of "belief" gradually falls off. If I rarely take relevant action without consulting my Filofax, for example, its status within my cognitive system will resemble that of the notebook in Otto's. But if I often act without consultation—for example, if I sometimes answer relevant questions with "I don't know"—then information in it counts less clearly as part of my belief system. The Internet is likely to fail on multiple counts, unless I am unusually computer-reliant, facile with the technology, and trusting, but information in certain files on my computer may qualify. In intermediate cases, the question of whether a belief is present may be indeterminate, or the answer may depend on the varying standards that are at play in various contexts in which the question might be asked. But any indeterminacy here does not mean that in the central cases, the answer is not clear.

What about socially extended cognition? Could my mental states be partly constituted by the states of other thinkers? We see no reason why not, in principle. In an unusually interdependent couple, it is entirely possible that one partner's beliefs will play the same sort of role for the other as the notebook plays for Otto.[7] What is central is a high degree of trust, reliance, and accessibility. In other social relationships these criteria may not be so clearly fulfilled, but they might nevertheless be fulfilled in specific domains. For example, the waiter at my favorite restaurant might act as a repository of my beliefs about my favorite meals (this might even be construed as a case of extended desire). In other cases, one's beliefs might be embodied in one's secretary, one's accountant, or one's collaborator.[8]

In each of these cases, the major burden of the coupling between agents is carried by language. Without language, we might be much more akin to discrete Cartesian "inner" minds, in which high-level cognition relies largely on internal resources. But the advent of language has allowed us to spread this burden into the world. Language, thus construed, is not a mirror of our inner states but a complement to them. It serves as a tool whose role is to extend cognition in ways that on-board devices cannot. Indeed, it may be that the intellectual explosion in recent evolutionary time is due as much to this linguistically-enabled extension of cognition as to any independent development in our inner cognitive resources.

What, finally, of the self? Does the extended mind imply an extended self? It seems so. Most of us already accept that the self outstrips the boundaries of consciousness; my dispositional beliefs, for example, constitute in some deep sense part of who I am. If so, then these boundaries may also fall beyond the skin. The information in Otto's notebook, for example, is a central part of his identity as a cognitive agent. What this comes to is that Otto *himself* is best regarded as an extended system, a coupling of biological organism and external resources. To consistently resist this conclusion, we would have to shrink the self into a mere bundle of occurrent states, severely threatening its deep psychological continuity. Far better to take the broader view, and see agents themselves as spread into the world.

As with any reconception of ourselves, this view will have significant consequences. There are obvious consequences for philosophical views of the mind and for the methodology of research in cognitive science, but there will also be effects in the moral and social domains. It may be, for example, that in some cases interfering with someone's environment will have the same moral significance as interfering with their person. And if the view is taken seriously, certain forms of social activity might be reconceived as less akin to communication and action, and as more akin to thought. In any case, once the hegemony of skin and skull is usurped, we may be able to see ourselves more truly as creatures of the world.

Notes

INTRODUCTION

1. This exchange was first brought to my attention by Galen Strawson.
2. I here suppress, without a moment's real hesitation, all versions of Cartesian doubt. The embodied perspective is not meant as a solution to such problems, and their discussion would rapidly take us too far afield.
3. Esther Thelen, a much-loved colleague and an inspirational thinker, died in December 2004 at the age of 63. Her work on infant development, exemplified by Thelen and Smith (1994) and Thelen et al. (2001), stands as one of the key practical and theoretical demonstrations of the value and power of the embodied approach.
4. The term *cognizing* is here used to mark a notion of the mental that is broader than the one suggested by introspection and common sense alone. Where introspection and common sense might identify mind simply as a locus of beliefs, desires, hopes, fears, and so forth, the scope of the cognitive may include states and operations unearthed by science. Examples might include grammars (if psychologically real) and the states and operations implemented by low-level vision.
5. The reference here is to Clark and Chalmers's (1998) treatment called "The Extended Mind"; see the discussion in the text. This article is reproduced in the appendix.

CHAPTER 1

1. The "specific cost of transport" is calculated as (energy used)/(weight) (distance traveled). See Collins and Ruina (2005) for the detailed energy-efficiency comparisons mentioned in the text.
2. This notion is introduced in Clark (in press-b).
3. This principle is based on, but extends, the original formulation in Pfeifer and Scheier (1999, chap. 13).
4. Thus, nontriviality is entirely in the eye of the beholder. If you expected sex determination to be controlled by the temperature of the nest, there is causal spread alright, but only of the kind already (let's presume) factored into our best science and thinking about the target event.
5. For excellent discussion, see Pfeifer and Scheier (1999), Pfeifer (2000), Pfeifer and Bongard (2007). For the possible importance of truly bedrock building materials, see Brooks (2001).
6. See, e.g., Gibson (1979), Turvey and Carello (1986), Warren (2006).
7. Wheeler (2005, chap. 9) offers an elegant and insightful treatment of these themes, tracing the many links between issues concerning causal spread, "inhabited interaction" (though he does not use this term), and various aspects of Heideggerian phenomenology.
8. The robotic "third arm" of the performance artist Stelarc is a case in point; see Clark (2003) for a discussion.
9. For the classical AI version of functional decomposition, see, e.g., Block (1990), Cummins (1989), Pylyshyn (1984). For the broader version that I have in mind, see, e.g., Clark (1997a, chap. 8) and Clark (1998b).
10. Thanks to Bill Warren for drawing this to my attention.
11. The landmark publications here are O'Regan and Noë (2001) and Noë (2004). Historically, the view has roots that span science (especially ecological psychology; see Gibson 1979) and several influential philosophical traditions (ranging from Husserl 1907, Heidegger 1927/1961, and Merleau-Ponty 1945/1962, to Ryle 1949/1990, MacKay 1967, and on to the "enactive" approach of Varela, Thompson, and Rosch 1991). It is also consistent with (but goes far beyond) the project of understanding mind and cognition in ways that are heavily "action oriented" (Clark 1997a) and that stress the importance of body, action, and the canny use of environmental structure (e.g., Hurley 1998; Ballard et al. 1997; Hutchins 1995; Churchland, Ramachandran, and Sejnowski 1994; and Thelen and Smith 1994).
12. This was especially true in the early days of dynamical approaches to cognitive science (see, e.g., Van Gelder 1995; Thelen and Smith 1994; Port and Van Gelder 1995). But the habit lingers even today. See, for example, the entry for The Embodied Cognition Research Program in the online survey article journal Philosophy Compass at http://www.blackwell/compass.com/subject/philosophy/. I return to this topic in chapter 9.
13. See Norton (1995) and Abraham and Shaw (1992) for useful introductions.
14. For further mathematical detail, see Van Gelder (1995, 356-357).

15. For the last two cases, see Goodwin (1994, 60).

16. For instance, Van Gelder's comments (1995, 358) on tasks that may only initially appear to require "that the system have knowledge of and reason about, its environment," and Thelen and Smith's (1994, xix) stress on the brain as a thermodynamic system. By contrast, the dynamicist Scott Kelso (1995, 288) sees the key problem as "how *information* is to be conceived in living things, in general, and the brain in particular."

17. Sloman and Chrisley (2003) thus develop a form of "Virtual Machine Functionalism" (VMF). In VMF, mental states, though indeed realized by functional matrixes of inputs, internal state transitions and outputs, can be simultaneous and multiple, due to potentially independently varying complexes of linked (inner and/or outer) substates. VMF thus allows "co-existing, independently varying, interacting mental states" (Sloman and Chrisley 2003, 148). These interacting "parts" may be defined at many levels of abstraction and organization; that is, they may be interactions among "virtual machines."

18. I have in mind here the so-called gating hypothesis in Van Essen and Gallant (1994).

19. Similarly, in the Yu, Ballard, and Aslin (2005) work on word learning (sec. 1.6), we saw an informationally potent combination of dynamical and computational properties—namely, the active conjuring of time-locked flows of multimodal training data, leading to the formation of "grounded" internal representations.

20. Eliasmith (2003) provides a useful, if somewhat neurocentric, account of such dynamic functional roles.

21. Rockwell (2005a; see also Rockwell 2005b, chap. 10) applies such an analysis directly so as to reconstitute (in a dynamical framework) various constructs from symbolic AI. For the most part, I envisage something weaker than this: the use of dynamical approaches to reveal facts about the flow and transformation of information, leading to a nuanced rapprochement between representational and information-theoretic perspectives, on the one hand, and time-rich dynamical analyses, on the other.

22. In other cases, it might be that the coupled activity of certain elements is itself the realizer of a single distinct kind of encoding, operation, or content (for some examples, see Clark 1998b). In such cases, entire neural, or neural-bodily, or neural-bodily-environmental loops, involving multiple components in continuous reciprocal causal exchange, may themselves be the realizers of computationally salient operations or the vehicles of specifiable contents.

23. Thanks to Michael Wheeler for many invaluable discussions of this point.

24. Such a vision implies no commitment to the existence, in biological systems, of classical symbolic entities manipulated according to explicitly encoded rules, nor to the use of digital forms of encoding. To think so is

to mistake contingent features of some contemporary *computer models* for deep features of the much broader explanatory framework in which they have sometimes figured.

CHAPTER 2

1. In fact, it is rather doubtful that these kinds of Gibsonian invariant detection involve truly high-bandwidth coupling at all. But given the extreme difficulty of finding a noncontroversial measure of objective bandwidth, I am willing to grant this for the sake of argument. My point will be that such high-bandwidth coupling, even if present, does not undermine the idea of interfaces located at just those points.
2. A typical description reads: "Computational Grids enable the sharing, selection, and aggregation of a wide variety of geographically distributed computational resources (such as supercomputers, clusters, storage systems, data sources, instruments, people) and presents them as a single, unified resource for solving large-scale and data intensive computing applications" (quote taken from the GRID computing information center at http://www.gridcomputing.com/).
3. See http://www.stelarc.va.com.au and a full discussion in Clark (2003, chap. 5).
4. It is noteworthy, especially in the light of our previous discussion, that "any expansion of the vRF only followed active, intentional use of the tool not its mere grasping by the hand" (Berti and Frassinetti 2000, 81).
5. Gallagher (1998) expresses the difference like this: "Body schema can be defined as a system of preconscious, subpersonal processes that play a dynamic role in governing posture and movement.... There is an important and often overlooked conceptual difference between the subpersonal body schema and what is usually called *body image*. The latter is most often defined as a conscious idea or mental representation that one has of one's own body." See also Gallagher (2005, 17–20).
6. For a lovely example of this, see Gray and Fu (2004). This example is discussed later in chapter 6.
7. I explore these near-future themes in Clark (2003).

CHAPTER 3

1. An example of such a display would be the projection, on demand, of green arrows marking the route to a university library onto a glasses-mounted display. The arrows would appear overlaid upon the actual local scene and would update as the agent moves.
2. This picture fits nicely with Barsalou's account of the relation between public symbols and "perceptual symbol systems." See Barsalou (2003) and, for a fuller story about perceptual symbol systems, Barsalou (1999). For an excellent discussion of these issues, and their relation to claims concerning the "extended mind" (see chapter 4 following), see Logan (2007).

3. Here, too, as John Protevi (personal communication) reminds me, the impact is not always positive. We can just as easily derail our own performance by explicit reflection on our own shortcomings.

4. Sutton explores two detailed examples, one involving batting advice for cricketers and the other concerning instructional nudges for piano playing. Concerning the latter, he writes,

> The sociologist and jazz pianist David Sudnow [2001] describes how explicit verbal phrases and maxims actually became more useful as his skills in improvised jazz piano increased...Sudnow explains his [initial] frustration at his teacher's compressed sayings, such as 'sing while you're playing,' 'go for the jazz,' 'get the time into the fingers,' or especially just 'jazz hands.' These at first make no sense, as the novice pianist is all too conscious of the embodied insecurity of his playing: but...what seemed like just vague words to the novice has now become very detailed practical talk, a shorthand compendium of 'caretaking practices' for toning and reshaping the grooved routines. (Sutton 2007)

5. These formulations are not yet precise enough. But I beg the reader's patience. Getting clear about the ways public language might reasonably be said to inform or transform thought and reason is the main topic of the chapter.

6. In partial support of this claim, notice that there is good evidence that children show attentional biases that are sensitive to the language they are learning (or have learned)—see Bowerman and Choi (2001), Lucy and Gaskins (2001), and Smith (2001). Smith (2001, 113) explicitly suggests that learned linguistic contexts come to "serve as cues that automatically control attention."

7. Gordon (2004) presents converging evidence from a tribe in Amazonia that uses only words for one, two, and many. Numerical cognition in this tribe was clearly affected, such that "performance with quantities greater than three was remarkably poor, but showed a constant coefficient of variation, which is suggestive of an analog estimation process" (496). Thanks to Keith Oatley for drawing this to my attention.

8. Those with deeper experience of numbers may come to have a richer mental representation of 98-ness, of course. But even for these agents, there will be thoughts (about other, much larger numbers perhaps) where this deeper grasp fails, and they only succeed in referring to a unique number thanks to the apparatus of the public number system itself.

9. Robert Rupert (personal communication) suggests that the Fodorian account has resources that could also explain the pattern of results we have been discussing. According to Rupert, the Fodorian need only claim that the number words of different languages, when learned by a single subject, receive different mentalese "translations" and that it is these differences in the associated mentalese terms that explain the differences in the subject's reactions and performances. Such a view, while clearly not ruled out, seems

to me less compelling than the alternative that takes shallow, imagistic inner encodings of the natural language items themselves (perhaps in the manner of Barsalou 2003 and Prinz 2004) to be playing the key cognitive role.

10. Elman cites Dave Rumelhart both for this phrasing and for the guiding conception of words as cues to meanings.

11. See Fodor (1981). Fodor energetically reaffirmed this view in a special session at the 2005 Cognitive Science Conference in Stresa, Italy. For a counterview, see Cowie (1999). For an excellent review of the territory, see Samuels (2004).

CHAPTER 4

1. For a host of other examples, see Laland et al. (2000) and Odling-Smee, Laland, and Feldman (2003). See also Dawkins (1982), Lewontin (1983), Odling-Smee (1988), and Turner (2000).

2. The idea of humans as cognitive niche constructors is familiar within cognitive science. Richard Gregory (1981) spoke of "cognition amplifiers," Don Norman (1993a, 1993b) of "things that make us smart," Kirsh and Maglio (1994) of "epistemic actions," and Daniel Dennett (1996) of "tools for thought."

3. In the paper, Tribble explicitly cites Hutchins's (1995) exploration of ship navigation as emergent from the complex interplay of artifacts and social practices as among the main inspirations for her approach.

4. The sense of constitution here in play is not, however, the strong sense of "being conceptually intertwined with" but the weaker (though still interesting and important) sense of "as it happens being part of the apparatus that implements."

5. Examples include Wilson (2004), Clark (1997a), Hurley (1998), Clark and Chalmers (1998), Dennett (1996), Donald (1991), Hutchins (1995), Menary (2007), Wheeler (2005), Sutton (2002b), and Rowlands (2006). See also Rockwell (2005b).

6. I shall focus, however, on a subclass of epistemic actions: the subclass involving "active dovetailing" via the use of multiple nested calls to the world during run-time processing.

7. The experiments used a restricted version of Tetris in which zoids are presented one at a time; see Maglio and Wenger (2000, 2002).

8. Experience is, of course, no *more* than a clue. I do not mean, here or elsewhere, to advance any arguments of the form "it seems to us as if we are/are not cognitively extended; therefore, we are/are not cognitively extended"!

9. It is true, of course, that we can feel like this about our own biological equipment, be it an injured leg or a malfunctioning biomemory. In such cases, it is rather as if we awoke to find some hard-to-use package permanently interfaced to our brain!

10. Thanks to Michael Wheeler for helping to clarify this issue.

11. Kirsh (2004) offers a complementary discussion of the many practical ways metacognition may be spread across neural and extraneural resources.

12. Donald's claim is not that *only* humans do this. Rather, it is a capacity that is present in other primates (at least) but pronounced in humankind. The differences are thus quantitative, not qualitative (see Donald 2001, 146).

13. Apart from "the extended mind," there are several other names currently on offer for the general claim that the mind and the cognitive processes that constitute it extend beyond the boundary of the skin of the individual agent. They include "locational externalism" (Wilson 2004), "environmentalism" (Rowlands 1999), and "vehicle externalism" (Hurley 1998). Similar claims are explored by John Sutton (2002a, 2002b) in his inspiring work on "porous memory." The phrase "the extended mind" was also coined, independently and at about the same time, by Robert Logan, whose work targets the links between human cognitive development, language, and culture (see Logan 2000, 2007).

14. This talk of "recruitment," though useful, needs careful handling. For it is in no way meant to suggest the deliberate gathering of resources by a thoughtful agent. That is, in fact, exactly the image we must avoid. Instead, the idea is that new problem-solving organizations emerge in conformity with some cost function (or functions) whose effect is to favor the inclusion of certain resources (be they neural, bodily, or bioexternal) and the exclusion of others. This cost function appears neutral (sec. 6.5) with regard to the location or nature of the resource except insofar as such matters make some functional difference—that is, except insofar as they are apt to impact the relative cost of one assembly over another. The question of how such functions might be computed is addressed, albeit in a rather preliminary fashion, in sections 6.5 and 9.8.

CHAPTER 5

1. These attributions are explicit but spread across the three papers by Adams and Aizawa (2001, in press-a, in press-b).

2. The need for some kind of "nontriviality clause" (to borrow a phrase from Rupert in press-b) is actually widely recognized in the literature on the extended mind. If it were not, then arguments for the extended mind could have been very short indeed! The requirement is made explicit in, for example, Wheeler and Clark (1999, 110).

3. Richard Samuels (personal communication) usefully notes that we do not encounter anything like Adams and Aizawa's demand for a "mark of the cognitive" in other scientific fields. Physicists do not worry about the mark of the physical, nor geologists about the mark of the geological. Working cognitive scientists are typically bemused by the demand for some general-purpose mark of the cognitive.

4. Thanks to Rob Wilson for the single-neuron comparison.

5. Thus, Ken Aizawa, after a long series of exchanges, asks, "So, you really agree with us that the notebook is non-cognitive?" implying that an affirmative answer must be incompatible with the Extended Mind Thesis. Yet insofar as the question is even intelligible, I would indeed concede that

the notebook, considered alone, is "non-cognitive," *just like a neuron or group of neurons.*

6. In the end, though it is not part of the present project to argue for this, empirical functionalism looks implausible as a story about the mental states themselves. For it deprives us of what was arguably the main reason to endorse a functional approach in the first place—namely, to leave room for alternative realizations of the very same mental states (see Braddon-Mitchell and Jackson 2007, chap. 5). We return to some of these issues in chapter 9.

7. Though allowing (for those states) conscious states to occur within the functional role itself.

8. This is fortunate because one of us (Clark) is tempted by such accounts, but the other (Chalmers) is not!

9. Rowlands (2006) argues that some of our world-involving bodily actions (what he calls "deeds") are best seen as vehicles of nonderived content in their own right. This means that they do not "derive their representational status from other, logically prior, representational states" (94). The representational status of certain actions, if this is correct, is not simply parasitic upon neural representations, and the vehicles of representation "do not, in general, stop at the skin" (17).

10. For some useful discussion of these kinds of issue, see Dennett's (1991b) thought experiment in which left-handed people turned out to have very different internal organizations to right-handers.

11. The most crucial features for achieving dense integration are, it seems to me (see sec. 2.6 and 3.8), fine temporal integration and subpersonal interweaving (these themes will resurface in chap. 6). For an extended treatment and defense of the notion of "cognitive integration," see Menary (2007); see also the discussion in Rowlands (1999, chap. 7). For an early statement of the integrationist perspective, see Rumelhart et al. (1986) and the discussion in Clark (1989, chap. 7).

12. It may even be (see 3.2, 3.4) that large chunks of the internal, biological processing that goes on in us humans (though not in other animals) consists in the manipulation of a variety of shallow imagistic renditions of external, public items such as tags, labels, and symbolic tokens. If this is so, then the kind of functional complementarity that (according to EXTENDED) explains the power of integrated systems of internal and external resources *also* explains much of the apparently unique power of purely *internal* human cognition. See Clark (2004, 2006).

13. In so doing, we apply to our own (extended) case the same kind of implicit grasp of the "realm of the cognitive" as we would to an alien species. In the latter case, we would not dream of insisting that only those aspects of alien processing that echo our own biological processing should count as aspects of alien cognition!

14. This worry also seems to be at work in Rupert (2004, in press-b).

15. For a useful survey, see Mundale (2001), and for more discussion, see Mundale (2002).

16. This is not quite true. Systems-level neuroscience could, for the most part, simply help itself to the idea of an individual, sufficiently unified cognizer. Extended mind theorists cannot. Instead, the incorporation of a nonbiological resource into the cognitive processing of an individual requires that certain kinds of reliable (enough) coupling between biological and nonbiological resources be present. In the absence of such reliable interpart coupling, of course, even inner biological goings-on (replete, let's assume, with all the currently available marks of the cognitive) would not count as part of the cognitive activity *of that very agent*. There could thus, in principle, be fully and permanently isolated neural events that in no way count as part and parcel of *my* cognizings. It is for this reason (as we saw earlier in sec. 5.3) that considerations of reliable coupling play a role (though not the one that Adams and Aizawa envisaged) in arguments for the extended mind.

CHAPTER 6

1. Though I do not take issue with this claim here, it is by no means obvious (see 5.9) that common sense itself is committed either to in-the-head or in-the-organism cognition. For some nice discussion, see Houghton (1997).
2. I have borrowed this locution from Rupert himself (personal communication).
3. This is obviously a loose though familiar usage. *Bodily* here means "gross bodily" (i.e., extraneural), whereas *worldly* means "extrabodily."
4. Reproduced as the appendix here.
5. For a similar point, see Rockwell (2005b, 18).
6. The notion of soft assembly is prominent in dynamical-systems influenced work in developmental psychology, where it is used to mean a temporary assembly of resources (perhaps spanning brain, body, and world) that arises in response to some opportunity or problem. See, for example, Thelen and Smith (1994, 86–88) and Clark (1997a, 42–45).
7. Related proposals include Damasio and Damasio's (1994) notion of "convergence zones," which are neuronal populations that likewise initiate and coordinate activity in multiple neuronal groups.
8. I mean the reader to take this phrase at face value. When Chairman Mao used the original "let a hundred flowers bloom, let a hundred schools of thought contend," the upshot, it seems, was not the happy flowering of heterogeneity I meant to suggest. Rather, the apparent amnesty in the summer of 1957 provided an opportunity to detect and destroy unwanted opposition that at last felt free to speak its mind.
9. The form of reasoning is thus parallel to that which led Dawkins (1982) to the notion of the web as part of the "extended phenotype" of the spider or J. Scott Turner (2000) to treat the sound amplifying ("singing") burrows of the mole cricket as external physiological organs (for more on this case, see Clark 2005b). In each case, we have a working sense of some baseline concept (phenotype, organ). We then notice that stuff that we do not ordinarily treat in those terms is playing the right kind of role to be considered as

belonging to that class. This is not about the new stuff working just like the old. There is no organ much like a burrow and no animal body much like a web. Nor does it require equal permanence: The web comes and goes in a way the spider body does not, and singing burrows, unlike inner organs, may be built, destroyed, and rebuilt in new locations.

10. Moreover, and contrary to the Rupert passage quoted at the end of section 6.2, EXTENDED offers the developmentalist no reason at all to be interested in Sally plus ball, Johnny plus book, and Terry plus stimulus. For as David Chalmers (personal communication) notes, there is no developmental path linking these together (and in any case, the tasks addressed are so radically different). What EXTENDED does suggest, however, is the potential value of looking at the development of, say, Sally's mathematical cognition under various conditions that may include the availability of fingers, abacus, calculator, and so on. To illustrate this, Chalmers suggests the following noncognitive analogy: We may study the development of Fred Astaire's dancing even though the dancing is itself instantiated, over time, by a variety of coupled systems (sometimes including Ginger Rogers, other times including Barrie Chase, etc.).

11. This is so in the case of all the nonmemory-test subjects, who had to pick up the information piecemeal during the course of the experiment.

12. Robert Rupert (personal communication) suggests that what the results actually show is a de facto bias to rely preferentially on internally stored information, since this is used even at the cost of performance errors when the access time (for the internally stored stuff) is faster. According to Rupert, interaction with the environment *typically* costs more, in terms of time, than inner store retrieval, and so there will be a de facto bias toward using the inner, even if the bias results from the application of a strictly location-neutral cost function (time to access). We can scout two points in reply. First, it is by no means obvious that the retrieval time constraint *will* systematically favor the use of the inner, as shown, for example, by recent ("second-generation") work on change blindness in which perfectly good internal representations of the altered elements can be shown to be present but simply not retrieved in response to the standard probes (see sec. 7.3). Second, all that really matters in any case is that given the strictly location-neutral cost function, inner and outer information stores are indeed on a par *as far as the recruitment process itself is concerned*. It would not affect our argument if, for example, the actual result of applying that cost function typically selected biointernal resources. For what is at issue is how to treat the cases (be they few or many) in which the upshot is instead a problem-solving assembly that criss-crosses brain, body, and world. More generally, to embrace EXTENDED is not to deny the existence of many important asymmetries in the actual nature and distribution of labor among brain, body, and world. We return to such issues in chapter 7.

13. Nothing in their story demands a single "central controller." But notice that even if there is such a controller, we would not be tempted to identify

that single inner element with the entire cognitive system of the agent at a given time for the reasons explored in section 7.8.

14. Gray and Veksler (2005, 809) depict the level playing field as populated by a set of possible "interactive routines." These are "a complex mixture of elementary cognitive, perceptual, and action operations [that] represent basic patterns of interactive behavior" and are compared to Ullman's visual routines (Hayhoe 2000; Ullman 1984).

15. Thanks to Paul Schweizer for pointing this out.

16. This talk of recruitment, as noted earlier (see ch. 4), needs careful handling. For it is in no way meant to suggest the deliberate gathering of resources by a thoughtful agent. Rather, new problem-solving organizations emerge in conformity with some cost function (or functions) whose effect is to favor the inclusion of certain resources (be they neural, bodily, or bioexternal) and the exclusion of others. This cost function appears to be neutral (sec. 6.5) with regard to the location or nature of the resource except insofar as such matters make some functional difference—that is, except insofar as they apt to impact the relative cost of one assembly over another. See also section 9.8.

17. In most real-world settings, of course, these two stages (though logically distinct) may be fully or partially temporally overlapping.

18. This is not to deny, of course, that much of the spinning is done by social groups of organisms spread out over long swaths of history.

19. One difference is that in the case of the webs of cognitive scaffolding, it is often the human organism acting in concert with existing webs of scaffolding that spins, selects, or maintains new layers of scaffolding, resulting in the powerful process that Sterelny (2004) dubs "incremental downstream epistemic engineering" (see sec. 4.4).

20. There is also some older work in which children were told to sit on their hands, thus effectively removing the gestural option without adding to the memory load!

21. Much of Goldin-Meadow (2003) is devoted to the task of attributing meaning to spontaneous free gestures. See also McNeill (1992, 2005).

22. Recall that Adams and Aizawa depict the neural as the seat of all truly cognitive activity. Rupert (wisely) prefers the whole organism. But by doing so, he puts a foot on a slippery slope. For once we allow cognitive processes to become sufficiently hybrid (allowing functional cognitive wholes to be made up of parts as heterogeneous as arm and hand motions plus neural activity), there seems no good reason to stop at the skin.

23. There is, unfortunately, substantial ambiguity in the notion of "thinking" invoked in these discussions of gesture because it can sometimes mean (a) "verbal thought," which is conceived, by Goldin-Meadow, as distinct from (though intertwined with) (b) the kinds of (holistic, imagistic) thinking specifically accomplished by gesture. Finally, there is (c) the overall cognitive state achieved by an agent who has engaged in some ongoing process

involving both gestural and verbal elements. To say that gesturing is part of the process that constitutes thinking is thus to say both that it helps mediate and inform the verbal thinkings and that in so doing it forms part of a larger integrated cognitive system.

24. The use of "thought" here is misleading (see n. 23). It reflects common usage rather than the actual model that McNeill and others develop. There is a similar ambiguity in the use of "language" because gesturing, on McNeill's account, is part of language. McNeill is aware of these infelicities but thinks the usage will do no harm; see Terminological Tango in McNeill (2005, 21).

25. A possible objection to this is that phantom limb patients sometimes report an ability to gesture with their phantom limbs (see Brugger et al. 2000; Ramachandran and Blakeslee 1998). These phantom gestures are likewise keyed to ongoing verbal discourse and problem solving. Does this show that all the real work is done by inner neural circuitry and that the actual arm and hand motions produced by ordinary speakers play no cognitive role after all? First, it is not yet known whether the phantom gesturing aids problem solving in any of the ways that Goldin-Meadow and McNeill describe. Second, even if the phantom gestures turned out to yield some degree of cognitive benefit, that would fall short of showing that the full range of such benefits was available (compare counting on your fingers to imagining so doing). The presence of gesture in the phantom cases is thus taken (see Goldin-Meadow 2003, 240–243; Gallagher 2005, 120–122; and McNeill 2005, 244–245) as just more evidence that gesturing forms an integral part of a coordinated brain–body system that has been selected for its overall cognitive virtues.

26. In the case of gesture, the relation between the self-created inputs and other processing elements also looks to involve the full complexities of continuous reciprocal causation (see sec. 1.7). In such cases, it is impossible to subsequently parcel out the contributions according to any simple model in which a self-contained reasoning agent does all the "real thinking" and then merely offloads information onto the environment for future use (as when we put a yellow sticky on the bathroom mirror to remind us of an important meeting the next day).

27. That is to say, one might endorse the idea of a central controlling locus while holding that, even internally, some states and processes outside that central locus count as among the agent's cognitive states and processes (examples might be some forms of memory and dispositional beliefs). What goes for inner states and processes must go for outer ones, too. It is thus open to even the staunchest fan of central control to endorse EXTENDED.

28. This description is nicely supported by recent results showing that thinking to ourselves in words correlates with increased activity in brain areas ordinarily involved in the production of overt speech and in brain areas ordinarily involved in the processing of auditory signals (see Smith 2000).

29. This need to avoid destructive interference has, in the case of gesture, an interesting counterpart. For part of the power of the gestural system seems to lie in the fact that we are not forced to consciously confront or even endorse our own gestured meanings, and this allows free exploration of ideas inconsistent with our verbal assertions. Otherwise put:

> gesture is not explicitly acknowledged. As a result, gesture can allow speakers to introduce into their repertoires novel ideas not entirely consistent with their current beliefs, without inviting challenge from a listener—indeed, without inviting challenge from their own self-monitoring systems…Once in, these new ideas could catalyze change. (Goldin-Meadow and Wagner 2004, 239)

30. For this to occur, ongoing control over the current degree of coupling, as in the "gated" self-cueing net, may well be crucial (see Philippides et al. 2005, 158).
31. See, for example, Dennett's (1998) description of a system in which it is "contention scheduling" (Norman and Shallice 1980) "all the way up."
32. For example, we decide to place that yellow sticky on the mirror reminding us of the important meeting. In such cases, an identifiable thinking agent offloads onto some environmental structure the semantically well-formed product of some recognizably cognitive activity, only to later reload it as needed to perform some task.
33. In the vexing case of Otto, the image of conscious choice and the perceived availability of an offload–reload parsing have haunted the discussion despite our best efforts (Clark and Chalmers 1998) to depict the use of the notebook as so well-practiced as to become automatic and unreflective.
34. See Sporns et al. (2004) for a nice account of the distinction between persisting structure and short-lived functional complexity in the brain.
35. The BIOS is a small (often just 512 byte) program that, as part of the basic input–output system (hence the name, BIOS), loads in the bigger ones that eventually comprise the whole up-and-running operating system.

CHAPTER 7

1. The latter is all that was required for our own appeal to change blindness in section 2.6.
2. That is, judging of two pairs of objects that the within-pair relations are the same or different across the two pairs; see section 3.2.
3. The idea here, which may seem elusive at first, is that such cases involve considering self-generated information about our own prior intentions. See Christoff et al. (2003, 1166).
4. Christoff et al. (2003, 1166) depict the self-generated information as abstract and contrast this with the case of attending to concrete cues or items. If Thompson, Oden, and Boysen (1997) are right, however, the internally generated targets here are shallow imagistic renditions of quite

concrete objects (the plastic tokens for sameness and difference) whose *contents* are nonetheless relatively abstract.

5. The relative size of the frontal lobes to the rest of the brain appears to be the same in humans and chimpanzees, but BA10 is twice as large, relative to the rest of the frontal lobe, in the human case. See Semendeferi et al. (2001, 2002).

6. In the token-training case, the conspiracy is a developmental one, as the external scaffolding eventually drops from view. In other cases, as we saw, there is continued reliance on the external scaffolding. In both cases, however, the picture will be one of key neural innovations combining with cultural ones to yield the capacities we most readily identify with minds like ours.

7. Nor should it be seen as "opposing the search for mechanisms in the head to explain cognitive activity" (Bechtel in press).

8. For the detailed story I favor, see Clark (1997a, 1997b).

9. For an update and review, see Kawato (1999).

10. This general idea is, of course, very familiar. See Campbell (1974) and Dennett (1996). What is novel in Grush's story is the appeal to motor emulation as the place this special trick got its foot in the evolutionary door.

11. Grush shows himself sensitive to this possibility in the Reply section of his 2004 article where he writes that "the skull is metaphysically inert" (428). Grush's account of the nature of representation is thus meant to be "transparent to organism boundaries" (429). Nonetheless, the thrust of the 2003 paper is to reinvent a fairly strong Cartesianism that places nearly all of the cognitive action, at least as a matter of contingent fact, inside the bounds of skin and skull. It is this emphasis only that I am seeking to resist.

12. There is, of course, considerable room for individual differences in these regards.

13. Notice that even supposing that the plug points *are* always explicitly represented as such by skilled users, this would still be consistent with the running, across the interfaces, of densely integrated problem-solving routines. High-bandwidth couplings, as Grush notes, may run across well-defined plug points. That being the case, there is no reason to suppose that such couplings cannot yield temporary information-processing wholes that, while up and running, are every bit as integrated as the underlying neural activity itself.

14. This is a view that I argue against at length in Clark (2003).

15. Thanks to Dave Chalmers for some useful discussion of this topic.

16. For example, by Ned Block at a recent meeting on these topics. I think, however, that Block now accepts that the vat scenarios cannot be used to challenge claims concerning the potentially extended nature of (at least nonconscious) mental states.

17. This modifier is meant to bracket questions concerning putative externalist criteria for the individuation of mental states (see comments in chap. 4 and the appendix) and to focus our attention on the question of what

local machinery implements the mental states, however they may be individuated.

18. For this notion of the constitutive, see, e.g., Block (2005).
19. More recent work (e.g., Thelen et al. 2001) seems rather more ecumenical in this regard.
20. For more on this antifunctionalist strand, see chapter 9.
21. For example, there is a greater use of "indexical-functional representations" such as "an arms reach straight ahead" (Agre 1995) or "the object in line with the direction I am headed and located between me and what I am looking at right now" (Pylyshyn 2001, 130). There is greater use, too, of encodings closely geared to the affordances of the current situation. For this general picture of an inner realm of "action-oriented representations," see Clark (1997a).
22. It is important, then, that we do not conflate the very idea of a stored program with the idea of a detailed instruction set that micromanages an activity (e.g., a full set of precise joint-angle control commands for fluent walking versus a much sparser control routine that makes the most of passive dynamic effects). See the discussions of so-called partial programs in Clark (1997a, 2001a).

CHAPTER 8

1. For an excellent, though itself skeptical, account of the traditional conception of qualia, see Pettit (2003).
2. For Noë's own take on such thought experiments, see, e.g., Noë (2004, 124).
3. See Bach y Rita and Kercel (2002) for a recent review.
4. Or at any rate, those elements in visual experience that drive verbal report. It is possible, of course, that conscious visual experience outruns report and perhaps outruns reportability itself, even in creatures capable of issuing such reports. For arguments to this effect, see Block (in press), and for some critical discussion of the complex issues here, see Dretske (2006), Clark (2007), Kiverstein and Clark (in press). For present purposes, I shall assume that the verbal reports of patients such as DF are a reliable indicator of their conscious visual experience.
5. Some evidence suggests that, in the Ponzo and Müller-Lyer cases, conscious visual illusions *do* influence grasp, although only to a small degree. Thus, according to Ellis, Flanagan, and Lederman (1999), the visual illusion, in these cases, *does* influence the action systems, but the action (grasp) system *also* has access to more veridical information. The results obtained then reflect the interaction between the two. In a similar fashion, Jeannerod (1997), Jacob and Jeannerod (2003), and Jeannerod and Jacob (2005) offer a variety of evidence favoring a greater degree of interaction between vision for perception and vision for action but without casting doubt on the general correctness the dual-systems perspective.

6. Sirigu et al. (1995) describe a patient who looks to have intact processing in both the dorsal and ventral streams but to suffer from impaired interaction between the two. This patient can grasp objects fluently and can name objects but will often display an efficient (well-calibrated) grip that is inappropriate to the object's use; see the brief discussion in Milner and Goodale (1995, 203) and the longer one in Jeannerod (1997, 91–93).

7. It also seems implicit in Matthen's (2005) account of the class of "descriptive sensory systems."

8. This general picture also looks to be a good fit with the so-called Theory of Event Coding (W. Prinz 1997; Hommel et al. 2001), according to which conscious perception and action planning share resources, working together as a kind of "distal-event system" that "cares about" the overall effects of action rather than the specifics of the action itself. See Jordan (2003) for a discussion.

9. As an aside, this same broad commitment to the constitutive role of whole organism activity probably leads to other oddities, such as Noë's later suggestion that a concert pianist, in losing his arms, would thereby (instantly, as what appears to be a matter of conceptual necessity) lose his know-how because "the knowledge was, precisely, arm-dependent" (Noë 2004, 121).

10. It remains possible that more neglected elements of experience, ones other than those concerning the typical qualia suspects such as shape, color, texture, and so on, may depend more directly on dorsal stream activity. Thus, Matthen (2005, 301) argues that the "feeling of presence" may depend on dorsal stream activity even if the other more descriptive elements do not.

11. I use this notion in the sense of Chalmers (2000)—that is, to refer to a system whose state is sufficient to ensure the presence of a target conscious state and none of whose proper parts can be in states sufficient for the obtaining of that state.

CHAPTER 9

1. The notion of information self-structuring can be found in Lungarella and Sporns (2005); see the discussion in sec. 1.5.

2. See the entry for The Embodied Cognition Research Program in the online journal *Philosophy Compass* at http://www.blackwellcompass.com/subject/philosophy/.

3. To be fair, Rohrer allows that the notions of functional and computational explanation might be broadened in many of the ways we have scouted. But such broadening, it seems to me, should not result in our putting the terms, as Rohrer then does, in scare quotes. Rather, to fail to recognize key events and processes as genuinely computational (because trafficking in representations, information, and information-based control) is to fail to

account for what is special about minds—what distinguishes them from volcanoes and other complex but noncognitive phenomena. See Clark (1997b) and the condensed discussion in sections 1.8 and 1.9.

4. In a similar vein, Alav Noë (2007, 537, emphasis in original) writes that "one deplorable legacy of functionalism is the idea that embodiment—the way we are put together, brains and body—is irrelevant to how our minds work. For functionalism, embodiment is just a matter of the way our mental functioning happens to be *implemented*." I shall try to show that while this is indeed true, it is by no means evidently "deplorable." Importantly, it is consistent with taking embodiment very seriously indeed. For insofar as certain key operations and encodings are accomplished by gross bodily (nonneural) means, features of embodiment (and action) turn out to provide the material means whereby minds like ours are realized. If embodiment thus turns out to be as important as (but no more important than) "embrainment," that would surely constitute a good reason to take embodiment seriously when pursuing the sciences of the mind.

5. That there is *something* problematic about this argument is evident in the tension between the easy use of a common notion of happiness and sadness in the first quoted sentence and the subsequent assertion that happy and sad would then "assume different meanings." But the point, in any case, is simply that arguments stressing the pervasive influence of embodiment on conceptualization look to be arguments against the ST because they assert the ineliminable involvement of bodily details in an account of mental states.

6. I use "bodily" here to refer to the gross physical body rather than to the (of course, equally bodily) brain.

7. Inimical to, but not inconsistent with. ST is said to be logically independent of Multiple Realizability Thesis (MRT) because "it is logically possible that a mind could be realized in a number of different kinds of structure, but that all of these structures are contained in similar sorts of bodies (and) it is logically possible that there is only one or a few ways of realizing a humanlike mind but that these few types of realizations can exist in many different sorts of bodies" (Shapiro 2004, 167). Such concessions make the intended force of the earlier arguments depicting physical structures as proper parts of psychological processes unclear, though Shapiro does add that he is willing to bet that "if there are but a few ways to realize a humanlike mind, probably there are but a few kinds of bodies that could contain such a mind" (167).

8. It is also compatible even with traditional forms of machine functionalism that, just as it happens, only one kind of stuff in the universe might be capable of implementing a given functional profile.

9. Taken to the extreme, one may here discern the possibility of what Wheeler (in press-b) describes as a form of "non-computational functionalism" that is nonetheless compatible with the multiple realizability of cognitive mechanisms.

10. Shapiro (personal communication) notes that on the account I favor, bodies *matter* because they can play certain roles in the processing cycles that constitute cognition, but in another sense, bodies *don't matter* because what matters is the resulting overall processing profile, not the presence of any specific bodily features per se nor the precise way that various operations are distributed among brain, body, and world. Shapiro fears that this robs the embodied approach of much of its distinctive appeal. I fear that the alternative buys bodily appeal at the price of scientific mystery.

11. That something might be awry with this latter picture is perhaps indicated by the simple fact that human bodies already come in a wide variety of shapes and forms. Just what then *is* "human embodiment" that it might so cleanly limn the space of "human mentality"?

12. Shapiro (personal communication) clarifies that the intended meaning was indeed the former (i.e., that the brain's algorithms factor in contingencies about the body). Given this reading, however, it seems unclear why facts about embodiment are taken to work against the Separability Thesis.

13. Thus, consider Flicker. Flicker is a creature with just one eye that moves very rapidly from side to side of its face, sending signals only while at the two locations that happen to match those of the human eyes. With some canny tweaks of the neural control and downstream sensory postprocessing circuitry, such a being could implement precisely the same basic stereo depth perception algorithm as humans. The situation would be not unlike the use of a fast serial computer to simulate a parallel processing device.

14. Noë may actually have an even more pervasive role for the body in mind. He writes that

> in general it is a mistake to think that we can sharply distinguish visual processing at the highly abstract algorithmic level, on the one hand, from processing at the concrete implementational level, on the other. The point is not that algorithms are constrained by their implementation, although that is true. The point, rather, is that the algorithms are actually, at least in part, formulated in terms of items at the implementational level. You might actually need to mention hands and eyes in the algorithms! (2004, 25)

It is unclear, though, just what Noë here has in mind. For some discussion, see Shapiro (in press).

15. Such an account, as we saw in chapter 8, makes it in principle impossible for a differently embodied being to fully share human perceptual experiences.

16. Thus, Noë (personal communication) does indeed assert that "you couldn't have the very same experience unless you have the same underlying sensorimotor exercise." This may turn out to be true, but it is not yet obvious to me why it should be true or how we can at this time know it to be true.

17. Notice, as an aside, that this may help explain why it often seems, phenomenologically speaking, as if the machinery of mind is all located within the bounds of the organism. For mind, intuitively, is that which mediates perception and action, and the body just *is* the place where perception and action meet. But it no more follows that the actual machinery of mind is body bound than it would follow that the control system of a mobile robot is located within the sensing and acting shell. In the case of the robot, the whole robot brain might be located elsewhere (a scenario neatly extended in Dennett 1981), to a science fiction scenario concerning a human agent whose brain, though still mediating the body's sensing and acting, is kept in a distant laboratory.

18. Notice that nothing here dictates a single persisting body in ordinary 3-space. Instead, there could be genuine but scattered forms of embodiment, embodiment in virtual or mixed realities, and multiple embodiments for a single intelligence (for more on these topics, see Clark 2003; Ismael 2006, in press).

19. An obvious contender here is the putative role of the body in the construction of emotional and affective response. For some treatments that explore this kind of possibility in various ways, see Damasio (1994, 1999); Colombetti and Thompson (in press); and Prinz (2004).

20. For an excellent account of multiple functionality in evolved systems, see Anderson (2007).

21. Which, in the case of the hand and finger system, are in turn connected to muscles (acting as contractive elements).

22. The coevolution of the tendon network and the neural control system may be relevant here, too, as showing not just that there is parity of actual role but also parity of selected role.

23. Notice that "action" here must play a dual role, both as practical action per se and as part of the information-processing routines that select other actions. This is, of course, exactly what we have found in a variety of cases ranging from the so-called epistemic actions in Tetris (sec. 4.6), to the role of speech and gesture in thought (sec. 6.7), and most recently, to the subtle twitches of the second-generation XOR robot.

24. Complexity is an especially interesting measure. It captures the degree to which a system is both functionally specialized and functionally integrated, a property that delivers maximum information-processing power. See Sporns (2002) for an accessible discussion.

APPENDIX

1. Much of the appeal of externalism in the philosophy of mind may stem from the intuitive appeal of active externalism. Externalists often make analogies involving external features in coupled systems, and appeal to the arbitrariness of boundaries between brain and environment. But these

252 NOTES TO PAGES 223-232

intuitions sit uneasily with the letter of standard externalism. In most of the Putnam/Burge cases, the immediate environment is irrelevant; only the historical environment counts. Debate has focused on the question of whether mind must be in the head, but a more relevant question in assessing these examples might be: is mind in the present?

2. Herbert Simon (1981) once suggested that we view internal memory as, in effect, an external resource upon which "real" inner processes operate. "Search in memory," he comments, "is not very different from search of the external environment." Simon's view at least has the virtue of treating internal and external processing with the parity they deserve, but we suspect that on his view the mind will shrink too small for most people's tastes.

3. Philosophical views of a similar spirit can be found in Haugeland (1995), McClamrock (1985), Varela et al. (1991), and Wilson (1994).

4. Or consider the following passage from a recent science fiction novel (McHugh 1992, 213): "I am taken to the system's department where I am attuned to the system. All I do is jack in and then a technician instructs the system to attune and it does. I jack out and query the time. 10:52. The information pops up. Always before I could only access information when I was jacked in, it gave me a sense that I knew what I thought and what the system told me, but now, how do I know what is system and what is Zhang?"

5. In the terminology of Chalmers's "The Components of Content," the twins in the Putnam and Burge cases differ only in their *relational* content, but Otto and his twin can be seen to differ in their *notional* content, which is the sort of content that governs cognition. Notional content is generally internal to a cognitive system, but in this case the cognitive system is itself effectively extended to include the notebook.

6. The constancy and past-endorsement criteria may suggest that history is partly constitutive of belief. One might react to this by removing any historical component (giving a purely dispositional reading of the constancy criterion and eliminating the past-endorsement criterion, for example), or one might allow such a component as long as the main burden is carried by features of the present.

7. From the *New York Times*, March 30, 1995, p. B7, in an article on former UCLA basketball coach John Wooden: "Wooden and his wife attended 36 straight Final Fours, and she invariably served as his memory bank. Nell Wooden rarely forgot a name—her husband rarely remembered one—and in the standing-room-only Final Four lobbies, she would recognize people for him."

8. Might this sort of reasoning also allow something like Burge's extended "arthritis" beliefs? After all, I might always defer to my doctor in taking relevant actions concerning my disease. Perhaps so, but there are some clear differences. For example, any extended beliefs would be grounded in an existing active relationship with the doctor, rather than in a histori-

cal relationship to a language community. And on the current analysis, my deference to the doctor would tend to yield something like a true belief that I have some other disease in my thigh, rather than the false belief that I have arthritis there. On the other hand, if I used medical experts solely as terminological consultants, the results of Burge's analysis might be mirrored.

References

Abraham, R., and C. Shaw. 1992. *Dynamics—The geometry of behavior*. Redwood City, CA: Addison-Wesley.

Adams, F., and K. Aizawa. 2001. The bounds of cognition. *Philosophical Psychology* 14, no. 1: 43–64.

———. in press-a. Defending the bounds of cognition. In *The extended mind*, ed. R. Menary. Aldershot, UK: Ashgate.

———. in press-b. Why the mind is still in the head. In *Cambridge handbook of situated cognition*, ed. M. Aydede and P. Robbins. New York: Cambridge University Press.

Aglioti, S., M. Goodale, and J. F. X. DeSouza, 1995. Size contrast illusions deceive the eye but not the hand. *Current Biology* 5: 679–685.

Agre, P. 1995. Computational research on interaction and agency. In *Computational theories of interaction and agency*, ed. P. Agre and S. Rosenschein. Cambridge, MA: MIT Press.

Alač, M., and E. Hutchins. 2004. I see what you are saying: Action as cognition in fMRI brain mapping practice. *Journal of Cognition and Culture* 4, no. 3: 629–661.

Anderson, M. 2007. The massive redeployment hypothesis and the functional topography of the brain. *Philosophical Psychology* 20, no. 2: 143–174.

————. in press. Cognitive science and epistemic openness. *Phenomenology and the Cognitive Sciences* 4, no. 4.

Bach y Rita, P., and S. W. Kercel. 2003. Sensory substitution and the human-machine interface. *Trends in Cognitive Sciences* 7, no. 12: 541–546.

Bach y Rita, P., M. Tyler, and K. Kaczmarek. 2003. Seeing with the brain. *International Journal of Human–Computer Interaction* 15, no. 2: 285–295.

Baddeley, A. 1986. *Working memory*. Oxford, UK: Clarendon Press.

Baker, S. C., R. D. Rogers, A. M. Owen, C. D. Frith, R. J. Dolan, R. S. J. Frackowiak, and T. W. Robbins. 1996. Neural systems engaged by planning: A PET study of the Tower of London task. *Neuropsychologia* 34, no. 6: 515–526.

Ballard, D., M. M. Hayhoe, and J. B. Pelz. 1995. Memory representations in natural tasks. *Journal of Cognitive Neuroscience* 7, no. 1: 66–80.

Ballard, D., M. Hayhoe, P. Pook, and R. Rao. 1997. Deictic codes for the embodiment of cognition. *Behavioral and Brain Sciences* 20: 723–767.

Bargh, J. A., and T. L. Chartrand. 1999. The unbearable automaticity of being. *American Psychologist* 54: 462–479.

Barr, M. 2002. Closed-loop control. *Embedded Systems Programming* (August): 55–56.

Barsalou, L. W. 1999. Perceptual symbol systems. *Behavioral and Brain Sciences* 22: 577–609.

————. 2003. Abstraction in perceptual symbol systems. *Philosophical Transaction of the Royal Society of London B Biological Sciences* 358: 1177–1187.

Beach, K. 1988. The role of external mnemonic symbols in acquiring an occupation. In *Practical aspects of memory*, Vol. 1, ed. M. M. Gruneberg and R. N. Sykes. New York: Wiley.

Bechtel, W. in press. Explanation: Mechanism, Modularity, and Situated Cognition in P. Robbins and M. Aydede (Eds.). *Cambridge handbook of situated cognition*. Cambridge: Cambridge University Press.

Beer, R. 1989. *Intelligence as adaptive behavior*. New York: Academic Press.

————. 2000. Dynamical approaches to cognitive science. *Trends in Cognitive Sciences* 4, no. 3: 91–99.

Berk, L. E. 1994. Why children talk to themselves. *Scientific American* (November): 78–83.

Bermudez, J. 2003. *Thinking without words*. New York: Oxford University Press.

Berti, A., and F. Frassinetti. 2000. When far becomes near: Re-mapping of space by tool use. *Journal of Cognitive Neuroscience* 12: 415–420.

Bingham, G. P. 1988. Task-specific devices and the perceptual bottleneck. *Human Movement Science* 7: 225–264.

Bisiach, E., and C. Luzzatti. 1978. Unilateral neglect of representational space. *Cortex* 14: 129–133.

Blake, A., and A. Yuille, eds. 1992. *Active vision*. Cambridge, MA: MIT Press.

Block, N. 1990. The computer model of the mind. In *An invitation to cognitive science: Thinking*, Vol. 3, ed. E. E. Smith and D. N. Osherson. Cambridge, MA: MIT Press.

————. 2005. Review of Alva Noë, "Action in perception." *Journal of Philosophy* 102, no. 5: 259–272.

———. in press. Consciousness, accessibility, and the mesh between psychology and neuroscience. *Behavioral and Brain Sciences*.

Bongard, J., V. Zykov, and H. Lipson. 2006. Resilient machines through continuous self-modeling. *Science* 314: 1118–1121.

Bowerman, M., and S. Choi. 2001. Shaping meanings for language: Universal and language-specific in the acquisition and shaping of semantic categories. In *Language acquisition and conceptual development*, ed. M. Bowerman and S. Levinson. Cambridge, UK: Cambridge University Press.

Boysen, S. T., G. Bernston, M. Hannan, and J. Cacioppo. 1996. Quantity-based inference and symbolic representation in chimpanzees (*Pan troglodytes*). *Journal of Experimental Psychology: Animal Behavior Processes* 22: 76–86.

Braddon-Mitchell, D., and F. Jackson. 2007. *The philosophy of mind and cognition*. 2nd ed. Oxford: Basil Blackwell.

Bradley, D. 1992. *From text to performance in the Elizabethan theatre: Preparing the play for the stage*. Cambridge, UK: Cambridge University Press.

Braitenberg, V. 1984. *Vehicles: Experiments in synthetic psychology*. Cambridge, MA: MIT Press.

Braver, T. S., and S. R. Bongiolatti. 2002. The role of frontopolar cortex in subgoal processing during working memory. *NeuroImage* 15: 523–536.

Bridgeman, B., and M. Mayer. 1983. Failure to integrate visual information from successive fixations. *Bulletin of the Psychonomic Society* 21: 285–286.

Brooks, R. 1991. Intelligence without representation. *Artificial Intelligence* 47: 139–159.

———. 2001. The relationship between matter and life. *Nature* 409: 409–411.

Brooks, R. A., C. Breazeal, M. Marjanovic, B. Scassellati, and M. M. Williamson. 1999. The Cog project: Building a humanoid robot. In *Computation for metaphors, analogy and agents*, Vol. 1562 of Springer Lecture Notes in Artificial Intelligence, ed. C. L. Nehaniv. Berlin: Springer-Verlag.

Brugger, P., S. S. Kollias, R. Müri, G. Crelier, M. C. Hepp-Reymond, and M. Regard. 2000. Beyond remembering: Phantom sensations of congenitally absent limbs. *Proceedings of the National Academy of Science* 97: 6167–6172.

Burge, T. 1979. Individualism and the mental. In *Midwest studies in philosophy*, Vol. 4, Metaphysics, ed. P. French, T. Uehling Jr., and H. Wettstein. Minneapolis: University of Minnesota Press.

———. 1986. Individualism and psychology. *Philosophical Review* 95: 3–45.

Burgess, P. W., A. Quayle, and C. D. Frith. 2001. Brain regions involved in prospective memory as determined by positron emission tomography. *Neuropsychologia* 39, no. 6: 545–555.

Burton, G. 1993. Non-neural extensions of haptic sensitivity. *Ecological Psychology* 5: 105–124.

Butler, K. 1998. *Internal affairs: A critique of externalism in the philosophy of mind*. Dordrecht, The Netherlands: Kluwer.

Campbell, D. T. 1974. Evolutionary epistemology. In *The philosophy of Karl R. Popper*, ed. P. A. Schilpp. LaSalle, IL: Open Court. Reprinted in *Methodology and epistemology for social sciences: Selected papers*, ed. E. S. Overman. Chicago: University of Chicago Press.

Campbell, J. 2002. *Reference and consciousness.* Oxford, UK: Oxford University Press.

Carey, D. 2001. Do action systems resist visual illusions? *Trends in Cognitive Sciences* 5, no. 3: 109–113.

Carmena, J., M. Lebedev, R. Crist, J. O'Doherty, D. Santucci, D. Dimitrov, P. Patil, C. Henriquez, and M. Nicolelis. 2003. Learning to control a brain-machine interface for reaching and grasping by primates. *Public Library of Sciences: Biology* 1, no. 2: 193–208.

Carrasco, M., S. Ling, and S. Read. 2004. Attention alters appearance. *Nature Neuroscience* 7: 308–313.

Carruthers, P. 1998. Thinking in language. In *Language and thought*, ed. J. Boucher and P. Carruthers. Cambridge, UK: Cambridge University Press.

———. 2002. The cognitive functions of language. *Behavioral and Brain Sciences* 25: 657–726.

Chalmers, D. 2000. What is a neural correlate of consciousness? In *Neural correlates of consciousness: Empirical and conceptual questions*, ed. T. Metzinger. Cambridge, MA: MIT Press.

———. 2005. MATRIX. In *Philosophers explore the matrix*, ed. C. Grau. New York: Oxford University Press.

Chapman, S. 1968. Trigonometric outfielding. *Scientific American* 220: 49–50.

Christoff, K., J. M. Ream, L. P. Geddes, and J. D. Gabrieli. 2003. Evaluating self-generated information: Anterior prefrontal contributions to human cognition. *Behavioral Neuroscience* 117, no. 6: 1161–1168.

Churchland, P. 1989. *The neurocomputational perspective.* Cambridge, MA: MIT/Bradford Books.

———. 1995. *The engine of reason, the seat of the soul.* Cambridge, MA: MIT Press.

Churchland, P., and Sejnowski, T. J. 1992. *The computational brain.* Computational Neuroscience Series, Cambridge, MA: MIT Press.

Churchland, P., V. Ramachandran, and T. Sejnowski. 1994. A critique of pure vision. In *Large-scale neuronal theories of the brain*, ed. C. Koch and J. Davis. Cambridge, MA: MIT Press.

Clark, A. 1989. *Microcognition: Philosophy, cognitive science and parallel distributed processing.* Cambridge, MA: MIT Press/Bradford Books.

———. 1993. *Associative engines: Connectionism, concepts and representational change.* Cambridge, MA: MIT Press/Bradford Books.

———. 1996. Connectionism, moral cognition and collaborative problem solving. In *Mind & morals*, ed. L. May, M. Friedman, and A. Clark. Cambridge, MA: MIT Press.

———. 1997a. *Being there: Putting brain, body and world together again.* Cambridge, MA: MIT Press.

———. 1997b. The dynamical challenge. *Cognitive Science* 21, no. 4: 461–481.

———. 1998a. Magic words: How language augments human computation. In *Language and thought: Interdisciplinary themes*, ed. P. Carruthers and J. Boucher. Cambridge, UK: Cambridge University Press.

———. 1998b. Twisted tales: Causal complexity and cognitive scientific explanation. *Minds and Machines* 8: 79–99. Reprinted in *Explanation and cognition*, ed. F. Keil and R. A. Wilson. Cambridge, MA: MIT Press, 2000.

———. 1999. Visual awareness and visuomotor action. *Journal of Consciousness Studies* 6, no. 11–12: 1–18.

———. 2000a. A case where access implies qualia? *Analysis* 60, no. 265: 30–38.

———. 2000b. Making moral space: A reply to Churchland. In *Moral epistemology naturalized: Canadian Journal of Philosophy*, Supp. Vol. 26, ed. R. Campbell and B. Hunter. Alberta, Canada: University of Calgary Press.

———. 2000c. Word and action: Reconciling rules and know-how in moral cognition. In *Moral epistemology naturalized: Canadian Journal of Philosophy*, Supp. Vol. 26, ed. R. Campbell and B. Hunter. Alberta, Canada: University of Calgary Press.

———. 2001a. *Mindware: An introduction to the philosophy of cognitive science.* New York: Oxford University Press.

———. 2001b. Reasons, robots, and the extended mind. *Mind and Language* 16: 121–145.

———. 2001c. Visual experience and motor action: Are the bonds too tight? *Philosophical Review* 110, no. 4: 495–519.

———. 2002. Is seeing all it seems? Action, reason and the grand illusion. *Journal of Consciousness Studies* 9, no. 5–6: 181–202. Reprinted in *Is the visual world a grand illusion?* ed. A. Noë. Thorverton, UK: Imprint Academic, 2002.

———. 2003. *Natural-born cyborgs: Minds, technologies, and the future of human intelligence.* New York: Oxford University Press.

———. 2004. Is language special? Some remarks on control, coding, and co-ordination. *Language Sciences*, Special issue on Distributed Cognition and Integrational Linguistics, ed. D. Spurrett, 26: no. 6.

———. 2005a. Beyond the flesh: Some lessons from a mole cricket. *Artificial Life* 11: 233–244.

———. 2005b. Intrinsic content, active memory, and the extended mind. *Analysis* 65, no. 1 (January): 1–11.

———. 2005c. The twisted matrix: Dream, simulation or hybrid? In *Philosophers explore the matrix*, ed. C. Grau. New York: Oxford University Press.

———. 2006. Language, embodiment and the cognitive niche. *Trends in Cognitive Sciences* 10, no. 8: 370–374.

———. 2007. What reaching teaches: Consciousness, control, and the inner zombie. *British Journal for the Philosophy of Science* 58, no, 3: 563–594.

———. in press-a. Memento's revenge: The extended mind, re-visited. In *The Extended Mind*, ed. R. Menary. Aldershot, UK: Ashgate.

———. in press-b. Re-inventing ourselves: The plasticity of embodiment, sensing, and mind. *Journal of Medicine and Philosophy*.

Clark, A., and D. Chalmers. 1998. The extended mind. *Analysis* 58, no. 1: 7–19. Reprinted in *The philosopher's annual*, Vol. 21, ed. P. Grim, 1998, and in *Philosophy of mind: Classical and contemporary readings*, ed. D. Chalmers. New York: Oxford University Press, 2002.

Clark, A., and R. Grush. 1999. Towards a cognitive robotics. *Adaptive Behavior* 7, no. 1: 5–16.

Clark, A., and A. Karmiloff-Smith. 1993. The cognizer's innards: A philosophical and psychological perspective on the development of thought. *Mind and Language* 8, no. 4: 487–519.

Clark, A., and P. Mandik. 2002. Selective representing and world-making. *Minds and Machines* 12: 383–395.

Clark, A., and C. Thornton. 1997. Trading spaces: Computation, representation, and limits of uninformed learning. *Behavioral and Brain Sciences* 20: 57–90.

Clark, A., and J. Toribio. 1994. Doing without representing? *Synthese* 101: 401–431.

———. 2001. Sensorimotor chauvinism? Commentary on O'Regan, J. K., and Noë, A. "A sensorimotor approach to vision and visual consciousness." *Behavioral and Brain Sciences* 24, no. 5: 979–980.

Clowes, R. 2007. The complex vehicles of human thought and the role of scaffolding, internalization, and semiotics in human representation. Target paper for web discussion at http://www.interdisciplines.org/ adaptation/papers/11.

Clowes, R. W., and A. F. Morse. 2005. Scaffolding cognition with words. In L. Berthouze, F. Kaplan, H. Kozima, Y. Yano, J. Konczak, G. Metta, J. Nadel, G. Sandini, G. Stojanov, and C. Balkenius, (eds.), *Proceedings of the Fifth International Workshop on Epigenetic Robotics: Modeling Cognitive Development in Robotic Systems*. Lund University Cognitive Studies, Lund, Sweden 101–105.

Collins, H. in press. The cruel cognitive psychology. Appears as part of a three-authored discussion by H. Collins, J. Shrager, and A. Clark entitled "Keeping the collectivity in mind?" Special issue of *Phenomenology and the Cognitive Sciences*, ed. E. Selinger.

Collins, S. H., and A. Ruina. 2005. A bipedal walking robot with efficient and human-like gait. *Proceedings IEEE International Conference on Robotics and Automation*, Barcelona, Spain.

Collins, S. H., A. L. Ruina, R. Tedrake, and M. Wisse. 2005. Efficient bipedal robots based on passive-dynamic walkers. *Science* 307: 1082–1085.

Collins, S. H., M. Wisse, and A. Ruina. 2001. A three-dimensional passive-dynamic walking robot with two legs and knees. *International Journal of Robotics Research* 20, no. 7: 607–615.

Colombetti, G., and E. Thompson. in press. The feeling body: Towards an enactive approach to emotion. In *Developmental perspectives on embodiment and consciousness*, ed. W. F. Overton, U. Müller, and J. Newman. Hillsdale, NJ: Erlbaum.

Cooney, J., and M. Gazzaniga. 2003. Neurological disorders and the structure of human consciousness. *Trends in Cognitive Sciences* 7, no. 4: 161–165.

Cowie, F. 1999. *What's within? Nativism reconsidered.* New York: Oxford University Press.

Cummins, R. 1983. *The nature of psychological explanation.* Cambridge, MA: Bradford Books/MIT Press.

————. 1989. *Meaning and mental representation*. Cambridge, MA: MIT Press.

Damasio, A. 1994. *Descartes' error*. New York: Grosset/Putnam.

————. 1999. *The feeling of what happens*. New York: Harcourt Brace.

————. 2000. Subcortical and cortical brain activity during the feeling of self-generated emotions. *Nature Neuroscience* 3: 1049–1056.

Damasio, A., and H. Damasio. 1994. Cortical systems for retrieval of concrete knowledge: The convergence zone framework. In *Large-scale neuronal theories of the brain*, ed. C. Koch. Cambridge, MA: MIT Press.

Dawkins, R. 1982. *The extended phenotype*. Oxford, UK: Oxford University Press.

de Villiers, J. G., and P. A. de Villiers. 2003. Language for thought: Coming to understand false beliefs. In *Language in mind: Advances in the study of language and thought*, ed. D. Gentner and S. Goldin-Meadow. Cambridge, MA: MIT Press.

Decety, J., and J. Grezes. 1999. Neural mechanisms subserving the perception of human actions. *Trends in Cognitive Sciences* 3, no. 5: 172–178.

Dehaene, S. 1997. *The number sense*. New York: Oxford University Press.

Dehaene, S., E. Spelke, P. Pinel, R. Stanescu, and S. Tviskin. 1999. Sources of mathematical thinking: Behavioral and brain imaging evidence. *Science* 284: 970–974.

Dennett, D. 1981. Where am I? In *Brainstorms*, ed. D. Dennett. Sussex, UK: Harvester Press.

————. 1987. *The intentional stance*. Cambridge, MA: MIT Press.

————. 1991a. *Consciousness explained*. Boston: Little, Brown.

————. 1991b. Real patterns. *Journal of Philosophy* 88: 27–51.

————. 1993. Learning and labeling (commentary on A. Clark and A. Karmiloff-Smith, "The cognizer's innards"). *Mind and Language* 8, no. 4: 540–547.

————. 1996. *Kinds of minds*. New York: Basic Books.

————. 1998. Reflections on language and mind. In *Language and thought: Interdisciplinary themes*, ed. P. Carruthers and J. Boucher. New York: Cambridge University Press.

————. 2000. Making tools for thinking. In *Metarepresentations: A multidisciplinary perspective*, ed. D. Sperber. Oxford, UK: Oxford University Press.

————. 2003. *Freedom evolves*. New York: Viking.

Densmore, S., and D. Dennett. 1999. The virtues of virtual machines. *Philosophy and Phenomenological Research* 59: 3: 747–761

Donald, M. 1991. *Origins of the modern mind*. Cambridge, MA: Harvard University Press.

————. 2001. *A mind so rare*. New York: Norton.

Dourish, P. 2001. *Where the action is: The foundations of embodied interaction*. Cambridge, MA: MIT Press.

Dretske, F. 1996. Phenomenal externalism, or if meanings ain't in the head, where are qualia? *Philosophical Issues* 7.

————. 2006. Perception without awareness. In *Perceptual Experience*, ed. T. Gendler and J. Hawthorne. New York: Oxford University Press, p. 147–180.

Dreyfus, H., and S. Dreyfus. 2000. *Mind over machine*. New York: Free Press.

Dyde, R. T., and A. D. Milner. 2002. Two illusions of perceived orientation: One fools all of the people some of the time; the other fools all of the people all of the time. *Experimental Brain Research* 144: 518–527.

Eliasmith, C. 2003. Moving beyond metaphors: Understanding the mind for what it is. *Journal of Philosophy* 100, no. 10: 493–520.

Ellis, R., J. Flanagan, and S. Lederman. 1999. The influence of visual illusions on grasp position. *Experimental Brain Research* 125: 109–114.

Elman, J. 1995. Language as a dynamical system. In *Mind as motion,* ed. R. Port and T. van Gelder. Cambridge, MA: MIT Press.

———. 2004. An alternative view of the mental lexicon. *Trends in Cognitive Sciences* 8, no. 7: 301–306.

———. 2005. Connectionist models of cognitive development: Where next? *Trends in Cognitive Sciences* 9: 111–117.

Feldman, M. W., and L. L. Cavalli-Sforza. 1989. On the theory of evolution under genetic and cultural transmission with application to the lactose absorption problem. In *Mathematical evolutionary theory,* ed. M. W. Feldman. Princeton, NJ: Princeton University Press.

Felleman, D. J., and D. C. Van Essen. 1991. Distributed hierarchical processing in primate cerebral cortex. *Cerebral Cortex* 1: 1–47.

Fisher, J. C. 2007. Why nothing mental is just in the head. *Nous* 41: 318–334.

Fitzpatrick, P., and A. Arsenio. 2004. Feel the beat: Using cross-modal rhythm to integrate perception of objects, others, and self. In *Proceedings of the fourth International Workshop on Epigenetic Robotics,* ed. L. Berthouze, H. Kozima, C. G. Prince, G. Sandini, G., G. Stojanov, G. Metta, and C. Balkenius. Lund, Sweden: Lund University Cognitive Studies.

Fitzpatrick, P., G. Metta, L. Natale, S. Rao, and G. Sandini. 2003. Learning about objects through action: Initial steps towards artificial cognition. In *2003 IEEE International Conference on Robotics and Automation* (ICRA), May 12–17, Taipei, Taiwan.

Fodor, J. A. 1981. *Representations: Philosophical essays on the foundations of cognitive science.* Cambridge, MA: MIT Press.

———. 1983. *The modularity of mind.* Cambridge, MA: MIT Press.

———. 1987. *Psychosemantics: The problem of meaning in the philosophy of mind.* Cambridge, MA: MIT Press.

———. 1994. *The elm and the expert.* Cambridge, MA: MIT Press.

———. 1998. Do we think in mentalese: Remarks on some arguments of Peter Carruthers. In *Critical condition: Polemical essays on cognitive science and the philosophy of mind,* ed. J. Foder. Cambridge, MA: MIT Press.

———. 2001. *The mind doesn't work that way.* Cambridge, MA: MIT Press.

———. 2004. Having concepts: A brief refutation of the twentieth century. *Mind and Language* 19, no. 1: 29–47.

Fowler, C., and M. T. Turvey. 1978. Skill acquisition: An event approach with special reference to searching for the optimum of a function of several variables. In *Information processing in motor control and learning,* ed. G. Stelmach. New York: Academic Press.

Frisch, K. von. 1975. *Animal architecture*. London: Hutchinson.

Fuller, R. 1961. Tensegrity. *Portfolio and Artnews Annual* 4: 112–127.

Gallagher, S. 1998. Body schema and intentionality. In *The body and the self*, ed. J. Bermudez. Cambridge, MA: MIT Press.

———. 2005. *How the body shapes the mind*. Oxford, UK: Oxford University Press.

Gazzaniga, M. 1998. *The mind's past*. Berkeley: University of California Press.

Gedenryd, H. 1998. *How designers work: Making sense of authentic cognitive activities*. Lund, Sweden: Lund University Cognitive Studies.

Gertler, B. 2007. Overextending the mind? In *Arguing about the mind*, ed. B. Gertler and L. Shapiro. New York: Routledge.

Gibbs, R. 2001. Intentions as emergent products of social interactions. In *Intentions and intentionality*, ed. B. Malle, F. Moses, J. Louis, and D. Bladwin. Cambridge, MA: MIT Press.

Gibson, J. J. 1979. *The ecological approach to visual perception*. Boston: Houghton-Mifflin.

Gleick, J. 1993. *Genius: The life and times of Richard Feynman*. New York: Vintage.

Goldin-Meadow, S. 2003. *Hearing gesture: How our hands help us think*. Cambridge, MA: Harvard University Press.

Goldin-Meadow, S., H. Nusbaum, S. Kelly, and S. Wagner. 2001. Explaining math: Gesturing lightens the load. *Psychological Science* 12: 516–522.

Goldin-Meadow, S., and S. Wagner. 2004. How our hands help us learn. *Trends in Cognitive Sciences* 9, no. 5: 234–241.

Goodale, M. 1998. Where does vision end and action begin? *Current Biology* R489–R491.

———. 2001. Real action in a virtual world. Commentary on O'Regan and Noë. *Behavioral and Brain Sciences* 24, no. 5: 984–985.

Goodale, M., and D. Milner. 2004. *Sight unseen: An exploration of conscious and unconscious vision*. Oxford, UK: Oxford University Press.

Goodale, M., and D. Westwood. 2004. An evolving view of duplex vision: Separate but interacting cortical pathways for perception and action. *Current Opinion in Neurobiology* 14: 203–221.

Goodwin, B. 1994. *How the leopard changed its spots*. London: Weidenfeld & Nicolson.

Gordon, P. 2004. Numerical cognition without words: Evidence from Amazonia. *Science* 306: 496–499.

Gray, W. D., and W.-T. Fu. 2004. Soft constraints in interactive behavior: The case of ignoring perfect knowledge in the world for imperfect knowledge in the head. *Cognitive Science* 28, no. 3: 359–382.

Gray, W. D., C. R. Sims, W.-T. Fu, and M. J. Schoelles. 2006. The soft constraints hypothesis: A rational analysis approach to resource allocation for interactive behavior. *Psychological Review* 113, no. 3: 461–482.

Gray, W. D., and V. D. Veksler. 2005. The acquisition and asymmetric transfer of interactive routines. In *27th annual meeting of the Cognitive Science Society*, ed. B. G. Bara, L. Barsalou, and M. Bucciarelli. Austin, TX: Cognitive Science Society.

Gregory, R. 1981. *Mind in science: A history of explanations in psychology.* Cambridge, UK: Cambridge University Press.

Grush, R. 1995. Emulation and cognition. PhD diss., University of California, San Diego.

———. 2003. In defence of some "Cartesian" assumptions concerning the brain and its operation. *Biology and Philosophy* 18: 53–93.

———. 2004. The emulation theory of representation: Motor control, imagery, and perception. *Behavioral and Brain Sciences* 27: 377–442.

Gusnard, D. A., E. Akbudak, G. L. Shulman, and M. E. Raichle. 2001. Medial prefrontal cortex and self-referential mental activity: Relation to a default mode of brain function. *Proceedings of the National Academy of Sciences, USA,* 98: 4259–4264.

Haugeland, J. 1991. Representational genera. In *Philosophy and connectionist theory,* ed. W. Ramsey, S. Stich, and J. McCelland. Hillsdale, NJ: Erlbaum. Reprinted in *Having thought: Essays in the metaphysics of mind,* ed. J. Haugeland. Cambridge, MA: Harvard University Press.

———. 1998. Mind embodied and embedded. In *Having thought: Essays in the metaphysics of mind,* ed. J. Haugeland. Cambridge, MA: Harvard University Press. This originally appeared in *Acta Philosophica Fennica* 58, 1995, a special issue on Mind and Cognition, ed. L. Haaparanta and S. Heinamaa.

Hayhoe, M. 2000. Vision using routines: A functional account of vision. *Visual Cognition* 7, no. 1–3: 43–64.

Heidegger, M. 1927/1961. *Being and time,* trans. J. Macquarrie and E. Robinson. New York: Harper & Row.

Henderson, J., and A. Hollingworth. 2003. Eye movements and visual memory: Detecting changes to saccade targets in scenes. *Perception and Psychophysics* 65, no. 1: 58–71.

Hermer-Vazquez, L., E. Spelke, and A. Katsnelson. 1999. Sources of flexibility in human cognition: Dual-task studies of space and language. *Cognitive Psychology* 39: 3–36.

Hirose, N. 2002. An ecological approach to embodiment and cognition. *Cognitive Systems Research* 3: 289–299.

Hollingworth, A., and J. M. Henderson. 2002. Accurate visual memory for previously attended objects in natural scenes. *Journal of Experimental Psychology: Human Perception and Performance* 28: 113–136.

Hollingworth, A., G. Schrock, and J. M. Henderson. 2001. Change detection in the flicker paradigm: The role of fixation position within the scene. Memory and Cognition 29: 296–304.

Hommel, B., Müsseler, J., Aschersleben, G., & Prinz, W. 2001. The theory of event coding (TEC). A framework for perception and action planning. *Behavioral and Brain Sciences,* 24, 849–937.

Houghton, D. 1997. Mental content and external representations. *Philosophical Quarterly* 47, no. 187: 159–177.

Hurley, S. 1998. *Consciousness in action.* Cambridge, MA: Harvard University Press.

————. in press. The varieties of externalism. In *The Cambridge handbook of situated cognition*, ed. M. Aydede and P. Robbins. Cambridge, UK: Cambridge University Press.

Husbands, P., T. Smith, N. Jakobi, and M. O'Shea. 1998. Better living through chemistry: Evolving GasNets for robot control. *Connection Science* 10, no. 4: 185–210.

Husserl, E. 1907. *Thing and space*, trans. R. Rojcewicz. Boston: Kluwer.

Hutchins, E. 1995. *Cognition in the wild*. Cambridge, MA: MIT Press.

————. in press. Material anchors for conceptual blends. *Journal of Pragmatics*.

Iida, F., and Pfeifer, R. 2004. Self-stabilization and behavioral diversity of embodied adaptive locomotion. In *Embodied artificial intelligence*, ed. F. Iida, R. Pfeifer, L. Steels, and Y. Kuniyoshi. Berlin, Springer.

Iizuka, H., and T. Ikegami. 2004. Simulating autonomous coupling in discrimination of light frequencies. *Connection Science* 16, no. 4: 283–300.

Irwin, D. 1991. Information integration across saccadic eye movements. *Cognitive Psychology* 23: 420–456.

Ismael, J. 2006. *The situated self*. Oxford, UK: Oxford University Press.

————. in press. Selves and self-organization. *Minds and Machines*.

Ito, M. 1984. *The cerebellum and neural control*. New York: Raven Press.

Iverson, J., and S. Goldin-Meadow. 1998. Why people gesture when they speak. *Nature* 396: 228.

————. 2001. The resilience of gesture in talk. *Developmental Science* 4: 416–422.

Iverson, J., and E. Thelen. 1999. Hand, mouth and brain. In *Reclaiming cognition: The primacy of action, intention and emotion*, ed. R. Núñez and W. J. Freeman. Bowling Green, OH: Imprint Academic.

Jackendoff, R. 1996. How language helps us think. *Pragmatics and Cognition* 4, no. 1: 1–34.

Jackson, S., and A. Shaw. 2000. The Ponzo illusion affects grip force but not grip-aperture scaling during prehension movements. *Journal of Experimental Psychology: Human Perception and Performance* 26: 418–423.

Jacob, P., and M. Jeannerod. 2003. *Ways of seeing: The scope and limits of visual cognition*. Oxford, UK: Oxford University Press.

Jeannerod, M. 1997. *The cognitive neuroscience of action*. Oxford, UK: Blackwell.

Jeannerod, M., and P. Jacob. 2005. Visual cognition. A new look at the two visual systems model. *Neuropsychologia* 43: 301–312.

Jordan, S. 2003. Emergence of self and other in perception and action: An event-control approach. *Consciousness and Cognition* 12: 633–646.

Kawato, M. 1990. Computational schemes and neural network models for formation and control of multijoint arm trajectory. In *Neural networks for control*, ed. W. T. Miller, R. Sutton, and P. Werbos. Cambridge, MA: MIT Press.

————. 1999. Internal models for motor control and trajectory planning. *Current Opinion in Neurobiology* 9: 718–727.

Kawato, M., K. Furukawa, and R. Suzuki. 1987. A hierarchical neural network model for control and learning of voluntary movement. *Biological Cybernetics* 57: 447–454.

Kelso, S. 1995. *Dynamic patterns*. Cambridge, MA: MIT Press.

Kirsh, D. 1995a. Complementary strategies: Why we use our hands when we think. In *Proceedings of the 17th annual conference of the Cognitive Science Society*. Hillsdale, NJ: Erlbaum.

———. 1995b. The intelligent use of space. *Artificial Intelligence* 73, no. 1–2: 31–68.

———. 2004. Metacognition, distributed cognition and visual design. In *Cognition, education and communication technology*, ed. P. Gardinfors and P. Johansson. Hillsdale, NJ: Erlbaum.

Kirsh, D., and P. Maglio. 1992. Reaction and reflection in Tetris. In *Artificial intelligence planning systems: Proceedings of the first annual conference AIPS*, ed. J. Hendler. San Mateo, CA: Morgan Kaufmann.

———. 1994. On distinguishing epistemic from pragmatic action. *Cognitive Science* 18: 513–549.

Kiverstein, J., and A. Clark. in press. Experience and agency: Slipping the mesh. Commentary on N. Block, "Consciousness, accessibility, and the mesh between psychology and neuroscience." *Behavioral and Brain Sciences*.

Koch, C. 2004. *The quest for consciousness*. New York: Roberts.

Kravitz, J. H. 1972. Conditioned adaptation to prismatic displacement. *Perception and Psychophysics* 11: 38–42.

Kroliczak, G., P. F. Heard, M. A. Goodale, and R. L. Gregory. 2006. Dissociation of perception and action unmasked by the hollow-face illusion. *Brain Research* 1080, no. 1: 1–16.

Kuniyoshi, Y., Y. Ohmura, K. Terada, A. Nagakubo, S. Eitoku, and T. Yamamoto. 2004. Embodied basis of invariant features in execution and perception of whole body dynamic actions—Knacks and focuses of roll-and-rise motion. *Robotics and Autonomous Systems* 48, no. 4: 189–201.

Lakoff, G., and M. Johnson. 1980. *Metaphors we live by*. Chicago: University of Chicago Press.

———. 1999. *Philosophy in the flesh: The embodied mind and its challenge to Western thought*. New York: Basic Books.

Laland, K. N., J. Odling-Smee, and M. W. Feldman. 2000. Niche construction, biological evolution and cultural change. *Behavioral and Brain Sciences* 23, no. 1: 131–146.

Lee, D., and P. Reddish. 1981. Plummeting gannets: A paradigm of ecological optics. *Nature* 293: 293–294.

Levy, N. in press. *Neuroethics: Challenges for the twenty-first century*. Cambridge, UK: Cambridge University Press.

Lewontin, R. C. 1983. Gene, organism, and environment. In *Evolution from molecules to men*, ed. D. S. Bendall. Cambridge, UK: Cambridge University Press.

Logan, R. 2000. *The sixth language*. Toronto: Stoddart Publishing.

———. 2007. *The extended mind: The emergence of language, the human mind, and culture*. Toronto: University of Toronto Press.

Lucy, J., and S. Gaskins. 2001. Grammatical categories and the development of classification preferences: A comparative approach. In *Language acquisition and conceptual development*, ed. M. Bowerman and S. Levinson. Cambridge, UK: Cambridge University Press.

Lungarella, M., T. Pegors, D. Bulwinkle, and O. Sporns. 2005. Methods for quantifying the information structure of sensory and motor data. *Neuroinformatics* 3, no. 3: 243–262.

Lungarella, M., and O. Sporns. 2005. Information self-structuring: Key principles for learning and development. *Proceedings 2005 IEEE International Conference on Development and Learning*: 25–30.

Lungarella, M., O. Sporns, and Y. Kuniyoshi. 2008. Candidate principles of development in natural and artificial systems. Unpublished manuscript.

MacKay, D. 1967. Ways of looking at perception. In *Models for the perception of speech and visual form*, ed. W. Wathen-Dunn. Cambridge, MA: MIT Press.

Maglio, P., T. Matlock, D. Raphaely, B. Chernicky, and D. Kirsh. 1999. Interactive skill in Scrabble. In *Proceedings of 21st annual conference of the Cognitive Science Society*. Mahwah, NJ: Erlbaum.

Maglio, P. P., and M. J. Wenger. 2000. Two views are better than one: Epistemic actions may prime. In *Proceedings of the 22nd annual conference of the Cognitive Science Society*. Mahwah, NJ: Erlbaum.

———. 2002. On the potential of epistemic actions for self-cuing: Multiple orientations can prime 2D shape recognition and use. In *Proceedings of the 24th annual conference of the Cognitive Science Society*. Mahwah, NJ. Erlbaum.

Maglio, P. P., M. J. Wenger, and A. M. Copeland. 2003. The benefits of epistemic action outweigh the costs. In *Proceedings of the 25th annual conference of the Cognitive Science Society*. Hillsdale, NJ: Erlbaum.

Maravita, A., and A. Iriki. 2004. Tools for the body (schema). *Trends in Cognitive Sciences* 8, no. 2: 79–86.

Martin, M. G. F. 2004. The limits of self-awareness. *Philosophical Studies* 120: 37–89.

Matthen, M. 2005. *Seeing, doing and knowing*. Oxford, UK: Oxford University Press.

Maturana, H. 1980. Biology of cognition. In *Autopoiesis and cognition*, ed. H. Maturana, R. Humberto, and F. Varela. Dordrecht, The Netherlands: Reidel.

McBeath, M., D. Shaffer, and M. Kaiser. 1995. How baseball outfielders determine where to run to catch fly balls. *Science* 268: 569–573.

McClamrock, R. 1995. *Existential cognition*. Chicago: University of Chicago Press.

McClelland, J. L., D. E. Rumelhart, and G. E. Hinton. 1986. The appeal of parallel distributed processing. In *Parallel distributed processing*, Vol. 2, ed. J. L. McClelland and D. E. Rumelhart. Cambridge, MA: MIT Press.

McConkie, G. W. 1991. Perceiving a stable visual world. In *Proceedings of the sixth European Conference on Eye Movements*, ed. J. Van Rensbergen, M. Devijver, and G. d'Ydewalle. Belgium: University of Leuven.

McConkie, G. W., and D. Zola. 1979. Is visual information integrated across successive fixations in reading? *Perception and Psychophysics* 25: 221–224.

McGeer, T. 1990. Passive dynamic walking. *International Journal of Robotics Research* 9, no. 2: 68–82.

McHugh, M. 1992. *China Mountain Zhang*. New York: Tom Doherty.

McLeod, P., N. Reed, and Z. Dienes. 2001. Toward a unified fielder theory: What we do not yet know about how people run to catch a ball. *Journal of Experimental Psychology: Human Perception and Performance* 27: 1347–1355.

———. 2002. The optic trajectory is not a lot of use if you want to catch the ball. *Journal of Experimental Psychology: Human Perception and Performance* 28: 1499–1501.

McNeill, D. 1992. *Hand and mind*. Chicago: University of Chicago Press.

———. 2005. *Gesture and thought*. Chicago: University of Chicago Press.

Mead, G. H. 1934. *Mind, self, and society*, ed. C. W. Morris. Chicago: University of Chicago Press.

Meijer, P. B. L. 1992. An experimental system for auditory image representations. *IEEE Transactions on Biomedical Engineering* 39, no. 2: 112–121.

Meltzoff, A. N., and M. K. Moore. 1997. Explaining facial imitation: A theoretical model. *Early Development and Parenting* 6: 179–192.

Menary, R. 2007. *Cognitive integration: Attacking the bounds of cognition*. New York: Palgrave Macmillan.

Merleau-Ponty, M. 1945/1962. *The phenomenology of perception*, trans. C. Smith. London: Routledge and Kegan Paul.

Metta, G., and Fitzpatrick, P. 2003. Early integration of vision and manipulation. *Adaptive Behavior* 11, no. 2: 109–128.

Milner, D., and R. Dyde. 2003. Why do some perceptual illusions affect visually guided action, when others don't? *Trends in Cognitive Sciences* 7: 10–11.

Milner, D., and M. Goodale. 1995. *The visual brain in action*. New York: Oxford University Press.

———. 2006. *The visual brain in action*, 2nd ed. Oxford, UK: Oxford University Press.

Mitroff, S., D. Simons, and D. Levin. 2004. Nothing compares two views: Change blindness can occur despite preserved access to the changed information. *Perception and Psychophysics* 66, no. 8: 1268–1281.

Mundale, J. 2001. Neuroanatomical foundations of cognition: Connecting the neuronal level with the study of higher brain areas. In *Philosophy and the neurosciences: A reader*, ed. W. Bechtel, P. Mandik, J. Mundale, and R. S. Stufflebeam. Oxford, UK: Basil Blackwell.

———. 2002. Concepts of localization: Balkanization in the brain. *Brain and Mind* 3: 1–18.

Mussa-Ivaldi, F., and L. Miller. 2003. Brain-machine interfaces: Computational demands and clinical needs meet basic neuroscience. *Trends in Cognitive Sciences* 26, no. 6: 329–334.

Namy, L., L. Smith, and L. Gershkoff-Stowe. 1997. Young children's discovery of spatial classification. *Cognitive Development* 12, no. 2: 163–184.

Neth, H., and S. J. Payne. 2002. Thinking by doing? Epistemic actions in the Tower of Hanoi. In *Proceedings of the 24th annual conference of the Cognitive Science Society*, ed. W. D. Gray and C. D. Schunn. Mahwah, NJ: Erlbaum.

Nilsson, N. J. 1984. Shakey the robot (Technical Note 323). Menlo Park, CA: AI Center, SRI International. Available on the Web at http://www.ai.sri .com/shakey/.

Noë, A. 2004. *Action in perception*. Cambridge, MA: MIT Press.

———. 2006. Experience without the head. In *Perceptual experience*, ed. T. S. Gendler and J. Hawthorne. New York: Oxford University Press.

———. 2007. Understanding *Action in perception:* Reply to Hickerson and Keijzer. *Philosophical Psychology* 20, no. 4: 531–538.

Norman, D. 1993a. Cognition in the head and in the world. *Cognitive Science* 17, no. 1: 1–6.

———. 1993b. *Things that make us smart*. Cambridge, MA: Perseus Books.

———. 1999. *The invisible computer*. Cambridge, MA: MIT Press.

Norman, D., and T. Shallice. 1980. Attention to action: Willed and automatic control of behavior. *Center for Human Information Processing Technical Report 99*. Reprinted in revised form in *Consciousness and self-regulation*, Vol. 4, ed. R. J. Davidson, G. E. Schwartz, and D. Shapiro. New York: Plenum Press, 1986.

Norton, A. 1995. Dynamics: An introduction. In *Mind as motion: Dynamics, behavior, and cognition*, ed. R. Port and T. Van Gelder. Cambridge, MA: MIT Press.

O'Regan, J. K. 1992. Solving the "real" mysteries of visual perception: The world as an outside memory. *Canadian Journal of Psychology* 46, no. 3: 461–488.

O'Regan, J. K., and A. Noë. 2001. A sensorimotor approach to vision and visual consciousness. *Behavioral and Brain Sciences* 24, no. 5: 883–975.

O'Reilly, R., and Y. Munakata. 2000. *Computational explorations in cognitive neuroscience*. Cambridge, MA: MIT Press.

Odling-Smee, F. J. 1988. Niche constructing phenotypes. In *The role of behavior in evolution*, ed. H. C. Plotkin. Cambridge, MA: MIT Press.

Odling-Smee, J., K. Laland, and M. Feldman. 2003. *Niche construction*. Princeton, NJ: Princeton University Press.

Paul, C. 2004. Morphology and computation. In *From animals to animats: Proceedings of the eighth international conference on the Simulation of Adaptive Behavior, Los Angeles*, ed. S. Schaal, A. J. Ijspeert, A. Billard, S. Vijayakumar, J. Hallam, and J.-A. Meyer. Cambridge, MA: MIT Press.

———. 2006. Morphological computation: A basis for the analysis of morphology and control requirements. *Robotics and Autonomous Systems* 54: 619–630.

Paul C., F. J. Valero-Cuevas, and H. Lipson. 2006. Design and control of tensegrity robots. *IEEE Transactions on Robotics* 22, no. 5: 944–957.

Peck, A., R. Jeffers, C. Carello, and M. Turvey. 1996. Haptically perceiving the length of one rod by means of anotherr. *Ecological Psychology* 8: 237–258.

Pettit, P. 2003. Looks as powers. *Philosophical Issues* 13: 221–252.

Pfeifer, R. 2000. On the role of morphology and materials in adaptive behavior. In *From animals to animats 6. Proceedings of the sixth international conference on Simulation of Adaptive Behavior*, ed. J.-A. Meyer, A. Berthoz, D. Floreano, H. Roitblat, and S. W. Wilson. Cambridge, MA: MIT Press.

Pfeifer, R., and J. Bongard. 2007. *How the body shapes the way we think.* Cambridge, MA: MIT Press.

Pfeifer, R., M. Lungarella, O. Sporns, and Y. Kuniyoshi. 2006. On the information theoretic implications of embodiment principles and methods. Unpublished manuscript.

Pfeifer, R., and C. Scheier. 1999. *Understanding intelligence.* Cambridge, MA: MIT Press.

Philippides, A., P. Husbands, T. Smith, and M. O'Shea. 2005. Flexible couplings: Diffusing neuromodulators and adaptive robotics. *Artificial Life* 11: 139–160.

Pinker, S. 1997. *How the mind works.* London: Allen Lane/Penguin Press.

Port, R., and T. van Gelder. 1995. *Mind as motion: Dynamics, behavior, and cognition.* Cambridge, MA: MIT Press.

Prinz, J. 2000. The ins and outs of consciousness. *Brain and Mind* 1, no. 2: 245–256.

———. 2004. *Gut reactions: A perceptual theory of emotion.* New York: Oxford University Press.

Prinz, J., and A. Clark. 2004. Putting concepts to work: Some thoughts for the 21st century (a reply to Fodor). *Mind and Language* 19, no. 1: 57–69.

Prinz, W. 1997. Perception and action planning. *European Journal of Cognitive Psychology* 9, no. 2: 129–154.

Putnam, H. 1960. Minds and machines. In *Dimensions of mind*, ed. S. Hook. New York: New York University Press.

———. 1967. Psychological predicates. In *Art, mind and religion*, ed. W. Capitan and D. Merrill. Pittsburgh, PA: Pittsburgh University Press.

———. 1975a. The meaning of "meaning." In *Language, mind and knowledge*, ed. K. Gunderson. Minneapolis: University of Minnesota Press. Reprinted in *Mind, language, and reality: Philosophical papers*, Vol. 2, ed. H. Putnam. New York: Cambridge University Press.

———. 1975b. Philosophy and our mental life. In *Mind, language, and reality*, ed. H. Putnam. Cambridge, UK: Cambridge University Press.

Pylyshyn, Z. 1984. *Computation and cognition.* Cambridge, MA: MIT Press.

———. 2001. Visual indexes, preconceptual objects, and situated vision. *Cognition* 80: 127–158.

Ramachandran, V. S., and S. Blakeslee. 1998. *Phantoms in the brain: Probing the mysteries of the human mind.* New York: Morrow.

Reed, E. 1996. *Encountering the world: Toward an ecological psychology.* New York: Oxford University Press.

Reisberg, D. 2001. *Cognition.* New York: Norton.

Richardson, D. C., and R. Dale. 2004. Looking to understand: The coupling between speakers' and listeners' eye movements and its relationship to discourse comprehension. *Proceedings of the 26th annual meeting of the Cognitive Science Society.* Mahwah, NJ: Erlbaum.

Richardson, D. C., and N. Z. Kirkham. 2004. Multi-modal events and moving locations: Eye movements of adults and 6-month-olds reveal dynamic spatial indexing. *Journal of Experimental Psychology: General* 133, no. 1: 46–62.

Richardson, D. C., and M. J. Spivey. 2000. Representation, space and *Hollywood Squares:* Looking at things that aren't there anymore. *Cognition* 76: 269–295.

Rizzolatti, G., L. Fogassi, and V. Gallese. 2001. Neurophysiological mechanisms underlying the understanding and imitation of action. *Nature Reviews: Neuroscience* 2: 661–670.

Rockwell, T. 2005a. Attractor spaces as modules: A semi-eliminative reduction of symbolic AI to dynamical systems theory. *Minds and Machines* 15, no. 1: 23–55.

———. 2005b. *Neither brain nor ghost: A nondualist alternative to the mind-brain identity theory.* Cambridge, MA: MIT Press.

Rohrer, T. 2006. The body in space: Embodiment, experientialism and linguistic conceptualization. In *Body, language and mind,* Vol. 2, ed. J. Zlatev, T. Ziemke, R. Frank, and R. Dirven. Berlin: Mouton de Gruyter.

Rosenblatt, F. 1962. *Principles of neurodynamics.* New York: Spartan Books.

Rowlands, M. 1999. *The body in mind: Understanding cognitive processes.* Cambridge, UK: Cambridge University Press.

———. 2006. *Body language: Representing in action.* Cambridge, MA: MIT Press.

Rumelhart, D. E., P. Smolensky, J. L. McClelland, and G. E. Hinton. 1986. Schemata and sequential thought processes in parallel distributed processing. In *Parallel distributed processing: Explorations in the microstructure of cognition, Vol. 2: Psychological and biological models.* ed. D. E. Rumelhart, J. L. McClelland, and the PDP Research Group. Cambridge, MA: MIT Press.

Rupert, R. 2004. Challenges to the hypothesis of extended cognition. *Journal of Philosophy* 101, no. 8: 389–428.

———. 2006. Extended cognition as a framework for empirical psychology: The costs outweigh the benefits. Paper presented to American Philosophical Association central division meeting.

———. in press-a. Innateness and the situated mind. In *The Cambridge handbook of situated cognition,* ed. P. Robbins and M. Aydede. Cambridge, UK: Cambridge University Press.

———. in press-b. Representation in extended cognitive systems: Does the scaffolding of language extend the mind? In *The extended mind,* ed. R. Menary. Aldershot, UK: Ashgate.

Ryle, G. 1949/1990. *The concept of mind.* London: Penguin.

Salzman, E., and J. A. S. Kelso. 1987. Skilled actions: A task dynamic approach. *Psychological Review* 94: 84–106.

Salzman, L., and W. Newsome. 1994. Neural mechanisms for forming a perceptual decision. *Science* 264: 231–237.

Samuels, R. 2004. Innateness in cognitive science. *Trends in Cognitive Sciences* 8: 136–141.

Scaife, M., and Y. Rogers. 1996. External cognition: How do graphical representations work? *International Journal of Human-Computer Studies* 45: 185–213.

Schrope, M. 2001. Simply sensational. *New Scientist* (June): 30–33.

Semendeferi, K., E. Armstrong, A. Schleicher, K. Zilles, and G. W. Van Hoesen. 2001. Prefrontal cortex in humans and apes: A comparative study of area 10. *American Journal of Physical Anthropology* 114: 224–241.

Semendeferi, K., A. Lu, N. Schenker, and H. Damasio. 2002. Humans and great apes share a large frontal cortex. *Nature Neuroscience* 5: 272–276.

Shaffer, D. M., S. M. Krauchunas, M. Eddy, and M. K. McBeath. 2004. How dogs navigate to catch Frisbees. *Psychological Science* 15: 437–441.

Shaffer, D. M., and M. K. McBeath. 2005. Naive beliefs in baseball: Systematic distortion in perceived time of apex for fly balls. *Journal of Experimental Psychology: Learning, Memory, and Cognition* 31: 1492–1501.

Shaffer, D. M., M. K. McBeath, W. L. Roy, and S. M. Krauchunas. 2003. A linear optical trajectory informs the fielder where to run to the side to catch fly balls. *Journal of Experimental Psychology: Human Perception and Performance* 29, no. 6: 1244–1250.

Shallice, T. 2002. Fractionation of the supervisory system. In *Principles of frontal lobe function*, ed. D. T. Stuss and R. T. Knight. New York: Oxford University Press.

Shapiro, L. 2004. *The mind incarnate*. Cambridge, MA: MIT Press.

———. in press. Reductionism, embodiment, and the generality of psychology. In *Reductionism*, ed. H. Looren de Jong and M. Schouten. Oxford, UK: Blackwell.

Sheets-Johnstone, M. 1999. Emotion and movement: A beginning empirical-phenomenological analysis of their relationship. *Journal of Consciousness Studies* 6, no. 11–12: 259–277.

Shiffrin, R., and W. Schneider. 1977. Controlled and automatic human information processing: II. General theory. *Psychological Review* 82: 127–190.

Silverman, M., and A. Mack. 2001. Priming from change blindness [Abstract]. *Journal of Vision* 1, no. 3: 13a.

Simon, H. 1981. *The sciences of the artificial*. Cambridge, MA: MIT Press.

Simons, D. J., C. F. Chabris, T. T. Schnur, and D. T. Levin. 2002. Evidence for preserved representations in change blindness. *Consciousness and Cognition* 11: 78–97.

Simons, D., and D. Levin. 1997. Change blindness. *Trends in Cognitive Sciences* 1, no. 7: 261–267.

Simons, D., and R. Rensink. 2005. Change blindness: Past, present and future. *Trends in Cognitive Sciences* 9, no. 1: 16–20.

Sirigu, A., L. Cohen, J. R. Duhamel, B. Pillon, B. Dubois, and Y. Agid. 1995. A selective impairment of hand posture, for object utilization in apraxia. *Cortex* 31: 41–55.

Sloman, A. 1993. The mind as a control system. In *Philosophy and cognitive science: Royal Institute of Philosophy Supplement 34*, ed. C. Hookway and D. Peterson. Cambridge, UK: Cambridge University Press.

Sloman, A., and R. Chrisley. 2003. Virtual machines and consciousness. *Journal of Consciousness Studies* 10, no. 4–5: 133–172.

Smith, E. 2000. Neural bases of human working memory. *Current Directions in Psychological Science* 9: 45–49.

Smith, L. 2001. How domain-general processes may create domain-specific biases. In *Language acquisition and conceptual development*, ed. M. Bowerman and S. Levinson. Cambridge, UK: Cambridge University Press.

Smith, L., and M. Gasser. 2005. The development of embodied cognition: Six lessons from babies. *Artificial Life* 11, no. 1: 13–30.

Smitsman, A. 1997. The development of tool use: Changing boundaries between organism and environment. In *Evolving explanations of development: Ecological approaches to organism–environment systems*, ed. C. Dent-Read and P. Zukow-Goldring. Washington, DC: American Psychological Association.

Spencer, J. P., and G. Schöner. 2003. Bridging the representational gap in the dynamical systems approach to development. *Developmental Science* 6: 392–412.

Sperber, D. 2001. An evolutionary perspective on testimony and argumentation. *Philosophical Topics* 29: 401–413.

Spivey, M. J., D. C. Richardson, and S. Fitneva. in press. Memory outside of the brain: Oculomotor indexes to visual and linguistic information. In *Interfacing language, vision, and action*, ed. F. Ferreira and J. Henderson. San Diego, CA: Academic Press.

Sporns, O. 2002. Network analysis, complexity and brain function. *Complexity* 8: 56–60.

Sporns, O., D. Chialvo, M. Kaiser, and C. C. Hilgetag. 2004. Organization, development and function of complex brain networks. *Trends in Cognitive Sciences* 8: 418–425.

Sporns, O., and M. Lungarella. 2006. Evolving coordinated behavior by maximizing information structure. In *Proceedings of the 10th international conference on artificial life*. Cambridge, MA: MIT Press.

Sterelny, K. 2003. *Thought in a hostile world: The evolution of human cognition.* Oxford, UK: Blackwell.

———. 2004. Externalism, epistemic artefacts, and the extended mind. In *The externalist challenge*, ed. Richard Schantz. New Studies on Cognition and Intentionality. New York: de Gruyter.

Sterling, B. 2004. Robots and the rest of us: Fear and loathing on the human-machine frontier. *WIRED* (May): 116.

Suchman, L. 1987. *Plans and situated actions.* Cambridge, UK: Cambridge University Press.

Sudnow, D. 2001. *Ways of the hand: A rewritten account.* Cambridge, MA: MIT Press.

Sur, M., A. Angelucci, and J. Sharma. 1999. Rewiring cortex: The role of patterned activity in development and plasticity of neocortical circuits. *Journal of Neurobiology* 41, no. 1: 33–43.

Sutton, J. 2002a. Cognitive conceptions of language and the development of autobiographical memory. *Language and Communication* 22: 375–390.

———. 2002b. Porous memory and the cognitive life of things. In *Prefiguring cyberculture: An intellectual history*, ed. D. Tofts, A. Jonson, and A. Cavallaro. Cambridge, MA: MIT Press/Power Publications.

———. 2007. Batting, habit, and memory: The embodied mind and the nature of skill. *Sport in Society* 10, vol. 5: 763–786.

Szucs, A., P. Varona, A. Volkovskii, H. Arbanel, M. Rabinovich, and A. Selverston. 2000. Interacting biological and electronic neurons generate realistic oscillatory rhythms. *NeuroReport* 11: 1–7.

Thelen, E. 2000. Grounded in the world: Developmental origins of the embodied mind. *Infancy* 1, no. 1: 3–28.

Thelen, E., G. Schöner, C. Scheier, and L. B. Smith. 2001. The dynamics of embodiment: A field theory of infant perseverative reaching. *Behavioral and Brain Sciences* 24: 1–86.

Thelen, E., and L. Smith. 1994. *A dynamic systems approach to the development of cognition and action.* Cambridge, MA: MIT Press.

Thompson, A. 1998. *Hardware evolution: Automatic design of electronic circuits in reconfigurable hardware by artificial evolution.* Berlin: Springer Verlag.

Thompson, A., I. Harvey, and P. Husbands. 1996. Unconstrained evolution and hard consequences. In *Towards evolvable hardware*, ed. E. Sanchez and M. Tomassini. Berlin: Springer-Verlag.

Thompson R. K. R., and D. L. Oden. 2000. Categorical perception and conceptual judgments by nonhuman primates: The paleological monkey and the analogical ape. *Cognitive Science* 24: 363–396.

Thompson, R. K. R., D. L. Oden, and S. T. Boysen. 1997. Language-naive chimpanzees (*Pan troglodytes*) judge relations between relations in a conceptual matching-to-sample task. *Journal of Experimental Psychology: Animal Behavior Processes* 23: 31–43.

Tooby, J., and L. Cosmides. 1990. The past explains the present: Emotional adaptations and the structure of ancestral environments. *Ethology and Sociobiology* 11: 375–424.

Townsend, J. T., and F. G. Ashby. 1978. Methods of modeling capacity in simple processing systems. In *Cognitive theory*, Vol. 3, ed. J. Castellan and F. Restle. Hillsdale, NJ: Erlbaum.

Townsend, J. T., and G. Nozawa. 1995. On the spatiotemporal properties of elementary perception: An investigation of parallel, serial, and coactive theories. *Journal of Mathematical Psychology* 39: 321–359.

Treue, S. 2004. Perceptual enhancement of contrast by attention. *Trends in Cognitive Sciences* 8, no. 10: 435–437.

Triantafyllou, M., and G. Triantafyllou. 1995. An efficient swimming machine. *Scientific American* 272, no. 3: 64–70.

Tribble, E. 2005. Distributing cognition in the globe. *Shakespeare Quarterly* 56, no. 2: 135–155.

Tucker, V. A. 1975. The energetic cost of moving about. *American Scientist* 63, no. 4: 413–419.

Turner, S. J. 2000. *The extended organism: The physiology of animal-built structures.* Cambridge, MA: Harvard University Press.

Turvey, M., and C. Carello. 1986. The ecological approach to perceiving-acting: A pictorial essay. *Acta Psychologica* 63: 133–155.

Ullman, S. 1984. Visual routines. *Cognition* 18, no. 1–3: 97–159.

Ullman, S., and W. Richards. 1984. *Image understanding*. Norwood, NJ: Ablex.

Valero-Cuevas, F. J., J. W. Yi, D. Brown, R. V. McNamara. C. Paul, and H. Lipson. 2007. The tendon network of the fingers performs anatomical computation at a macroscopic scale. *IEEE Transactions on Biomedical Engineering* 54, no. 6: 1161–1166.

Van Essen, D. C., C. H. Anderson, and B. A. Olshausen. 1994. Dynamic routing strategies in sensory, motor, and cognitive processing. In *Large scale neuronal theories of the brain*, ed. C. Koch and J. Davis. Cambridge, MA: MIT Press.

Van Essen, D., and J. Gallant. 1994. Neural mechanisms of form and motion processing in the primate visual system. *Neuron* 13: 1–10.

Van Gelder, T. 1995. What might cognition be, if not computation? *Journal of Philosophy* 92, no. 7: 345–381.

Van Gelder, T., and R. Port, eds. 1995. It's about time: An overview of the dynamical approach to cognition. In *Mind as motion: Explorations in the dynamics of cognition*, ed. R. Port and T. Van Gelder. Cambridge, MA: MIT Press.

Varela, F., E. Thompson, and E. Rosch. 1991. *The embodied mind*. Cambridge, MA: MIT Press.

Vygotsky, L. S. 1962/1986. *Thought and language*, trans. A. Kozulin. Cambridge, MA: MIT Press.

Wagner, S. M., H. C. Nusbaum, and S. Goldin-Meadow. 2004. Probing the mental representation of gesture: Is handwaving spatial? *Journal of Memory and Language* 50: 395–407.

Warren, W. 2006. The dynamics of action and perception. *Psychological Review* 113, no. 2: 358–389.

Webb, B. 1996. A cricket robot. *Scientific American* 275: 62–67.

Wegner, D. M. 2005. Who is the controller of controlled processes? In *The new unconscious*, ed. R. Hassin, J. S. Uleman, and J. A. Barg. New York: Oxford University Press.

Wenger, M. J., and J. T. Townsend. 2000. Basic response time tools for studying general processing capacity in attention, perception, and cognition. *Journal of General Psychology* 127: 67–99.

Wheeler, M. 2004. Is language the ultimate artifact? In *Language Sciences*, special issue on Distributed Cognition and Integrational Linguistics, ed. D. Spurrett, 26, no. 6.

———. 2005. *Reconstructing the cognitive world*. Cambridge, MA: MIT Press.

———. in press-a. Continuity in question: An afterword to "Is language the ultimate artifact?" In *The mind, the body and the world: Psychology after cognitivism*, ed. B. Wallace, A. Ross, J. Davies, and T. Anderson. Bowling Green, OH: Imprint Academic.

———. in press-b. Minds, things and materiality. In *The cognitive life of things*, ed. C. Renfrew and L. Malafouris. Cambridge, UK: McDonald Institute for Archaelogical Research.

Wheeler, M., and A. Clark. 1999. Genic representation: Reconciling content and causal complexity. *British Journal for the Philosophy of Science* 50, no. 1: 103–135.

Wilson, M. 2002. Six views of embodied cognition. *Psychonomic Bulletin and Review* 9, no. 4: 625–636.

Wilson, R. A. 1994. Wide computationalism. *Mind* 103: 351–372.

———. 2004. *Boundaries of the mind: The individual in the fragile sciences—Cognition.* Cambridge, UK: Cambridge University Press.

Wolpert, D. M., R. C. Miall, and M. Kawato. 1998. Internal models in the cerebellum. *Trends in Cognitive Sciences* 2: 338–347.

Yu, C., D. Ballard, and R. Aslin. 2005. The role of embodied intention in early lexical acquisition. *Cognitive Science* 29, no. 6: 961–1005.

Index

Made in the USA
Lexington, KY
09 January 2014